THE UNADJUSTED GIRL

Publication No. 26: Patterson Smith Reprint Series in Criminology, Law Enforcement, and Social Problems

THE UNADJUSTED GIRL

WITH CASES AND STANDPOINT
FOR BEHAVIOR ANALYSIS

BY

WILLIAM I. THOMAS

FOREWORD BY

Mrs. W. F. DUMMER

HV
6046
T4
1969

141102

Montclair, New Jersey
PATTERSON SMITH
1969

EDITORIAL ANNOUNCEMENT

The rapid development of criminological research in this country since the organization of the American Institute of Criminal Law and Criminology, has made a place in America for this series of Criminal Science Monographs. Their publication is authorized by the American Institute of Criminal Law and Criminology. They appear as supplements to the Journal of the Institute. We believe the present number will satisfy a real need in America.

ROBERT H. GAULT,
Chairman, Editor of the Journal of Criminal Law and Criminology.

FREDERIC B. CROSSLEY,
Northwestern University.

ROBERT W. MILLAR,
Northwestern University.

JOHN H. WIGMORE,
Northwestern University.

JOEL D. HUNTER,
Superintendent Chicago United Charities.

Committee on Publications of the American Institute of Criminal Law and Criminology.

FOREWORD

MODERN psychology is throwing so much light upon human behavior that concerning delinquency one cannot do better than follow the teaching of Spinoza, "Neither condemn nor ridicule but try to understand." Such an attitude led to the establishment of the first mental clinic in connection with a court, where Doctor William Healy revealed astonishing facts regarding causes and cures of delinquency; such an attitude led to this sociological study of delinquency.

Having learned from Doctor Healy the relation between mental conflict and misconduct and the possibility of cure by the freeing of blocked emotion, social workers were somewhat prepared for one of the unusual situations brought about by the war, — namely, the wholesale arrests of girls and women on suspicion of venereal disease, with effort on the part of the government not only to cure the physical disease but to rehabilitate the individual. The gathering of data by the Girls' Protective Bureau of the United States Interdepartmental Social Hygiene Board gave a basis for study which years of private practice or philanthropy could not assemble. One felt about these young prostitutes that mere suppression by force would not reach the root of the matter, — that causes and conditions must be studied. With this in mind certain lines of research were undertaken, primarily to gather and interpret data which would lead to less unjust treatment than is at present accorded so-called delinquent women, by changing public opinion and especially altering procedure in our courts, jails and hospitals. It was hoped that such data might also tend toward a better understanding of human relations and indicate marriage standards based upon biology and psychology rather than on economics.

A profound statement of Mr. Thomas's is, "Statistics in themselves are nothing more than the symptoms of unknown causal processes. A social institution can be understood and modified only if we do not limit ourselves to the study of its formal organization but analyze the way in which it appears in the personal experience of various members of the group and follow the influence it has on their lives." It was just the sudden knowledge of the effect of our custom, law and court procedure as they influenced the lives of individual girls which brought critical questioning of such justice as had been meted out to them. It seemed as if society had been systematically wrecking women.

The government program acted as a searchlight flashed upon the farce of our dual system of morality. In the case of a child suffering assault or rape she might be detained in an old type of reform school till her majority gave her freedom — a poor preparation for later life — while the man, were he convicted, rarely had a long sentence. Of two parents of a child conceived out of wedlock, for the girl abortion is classed as crime; motherhood brings shame and condemnation; while the part of the man passes as a biological necessity. Whereas in some hospitals fifty per cent of the women arrested on suspicion of disease were found to be not infected, it was suggested in one city that prophylactic stations be established in men's clubs and even in boys' schools, — the futility of fine and jail for the woman, freedom for the man.

This war measure brought hundreds of girls to our courts for whom in some States there was no proper provision. This emergency developed rapid establishment of correctional schools of most approved type, showing marked success in the rehabilitation of girls, even with some seeming psychopathic cases. Little girls unfortunate enough to have a sex experience called to the attention of the court, who in the past would have been confined behind bars, are now placed in the country, given good food and opportunity for free happy activity. Formerly for the unmarried mothers the psychological values of pregnancy were ignored, and in the effort to save the reputation by concealing motherhood the mind and character were often weakened.

If fear in soldiers could produce pathological symptoms both mental and physical, curable by psychiatry, might not some of this apparent feeble-mindedness be a hysteria resulting from shock? Most case histories showed early sex experience treated, especially when pregnancy resulted, with utmost scorn, contempt and condemnation. Surely the world offers to these little unmarried mothers as menacing a front as was faced by the soldiers in France. For girls passing through Juvenile Hall in Los Angeles, right environment is provided where they receive friendly care and encouragement. As a psychologist said of the soldiers, "Morale is pumped into them." The fact that they have shown during pregnancy an advance in intelligence quotient amounting in some cases to ten points demands a reconsideration of opinion till further data give scientific basis for judgment.

In the introduction to Kammerer's study of "The Unmarried Mother", Doctor Healy questions whether such a constructive act as bringing a child into the world should ever be classed as a crime. Life, legal or illegal, must be respected.

One grows to love the incorrigible girl. She has many fine qualities. A protective officer was escorting to a State institution a girl thought too bad for a House of the Good Shepherd. A train wreck occurred and she thought, "Here is where my girl escapes me." On the contrary, the "incorrigible" turned to and helped as many as possible of those injured. The biologist tells us it is just this superabundant vitality that is necessary for the evolution of higher types.

In the autumn of 1919 at the International Conference of Women Physicians held in New York under the auspices of the National Y. W. C. A. for discussion of the physical, mental and social health of women, many valuable contributions were made to our problem. The relation between sex shock and nervous disease was plainly given by the psychoanalysts, and their theory of retarded emotion and fixation of infantile affection explained varied phases of behavior. Most encouraging of all was Freud's hypothesis of sublimation.

Those who, in Freud's teaching of the danger of sex repression to mental health, find merely sanction for license miss the point of his wonderful message. This theory that life force, libido, creative energy, follows the Law of Conservation true of Physical force — that as motion may become heat, light or electricity, so this inner power may be transmuted from procreative effort to creative work of hand and brain — would seem to explain much of the modern success in the re-

habilitation of the young prostitute. This transmuta-
tion of sex force into art and religion had been noted
in the past by Jacob Boehme and James Hinton.
Myers hinted it in a line of poetry, "Forge and transform my passion into power", but it remained for
Freud to bring it to common understanding. James
Hinton, the English surgeon, said just after our Civil
War, "Prostitution will pass as has slavery when it
becomes too great a burden for humanity to carry."
That time has come and prostitution must pass. Prostitution and promiscuity will be eliminated not by force
but through sublimation.

Further analysis of this hypothesis of sublimation
shows that life energy or libido may be manifested
physically, psychically, socially, spiritually:

Physically in motion, eating, drinking and in sex
acts;

Psychically in art, science, literature, anything which
uses one's wits;

Socially in service to others;

Spiritually in meditating upon Infinite Power or
seeking one's relation to The Whole.

Though these divisions give somewhat roughly
general group types, humanity shows infinite variety
of expression, and individuals may change from time
to time according to influence and environment. Each
may be developed through her special abilities. One
notes with interest that associated with physical sex
expression there is frequently great cleverness in
cookery and crochet. Each must be stabilized on her
own level.

An interesting report comes from El Retiro, the
experimental school for correctional education established by the city and county of Los Angeles during

the war. Of two hundred girls passing through this
institution during the first three years, only two have
drifted to the underworld, these being drug addicts
when they came from the court. One hundred and
ninety-eight are functioning socially in the community.
These girls were all under twenty-one years. On
arriving at El Retiro each girl is studied by a group
consisting of the referee of the court, the psychologist,
the superintendent, the teacher and the head of student government. So soon as her interests and special
abilities are discovered, a project is chosen which will
prepare her for constructive living in the community.
The girls are stimulated to mental expression of energy, not set to hours of dull routine, scrubbing floors
or paring potatoes. Not punishment but responsibility develops power and leads to higher expression
and achievement. Science is teaching us that man is
an epitome of the past, — that in each human being
is retained the impress of prehuman behavior. As one
analyst puts it, "Each day is an adjustment between
the higher nerve centers and the spinal column." We
must study this conservation of life force that we may
strengthen those manifestations which show ascend-
ing effort and decrease the tendency to revert to action
patterns of earlier forms.

A dictum of the percipient mind of the biologist-
sociologist, Lester Ward, should startle us into fresh
appraisal of life's values. Shortly before his death
he said, "The day will come when society shall be as
much shocked at the crime of perpetuating the least
taint of hereditary disease, insanity or other serious
defect, as it is now at the comparatively harmless crime
of incest."

As an equation is solved more simply by algebra

than arithmetic, so any subject carried up into the next
higher universe of discourse becomes clarified, falls into
proper perspective, and is more easily understood.
This thought in conjunction with the statement of
Lester Ward shows the need of extending our discussion to include women both in and out of wedlock, and
instead of differentiating the good from the bad by
legal definition, the ethics of human mating must be
based upon those laws of nature which secure the finest
human values, the essential aim being an ever better
next generation.

The fundamental function of woman being motherhood, this with its secondary manifestations explains
much of her behavior. The devotion of the young
girl to the cadet who enslaves her reveals the same instinct which holds a wife faithful through difficulties
and degradation, — the instinct from which have developed the virtues of loyalty, endurance and self-
sacrifice. The period of pregnancy should be (if the
imagination be not filled with old wives' tales) one of
health, exhilaration, development of psychic values
and social consciousness. Any woman experiencing
this wonderful functioning should be aided to as complete psycho-biological fulfillment as her personality
and the social situation permit. Should the higher
love and association of the father of her child be lacking,
so much the greater is her need of genuine help and encouragement. Given this, she may be strengthened
and stabilized whether the man desert or become dis-
affected before or after a legal ceremony.

Though mating and its resulting responsibilities
have evolved our highest virtues, marriage is now
under attack. Not only are divorce and illegitimacy
evidenced as showing its failure, but intellectual women

are demanding freedom and self-expression which they
find doubtful in marriage. In Paris one woman who
believed the relation of the unmarried mother to her
child more ethical under French law than that of
the married mother, lived out of wedlock for years of
monogamous mating, her daughter bearing her name.
She and the father of her child were leaders in La Ligue
pour le Droit des Femmes, of which Victor Hugo was
an early president. Fundamentally this attack is
encouraging, indicating effort to bring law up to newer
ideals of ethical mating. Man's marriage law was
based upon economics, upon the idea of possession
and inheritance of possessions. In Scandinavia, where
woman has for some time been voting, there is a tendency to make the law conform to biology. In Nor-
way all births are registered. The father as well as
the mother must be held responsible and there are no
illegitimate children. Under their law for children
born out of wedlock which went into effect in 1915, in
only nine out of the first five thousand cases was paternity contested. Here law is conforming to biologic
fact. Before science can offer a new marriage law the
psychology of mating must be further studied. Women are classifying as prostitution a marriage in which
psychical values are ignored. They seek chastity in
marriage according to the definition given in Doctor S.
Herbert's Fundamentals in Sexual Ethics, "Chastity —
true chastity — has reference not so much to actions
as to feelings and motives. It is the quality of the
emotion in relation to sexual acts that constitutes a
state of purity or impurity."

Mr. Thomas's study quite disproves the former
theory of psychologists and criminologists that the
prostitute is a type and can live no other way. Girls

may come through a measure of prostitution, marry and make successes of their lives. In China a girl will sometimes earn through prostitution the money which makes marriage possible. In that country, where the seclusion of wives necessitates the entertainment of men guests at public places, the so-called prostitute may be called to act as hostess at dinner, to provide music or dancing at regular stipulated prices, according to the class to which she belongs, this not necessarily including the barter of the body. Even dominoes are played at so much a game. It would seem strange to our Y. W. C. A. hostesses at the army camps that their hospitality to the soldiers would in China have been classed as activities of the prostitute.

One of the surprises of the war work was the definite number of married women carrying on not commercial prostitution, but clandestine relationships. They were not vicious but immature. Their husbands being away, they seemed unable to get on without the aid of a friendly man. The need was not money but affectionate companionship. In some cases women were glad to escape from conditions of marital cruelty, yet they were so simple-minded as to accept instead most casual relationships.

Few people are able to live without some affectional alliance. An unmarried woman may establish a permanent friendship with another woman; one of less stable personality may pass from one "crush" to another, leaving havoc in her wake as does the promiscuous male, yet for this she may not be haled into court. If affection be lacking it takes a strong purpose in life to steady either a man or woman.

To claim that a girl need not be ruined or may recover from sex conflict expressed or repressed is not

advocating promiscuity. Far from it. Nor in this
effort of women to free themselves from the blunders
hidden under the sanction of marriage should young
people be encouraged to believe that to repeat those
same blunders freely is the ideal of mating. Much
nervous disease and delinquency are traceable to early
emotional shock. Each case requires special study of
personality. The results of any conflict are dependent
upon previous environment, training, characteristics,
interests, ideals. Freud says that if two little girls,
one the daughter of intellectual parents, the other
the child of the janitor, should have some sex experience, the former might later suffer neurosis while the
latter would probably be unharmed. Cases of disease
and of delinquency show the persistence of the association of idea, the strange continuance of symptoms
fixed as conditioned reflexes which hamper a human
being for years. Recent study of pre-delinquent groups
has revealed children "with normal or even superior
native endowment who are prevented from showing
their ability by factors acting upon their feelings."
These illustrate the dangers of affectional wound, —
the sensitivity of personality to emotional shock. A
conflict may make or break an individual.

Just what is it which differentiates between two lives
of similar asocial behavior or suffering affectional
wounds, one becoming disorganized, the other attain-
ing higher levels of mental and social integration?
Certain psychanalytic biographies show struggles of
eminent men and women who passed through periods
of mental strain or moral failure, yet rose superior to
and even strengthened by their wrestling with life.
Our revered Abraham Lincoln not only kept bride
and guests waiting on the first date set for his wedding,

but disappeared from family and friends for three days. Imagine the frenzy of the modern press over such an event.

Psychiatrists are interpreting to nervous patients symptoms of strain and sorrow, assisting them to assimilate such emotional experience and to regain poise. It is possible to minimize sexual blunder as unfortunate but not irreparable. One recovers from disease, from disappointment. One lie told may bring from the parent an explanation of the importance of truth and be a milestone on the upward path. Such lesson, however, should never be based on condemnation but must be linked with idealism. A wise physician said, "Nature tends toward meliorism." This accounts for the success of girls who pull themselves up without aid.

That nature has brought us up from the amœba to man should give us confidence in Life Force. Life is not so simple as to have one "definition of the situation" solve the whole problem. This will take further trial and error. The scientific mind observes, differentiates, finds contrasts and resemblances. Bits of inorganic elements may be identical, but in the study of living organisms the higher the type the greater the possibility of variation, till in man no two are identical in finger print, still less so in emotional reaction. Even when a new period of socialization shall have simplified life, each individual must still be considered separately, each personality approached with utmost reverence, accepted for values and possibilities which when developed displace asocial behavior. The problems of sexual disharmony, retarded emotion, affectional distress, which send people of wealth to the sanitarium or divorce court, lead the poor to delinquency. The future court of domestic relations may become a clinic for all.

On the whole this period of individualization is more fortunate for women than otherwise. Their struggle for independence is winning higher standards of affectional association in friendships with both sexes, higher psychic and social levels of group coöperation. Though one deplores the necessity of divorce one watches its increase with the feeling that consecutive marriages are an advance upon simultaneous promiscuity. From marriage based upon possession there is evolving a fine comradeship in which psychic fertilization becomes ever more significant as is seen in the collaboration of man and woman in art, science, literature and social service. While marriage within the law may attain the highest level of human mating known today, and social sanction is necessary for right environment for children, it is not law which achieves this result but the ever evolving adjustments of fine personality shown by men and women in whom emotion and intellect and will have matured harmoniously and in whose lives sublimation begun in childhood has given stability.

Sex has always baffled humanity. Alternately it has been considered sacred and sinful, attached to temple worship or cast beyond the pale. In this day of scientific synthesis we are solving some at least of the fundamentals of this Welträtsel.

This present research of William I. Thomas with his trenchant sociological analysis is a distinct contribution not only to the study of delinquency but to educational and industrial problems. As his conclusions point toward the practice of the most advanced experimental schools and also conform to the theories of certain leading psychiatrists, this triple concurrence of opinion indicates approach to scientific truth. Mr.

Thomas's interpretation of today's unrest as a "period of individualization following and preceding periods of socialization" emphasizes our present opportunity to reorganize the administration of justice. Let such reorganization be based upon that emergent truth which Dean Pound has called "the most important change of the century, — the transference of the sense of value from property to humanity."

ETHEL S. DUMMER

CONTENTS

THE UNADJUSTED GIRL

CHAPTER I

THE WISHES

It is impossible to understand completely any human being or any single act of his behavior, just as it is impossible to understand completely why a particular wild rose bloomed under a particular hedge at a particular moment. A complete understanding in either case would imply an understanding of all cosmic processes, of their interrelations and sequences. But it is not harder to comprehend the behavior of the "unadjusted" or "delinquent" person, say the vagabond or the prostitute, than that of the normally adjusted person, say the business man or the housewife.

In either case we realize that certain influences have been at work throughout life and that these are partly inborn, representing the original nature of man, the so-called instincts, and partly the claims, appeals, rewards, and punishments of society, — the influences of his social environment. But if we attempt to determine why the call of the wild prevails in the one case and the call of home, regular work, and "duty" in the other, we do not have different problems but aspects of the same general problem. It is only as we understand behavior as a whole that we can appreciate the failure of certain individuals to conform to the usual standards. And similarly, the unrest and maladjustment of the girl can be treated only as specifications of the general unrest and maladjustment.

In this connection students of psychology and education have been particularly interested in determining what the inborn tendencies really are. There was however no scientifically controlled work on the point until Watson undertook his experiments on newborn babies. At the time his work was interrupted he had found only three "instincts" present in the child at birth:

We are inclined now to believe that the fundamental emotional reactions can be grouped under three general divisions: those connected with fear; those connected with rage; those connected with what, for lack of a better term, we may call joy or love. These at least deserve the name of major emotions. Whether or not other types of emotional reactions are present we cannot yet determine. . . . The principal situations which call out fear responses are as follows: (1) To suddenly remove from the infant all means of support, as when one drops it from the hand to be caught by an assistant. . . . (2) By loud sounds. (3) Occasionally when an infant is just falling asleep the sudden pulling of the blanket upon which it is lying will produce the fear response. (4) Finally, again, when the child has just fallen asleep or is just ready to awake a sudden push or a slight shake is an adequate stimulus. The responses are a sudden catching of the breath, clutching randomly with the hands (the grasping reflex invariably appearing when the child is dropped), blinking of the eyelids, puckering of the lips, then crying; in older children, flight and hiding.

Observations seem to show that the hampering of the infant's movements is the factor which apart from all training brings out the movements characterized as rage. If the face or head is held, crying results, quickly followed by screaming. The body stiffens and fairly well coördinated slashing or striking movements of the hands and arms result; the feet and legs are drawn up and down; the breath is held until the child's face is flushed. In older children the slashing movements of the arms and legs are better coördinated and appear as kicking, slapping, biting, pushing, etc. These reactions continue until the irritating situation is removed, and sometimes do not cease then. Almost any child from birth can be thrown into a rage if its arms are held tightly to its sides. . . . Even the best-natured child shows rage if its nose is held for a few seconds. . . .

The original stimuli for bringing out the earliest manifestations of joy or love seem to be as follows: gentle stroking and soft tickling of the infant's body, patting, gentle rocking, turning upon the stomach across the attendant's knee, etc. The response varies: if the infant is crying, crying ceases and a smile may appear; finally a laugh, and extension of the arms. In older children and in adults this emotion, due both to instinctive and habit factors, has an extremely wide range of expression.[1]

We understand of course that these expressions of emotion mean a preparation for action which will be useful in preserving life (anger), avoiding death (fear), and in reproducing the species (love), but even if our knowledge of the nervous system of man were complete we could not read out of it all the concrete varieties of human experience. The variety of expressions of behavior is as great as the variety of situations arising in

[1] John B. Watson: "Practical and Theoretic Problems in Instinct and Habits", in "Suggestions of Modern Science Concerning Education", by H. S. Jennings, J. B. Watson, Adolf Meyer, W. I. Thomas, p. 63.

the external world, while the nervous system represents only a general mechanism for action. We can however approach the problem of behavior through the study of the forces which impel to action, namely, the wishes, and we shall see that these correspond in general with the nervous mechanism.

The human wishes have a great variety of concrete forms but are capable of the following general classification :

1. The desire for new experience.
2. The desire for security.
3. The desire for response.
4. The desire for recognition.

1. THE DESIRE FOR NEW EXPERIENCE. Men crave excitement, and all experiences are exciting which have in them some resemblance to the pursuit, flight, capture, escape, death which characterized the earlier life of mankind. Behavior is an adaptation to environment, and the nervous system itself is a developmental adaptation. It represents, among other things, a hunting pattern of interest. "Adventure" is what the young boy wants, and stories of adventure. Hunting trips are enticing; they are the survival of natural life. All sports are of the hunting pattern; there is a contest of skill, daring, and cunning. It is impossible not to admire the nerve of a daring burglar or highwayman. A fight, even a dog fight, will draw a crowd. In gambling or dice throwing you have the thrill of success or the chagrin of defeat. The organism craves stimulation and seeks expansion and shock even through alcohol and drugs. "Sensations" occupy a large part of the space in newspapers. Courtship has in it an element of "pursuit." Novels, theaters, motion pic-

tures, etc., are partly an adaptation to this desire, and their popularity is a sign of its elemental force.

1. When 11 years old Walter McDermott was brought to court in company with three other boys, accused of breaking a padlock on a grocery store and attempting to enter the store at four o'clock A.M., March 3, 1909, and also of breaking a padlock on the door of a meat-market and stealing thirty-six cents from the cash till. Put on probation. August 19, 1910, brought to court for entering with two other boys a store and stealing a pocket-book containing $3.00. He admitted to the officers he and his company were going to pick pockets down town. He is the leader of the gang. . . .

Sent to St. Charles. Ran away March 17, 1913. By breaking a window got into a drug store, with two other boys, and stole a quantity of cigars and $1.61. Having taken the money, he gave one boy ten cents and another five cents. He gave away the cigars — eight or nine boxes — to "a lot of men and some boys." Spent the money "on candy and stuff." Committed to John Worthy School . . . October 27. His conduct has improved greatly; released on probation . . .

December 23, 1913, accused of having broken, with an adult boy (19), into a clothing store and filled a suit case they found in the store with clothing and jewelry. Caught in shop. The officer said, "He would like to imitate Webb. He would like to kill some boy." According to his own confession, "It was six o'clock at night. I was going to confession. I met a boy and he said, 'Come out with me.' About nine o'clock we came to a clothing store, and we walked to the back, and seen a little hole. We pulled a couple of the laths off and as soon as we got in we got caught." But the officer said that previous to this they had burglarized a butcher's store and took from there a butcher's steel, and bored a hole in the wall with it. Committed to John Worthy School. Released June 26th, 1914. . . .

July 19, shot in a back alley twice at a little boy and once hit him. Broke with two other boys at night into Salvation

Army office, broke everything he could and "used the office as a toilet room." Next day broke into a saloon, broke the piano, took cigars. Before this, July 14th, broke a side window of a saloon, stole $4.00 and a revolver. At the hearing Walter said about shooting the boy : "That boy was passing and I asked him for a match, and I heard this boy holler. I took a revolver off (his companion) and fixed a shot and hit the boy." His mother testified that he had spent only three nights at home since the time of his release from John Worthy School. He was arrested after the first offense, but escaped from the detention home. Committed to John Worthy School. . . .

Released after March 26. Committed a burglary in a grocery store, April 7th. Shot a man with a revolver in the left arm April 4th. Held up, with three other boys, a man on April 11, and robbed him of $12.00. Caught later, while the other boys caught at once. Held to the grand jury, found "not guilty" and released June 16, 1915.[1]

Vagabondage secures a maximum of new experience by the avoidance of the routine of organized society and the irksomeness at labor to which I will refer presently. In the constitutional vagabond the desire for new experience predominates over the other wishes and is rather contemplative and sensory, while in the criminal it is motor. But the discouraged criminal is sometimes a vagabond.

2. I have known men on the road who were tramping purely and simply because they loved to tramp. They had no appetite for liquor or tobacco, so far as I could find, also were quite out of touch with criminals and their habits; but somehow or other they could not conquer that passion for roving. In a way this type of vagabond is the most pitiful that I have ever known; and yet is the truest type of the genuine voluntary vagrant. . . . The *Wanderlust*

---

[1] Records of the Juvenile Court of Cook County (Illinois).

vagrant . . . is free from the majority of passions common among vagrants and yet he is the most earnest vagrant of all. To reform him it is necessary to kill his personality, to take away his ambition — and this is a task almost superhuman. Even when he is reformed he is a most cast-down person.[1]

3. In view of the experience at home and abroad it is now proposed in France to place vagrants in solitary confinement. These vagrants are free-footed and irregular, devoted to the highway and an open-air life, and they are far less afraid of fatigue and hardship than of a steady and regular job. Advantage must be taken of their weak point by imposing solitary confinement; they must be subjected to what they most dread.[2]

4. Dear Brother Joe: I have decided to trop you a feiw lines and hope you are well and you family also. I have heart of your troubles but could not helpet. I have left Chi. and went tru Ky. Ind. N. Y. Pa. N. Jerrsey and bak. Mich. Ohio. Ill. Wisconsin Minnesota Iway. Mo. Kansas. Nebr. Colo. and I have not done any work since I left. I am hapy on the road and it is very fine, I feel like I never will work again onless I have seen all U. S. I am on my way to Californ but I take my time. I ant in horry, you have been traveling, but you have not seen anything yet and you have no experience about Ho Bo life a tall. gee it is fine to be on the Road. It is 10 weeks since I have no home but a Box Car. If you go on the Road again look for my Monogram in the Cars. I will not work very much this Sumer only to bull tru the Coast. It is blenty of work around here, but I dond feel like working yet. I wisht you vas not mareyt and could be with me. I bet you would engoeyet. I hav enofh to eet and a diferent place to sleep every night and feel healty.[3]

[1] Josiah Flynt: "How Men Become Tramps", *Century Magazine*, Vol. 50, p. 944 (October, 1895).

[2] R. Saleilles: "The Individualization of Punishment", p. 283.

[3] Letter from "Railroad Jack" (Manuscript).

5. Girl states that she has been a tramp since she was 15 years old, going from one place to another, usually on freight trains, part of the time dressed as a boy. . . . She has a child, two years old, which she had illegitimately. The Court had compelled the father of it to marry her. This statement was verified at this office on its communication with the Probate Judge at Moundsville, W. Va.

She says that both her parents died when she was a little girl, that she lived with her grandmother, who worked out for her living, leaving her to run the streets. She says that from earliest childhood she has had the wanderlust. She spoke of being as far west as Denver, and mentioned several army camps she had visited, always riding freight trains. Says that she never works except long enough to get what she can't beg. She says that she has no love for her child and that her grandmother takes care of it with money supplied by her husband. Her husband secured a divorce from her about three months after their marriage. The reason she asked to stay at the Detention Home over night was because she was going past the house in the alley and saw through the open door several young girls and thought it would be a nice place to stay all night.

Case was reported to office immediately after her admittance to the Detention Home. The next morning immediately after breakfast, while the Matron's back was turned, the girl escaped. The case was immediately reported to the Military and local police. The girl was picked up near camp, having had intercourse with several soldiers. Her appearance was the least attractive of any girl handled by this office. The little bundle of clothes she carried, tied in a bandanna handkerchief, was the dirtiest ever seen, and was burned at the Detention Home. At police headquarters she gave her age as 20 years but later told that she was but 17, which was verified from Moundsville. She was given $10.00 and thirty days and costs in the county jail, and while being taken from the jail to the clinic, by a policeman and Miss Ball, she, with another girl, escaped. Every effort was made to catch her, but she was as fleet as a deer. [1]

There is also in the hunting pattern of interest an intellectual element. Watson does not note curiosity among the instincts because it does not manifest itself at birth, but it appears later as the watchful and exploratory attitude which determines the character of action, — whether, for example, it shall be attack or flight. The invention of the bow and arrow, the construction of a trap, the preparation of poison, indicated a scientific curiosity in early man. Activities of this kind were interesting because they implied life or death. The man who constructed the poisoned arrow visualized the scene in which it was to be used, saw the hunt in anticipation. The preparation for the chase was psychologically part of the chase. The modern scientific man uses the same mental mechanism but with a different application. He spends long months in his laboratory on an invention in anticipation of his final "achievement." The so-called "instinct for workmanship" and the "creative impulse" are "sublimations" of the hunting psychosis. The making of a trap was a "problem", and any problem is interesting, whether the construction of a wireless or the solving of a puzzle. Modern occupations or "pursuits" are interesting or irksome to the degree that they have or have not a problematical element:

The convict makes bricks, digs the earth, builds, and all his occupations have a meaning and an end. Sometimes, even the prisoner takes an interest in what he is doing. He then wishes to work more skillfully, more advantageously. But let him be constrained to pour water from one vessel into another, or to transport a quantity of earth from one

[1] Records of the Girls' Protective Bureau (Manuscript).

place to another in order to perform the contrary operation
immediately afterwards, then I am persuaded that at the
end of a few days the prisoner would strangle himself or
commit a thousand crimes, punishable with death, rather than
live in such an abject condition and endure such torments. [1]

The following description of a scientific adventure
of a creative man, which I transcribe from an earlier
paper, illustrates perfectly the psychological identity
of a scientific quest with the pursuit of game :

6. Pasteur's first scientific success was in the study of
crystallization, and in this connection he became particularly interested in racemic acid. But this substance, produced first by Kestner in 1820 as an accident in the manufacture of tartaric acid, had in 1852 ceased to appear, in
spite of all efforts to obtain it. Pasteur and his friend
Mitscherlich suspected that the failure to get it was due to
the fact that the present manufacturers of tartaric acid were
using a different tartar. The problem became then to in-
spect all the factories producing tartaric acid and finally
to visit the sources from which the tartars came. This was
the quest, and the impatience which Pasteur showed to
begin it reminds us of a hound tugging at the leash. He
asked Biot and Dumas to obtain for him a commission from
the Ministry, or the Académie, but exasperated by the delay
he was on the point of writing directly to the President
of the Republic. "It is," he said, "a question that France
should make it a point of honor to solve through one of her
children." Biot counselled patience and pointed out that
it was not necessary to "set the government in motion for
this." But Pasteur would not wait. "I shall go to the end
of the world," he said. "I *must* discover the source of racemic acid," and started independently. I will excuse you
from following this quest in detail, but in a sort of diary
prepared for Mme. Pasteur he showed the greatest eagerness

[1] F. Dostoievsky : "The House of the Dead ", p. 25.

to have her share the joy of it. He went to Germany, to Vienna, to Prague, studied Hungarian tartars. "Finally," he said, "I shall go to Trieste, where I shall find tartars of various countries, notably those of the Levant, and those of the neighborhood of Trieste itself. . . . If I had money enough I would go to Italy; . . . I shall give ten years to it if necessary." And after eight months he sent the following telegram: ".I transform tartaric acid into racemic acid. Please inform MM. Dumas and Senarmont." He had made his kill.[1]

The craftsman, the artist, the scientist, the professional man, and to some extent the business man make new experience the basis of organized activity, of work, and produce thereby social values. The division of labor which removes the problematical from the various operations of the work makes the task totally unstimulating. The repudiation of work leads to the vagabondage just illustrated and to the antisocial attitudes described below:

7. We have in New York at present, and have had for some years past, an immense army of young men, boys between fifteen and twenty-six, who are absolutely determined that under no conditions will they do any honest work. They sponge on women, swindle, pick pockets, commit burglary, act as highwaymen, and, if cornered, kill, in order to get money dishonestly. How do they dispose of the vast sums they have already stolen? Gambling and women. They are inveterate gamblers.[2]

And similarly, among women we have the thief, the prostitute, the blackmailer, the vamp, and the "charity girl."

[1] "Primary-Group Norms in Present-Day Society", in "Suggestions of Modern Science Concerning Education", p. 162.

[2] Chief City Magistrate William McAdoo, in *New York World*, December 18, 1920.

2. THE DESIRE FOR SECURITY. The desire for security is opposed to the desire for new experience. The desire for new experience is, as we have seen, emotionally related to anger, which tends to invite death, and expresses itself in courage, advance, attack, pursuit. The desire for new experience implies, therefore, motion, change, danger, instability, social irresponsibility. The individual dominated by it shows a tendency to disregard prevailing standards and group interests. He may be a social failure on account of his instability, or a social success if he converts his experiences into social values, — puts them into the form of a poem, makes of them a contribution to science. The desire for security, on the other hand, is based on fear, which tends to avoid death and expresses itself in timidity, avoidance, and flight. The individual dominated by it is cautious, conservative, and apprehensive, tending also to regular habits, systematic work, and the accumulation of property.

The social types known as "bohemian" and "philistine" are determined respectively by the domination of the desire for new experience and the desire for security. The miser represents a case where the means of security has become an end in itself.

8. Mamie Reilly's mother viewed with increasing regret the effect of premature care and responsibility on her daughter. Mamie had been working five years since, as a child of thirteen, she first insisted on getting a job. "She's a good girl, Mame is, but y' never seen anything like her. Every pay night reg'lar she'll come in an' sit down at that table. 'Now Ma,' she'll say like that, 'what *are* you goin' to do? How ever are y' goin' t' make out in th' rent?' 'Land sakes,' I'll say, 'one w'd think this whole house was right there on your

shoulders. I'll get along somehow.' But y' can't make her
see into that. 'Now, what'll we do, how'll you manage, Ma?'
she'll keep askin'. She's too worrisome — that's what I tell
her. An' she don't care to go out. Mebbe she'll take a
walk, but like's not she'll say, 'What's th' use?' Night
after night she jest comes home, eats 'er supper, sits down,
mebbe reads a bit, an' then goes t' bed." [1]

Document 9 shows the desire for security in a person
who is temperamentally inclined to new experience, but
whose hardships call out the desire for security. The
whole life, in fact, of this man shows a wavering between the two wishes. The desire for a "secure existence" which he expresses here finally prevails and he
approaches the philistine type:

9. I had been ten weeks on the journey without finding
any work, and I had no idea how long I should still be obliged
to tramp about the world, and where was the end toward
which I was going. . . . I should have been very glad of
my visit to Stach had it not been for the thought of my wandering. If I had been going immediately to work from
Mokrsko I should certainly have fallen in love with some girl,
but the thought that I must tramp again about the world
destroyed my wish for anything. Moreover I wanted to
leave as soon as possible, for I could not look with dry eyes
on how he wallowed in everything and had whatever he
wanted. Everybody respected and appreciated him; every-
where doors were open for him, and he prized lightly everything he had, for he had never experienced any evil or misery.
For if I had only one half of what he owned, how grateful I
should be to God for his goodness. And tears flowed from
my eyes when I compared his lot with mine. Fortune, how
unjust you are! You drive one man about the world and
you have no pity on him though he is whipped with wind
and snow and cold stops his breath. People treat him worse

[1] Ruth True: "The Neglected Girl", p. 50.

than a dog and drive him away from their doors, without asking: "Have you eaten? have you a place to sleep?" And when he asks for anything they are ready to beat him, like that peasant who struck me with the whip. And what for? Perhaps this mayor would have acted likewise if he had met me somewhere on my journey, and today he sets tables for this same tramp.

What a difference between us! Why, we have the same parents, the same name! And perhaps he is better considered because he is better instructed than I? In my opinion, not even for that. Or perhaps because he is nobler and handsomer? No, not for that. He merits consideration only because he has a secure existence, because he has bread. Let him wander into an unknown country; would he be better considered than I? No, a thousand times No. So if I want to merit consideration and respect, I ought first to win this [secure] existence. And how shall I win it and where? Shall I find it in tramping about the world? No, I must work, put money together and establish my own bakery. Then I can say boldly that I have [a secure existence] and even a better one than a teacher.[1]

In case 10 the desire for security is very strong but is overwhelmed by the desire for new (sexual) experience of the type which I shall term presently the "desire for response."

10. I am a young woman of twenty-five, married seven years. I have a good husband and two dear children; also a fine home. I was quite happy until an unexpected misfortune entered my life, destroying my happiness.

I consider it important to state that as a child I conducted myself decently; people regarded me as a blessing and my parents were very proud of me. As a young girl I strove to marry some good young man and live contentedly.

[1] W. I. Thomas and Florian Znaniecki; "The Polish Peasant in Europe and America", in "Life Record of an Immigrant", Vol. 3, pp. 246 and 251.

I had no higher ambition. My dream was realized but unfortunately this did not last long.

Three years ago, my husband's cousin, a young man, came to us. He obtained employment in our town and lived with us. He stayed with us four months altogether. During the first three months he was not in my thoughts at all . . . but during the last month my heart began to beat for him. It was a novel sensation for me and I did not know the meaning of this attraction; I said to myself: I love my husband and my children, why then this strange fascination for my husband's cousin? He surely must have done something to me to arouse this feeling in me, I thought. Fortunately, the young man soon lost his position and left for some distant place. I felt very happy at his departure, though I longed for him very much.

Two years passed thus, during which I resumed my former contented life with my husband until one day my husband informed me that his cousin had returned and planned to live in our town. I had a presentiment of dark clouds that would soon gather over my head, so I requested my husband to find other quarters than our own for his relative, on the pretext that I was not well enough to care for another person in the family. But as my husband reproached me and charged me with lack of interest in his relatives, I had to yield and give my permission for the man to stay with us.

I had decided to be indifferent and act as a stranger toward the boarder that was thrust upon me, so as to avoid trouble. I did not wish to ignite the feeling in my heart toward him by too close contact. I almost never spoke to him, and never came near him. God only knows how much these efforts cost me, but with all my energy I fought against the diabolic feeling in my heart. Unfortunately, my husband misinterpreted my behavior as a lack of hospitality. His resentment compelled me to assume a more friendly attitude toward his relative, as I wished to avoid quarrelling. What followed may easily be inferred. From amiability I passed to love until he occupied my whole mind and everybody else was non-existent for me. Of course no one was aware of my predicament.

One day I decided to put an end to my sufferings by confessing all to my boarder and requesting him to go away or at least leave our house and avert a scandal. Unfortunately, my hope of a peaceful life was not fulfilled, following my confession to the cousin. He remained in our home and became more friendly than ever towards me. I began to love him so intensely that I hardly noticed his growing intimacy with me and as a result I gave birth to a baby whose father is my husband's cousin. . . .

I am unable to describe to you one hundredth part of the misery this has caused me. I always considered an unfaithful wife the worst creature on earth and now . . . I am myself a degraded woman. . . . The mere thought of it drives me insane. My husband, of course, knows nothing about the incident. When the child was born he wanted to name it after one of his recently deceased relatives but . . . I felt as if this would desecrate the grave of his late relative. After oceans of tears, I finally induced him to name the child after one of my own relatives.

But my troubles did not end here. Every day in the week is a day of utter anguish for me and every day I feel the tortures of hell. . . . I can not stand my husband's tenderness toward the child that is mine but not his. When he gives the baby a kiss it burns me like a hot coal dropped in my bosom. Every time he calls it his baby I hear some one shouting into my ear the familiar epithet thrown at low creatures like me . . . and every time he takes the child in his arms I am tempted to tell him the terrible truth. . . . And so I continue to suffer. When my husband is not at home I spend my time studying the face of my child, and when I think it appears to resemble its father at such a moment I become terrified at the possibility of the baby's growing up into a real likeness to its father. What would my husband say and do when he noticed the similarity between my baby and his cousin? It is this thought that is killing me. . . . [If I should tell my husband I am sure he would drive me away.] I do not care for myself so much as for the child who would be branded with the name given all such children and this would remain a stain upon him for the rest of his life. . . . It is this fear that prevents me from revealing to my husband my crime against him. But how much longer shall I be able to bear the pain and wretchedness? [1]

3. THE DESIRE FOR RESPONSE. Up to this point I have described the types of mental impressionability connected with the pursuit of food and the avoidance of death, which are closely connected with the emotions of anger and fear. The desire for response, on the other hand, is primarily related to the instinct of love, and shows itself in the tendency to seek and to give signs of appreciation in connection with other individuals.

There is first of all the devotion of the mother to the child and the response of the child, indicated in the passage from Watson above, and in the following passage from Thorndike.

All women possess originally, from early childhood to death, some interest in human babies, and a responsiveness to the instinctive looks, calls, gestures and cries of infancy and childhood, being satisfied by childish gurglings, smiles and affectionate gestures, and moved to instinctive comforting acts by childish signs of pain, grief and misery. Brutal habits may destroy, or competing habits overgrow, or the lack of exercise weaken, these tendencies, but they are none the less as original as any fact in human nature.[2]

[1] From the section entitled "A Bintel Brief" in *Forward* (a New York newspaper in the Yiddish language), April 12, 1920.
[2] E. L. Thorndike: "The Original Nature of Man", p. 81.

This relation is of course useful and necessary since the child is helpless throughout a period of years and would not live unless the mother were impelled to give it her devotion. This attitude is present in the father of the child also but is weaker, less demonstrative, and called out more gradually.

In addition, the desire for response between the two sexes in connection with mating is very powerful. An ardent courtship is full of assurances and appeals for reassurance. Marriage and a home involve response but with more settled habits, more routine work, less of new experience. Jealousy is an expression of fear that the response is directed elsewhere. The flirt is one who seeks new experience through the provocation of response from many quarters.

In some natures this wish, both to receive and to give response, is out of proportion to the other wishes, "over-determined", so to speak, and interferes with a normal organization of life. And the fixation may be either on a child or a member of either sex. The general situation is the same in the two cases following.

11. I am the unhappy mother of a dear little son, eight years old. You ask the cause of my unhappiness? I ought to be happy with such a dear treasure? But the answer is, I love my child too much. My love to my son is so great, so immeasurably deep, that I myself am worthless. My own person has not a trace of worth for me. I am as it were dead to all and everything. My thoughts by day and by night are turned toward my child. I see nothing in the world except my beloved child. Nothing exists for me except him. Every one of my thoughts, every desire and wish that awakens in me, turns around the child of my heart. I am nothing. I do not live, I do not exist. I forget myself

as I forget all and everything in the world. I go around the whole day without eating and feel no hunger. I forget that I must eat. I go around often a whole day in my night-clothes because I forget that I have to dress. With soul and body, with mind and spirit I am wrapt up in my child. I have no thought for myself at all.

If clothes come to my mind, I am thinking of a new suit for my boy. I am nothing. And if I think of shoes, I imagine a pair of little shoes on the feet of my dear little boy. I myself am the same as dead. If I go to the country in the summer, I come home on account of my child. I myself do not exist. Every enjoyment in life, every happiness to which I give a thought is connected in my mind with my little boy. I myself am as if I were never at all in the world. The child is everything — my soul and my spirit, my breath and my life. He is the air I breathe. I am nothing. I don't consider myself, I don't think of myself, just as if I had never been in the world.

And so it is when my child is not well, when he has perhaps scratched his finger. . . . Oh, how I suffer then. No pen in the world can describe the terrible despair I feel. I live then as it were in a cloud, I cannot at all understand how my soul then remains in my body. My pain is then indescribable, greater than any can understand. . . . When my child is well again and his round, rosy cheeks bloom like the flowers in May and he is joyous and full of life and leaps and dances, then I myself look as if I had just recovered from a fever sickness.

Tell me, I beg you, dear editor, what can such a mama do that her dear child shall not become a lonely orphan. For I feel that I cannot continue long as it is. My strength is not holding out and a time must come when no strength to live will remain in me.[1]

12. I beg you to advise me, dear editor, how to stop loving. It is perhaps a ridiculous question but for me it is a

[1] *Forward*, February 8, 1922.

very sad one. It is almost a question of life and death. It is so: I love a person who is not in a position to return my love. It is certain that we can never be united. . . . My love is hopeless but I cannot give it up. I run after the person I love, I follow his steps, knowing that it will do me no good. I have simply attached myself to an innocent person and distress him. My conscience tells me that it is not right. I suffer needlessly and I make suffering for another, but I simply have no inclination to stop.

I cannot live without my lover. When I don't see him at the expected moment I am wild, and I am ready to commit the greatest crime in order to accomplish my purpose. He runs away from me and I chase after him. When he goes away to another city I feel sure that I cannot live another twenty-four hours without him. I feel like throwing myself from a roof. I feel that I am capable of doing any evil deed on account of my love.

Do not think, dear editor, that I pride myself for having such a feeling. No, I do not compliment myself at all. I am provoked with myself, I am ashamed of myself and I hate myself. How can a person be such a rag? I argue with myself, how can I permit my mind to have no control over my heart? But my arguments with myself do me no good at all. It is work thrown away. I can love no one except him, the only one who has captured my heart and soul. I cannot even entertain the thought of ceasing to love him. It is simply impossible.

By what name would you call such a person as I am, dear editor? Perhaps I have gone out of my senses. So give me a word of advice as to how I may become sane again. I neglect everything in the world. Nothing remains in my thoughts except him. Without him everything is dark.

He is also unhappy on account of me. I don't let him breathe freely. He might have been happy with another, but I give him no chance. I disturb his life. I will add that this condition has gone on now for several years and there is no prospect of its ending.

Dear editor, give me an advice before I commit a deed after which marriage is impossible. I wait for your wise advice. Perhaps you will be my savior.[1]

The varieties of love in women are greater than in men, for we are to include here not only physical passion but parental feeling — that fund of emotion which is fixed on the child. The capacity of response to the child, mother love, is notorious and is painfully evident in document 11, p. 18, where the mother has no thought left for anything but the child. The mother is one who does not refuse. She does not refuse the breast to the lusty child even when she is herself ailing. And while this feeling is developed as a quality of motherhood it is present before motherhood and is capable of being transferred to any object calling for sympathy, — a doll, a man, or a cause. The women of the Malay Peninsula suckle little wild pigs when these are found motherless.

I have seen (through the kindness of Hutchins Hapgood) the life history of a woman who has had sexual relations with numbers of men. At the same time she has always fed men. She has kept a restaurant, partly I think to feed men. When one of her friends committed suicide she dreamed of him for months and always dreamed that she was feeding him. While she was sexually passionate her concern was mainly to satisfy the sexual hunger of others, as she satisfied their food-hunger. When two of her lovers were jealous, unhappy, and desperate, she ran from one to the other like a mother visiting two sick children in different hospitals. More than once she attempted suicide. When she tried to explain herself to me she

---

[1] *Forward*, March 8, 1922.

said that without some human relationship she felt
unbearably lonely, and that she was drawn to lonely
men without regard to their social condition. Many
of her friends were criminals and she would speak to
any bum on a park bench. She was never a prostitute.
One of her friends said, "Martha is a woman to whom
everything has happened that should logically break
a woman's character and spirit. She ought to be a
demoralized victim of society. She has done nearly
everything that is supposed to ruin and destroy a person, especially a woman, but she is not a bit destroyed.
She knows the so-called lowest things in life, but she
wants the best and feels it. She feels what is beautiful
and fine and loves it. She does things that sometimes
mean sordidness in others but not in her. She gets
drunk, but is not drunken. She is loose sexually in
her acts, but her spirit is as simple as the flowers."

A touching expression of response from a man, a
devotion to a parent as deep as mother love, is found
in a letter of the psychologist William James, written
to his father from England when the death of the
latter was anticipated.

13. My blessed old Father: I scribble this line (which
may reach you, though I should come too late) just to tell
you how full of the tenderest memories and feelings about
you my heart has for the last few days been filled.   In that
mysterious gulf of the past, into which the present will soon
fall and go back and back, yours is still for me the central
figure.   All my intellectual life I derive from you; and
though we have often seemed at odds in the expression
thereof, I'm sure there's a harmony somewhere and that our
strivings will combine.   What my debt to you is goes beyond all my power of estimating — so early, so penetrating
and so constant has been the influence.

You need be in no anxiety about your literary remains. I will see them well taken care of, and that your words shall not suffer from being concealed. At Paris I heard that Milsand, whose name you may remember is in the *Revue des Deux Mondes* and elsewhere, was an admirer of the *Secret of Swedenborg*, and Hodgson told me your last book had deeply impressed him. So will it be. . . .

As for us, we shall live on, each in his way — feeling somewhat unprotected, old as we are, for the absence of the parental bosoms as a refuge, but holding fast together in that common sacred memory. We will stand by each other and by Alice, try to transmit the torch in our offspring as you did in us, and when the time comes for being gathered in, I pray we may, if not all, some at least, be as ripe as you.

As for myself, I know what trouble I've given you at various times through my peculiarities; and as my own boys grow up I shall learn more and more of the kind of trial you had to overcome in superintending the development of a creature different from yourself, for whom you felt responsible. I say this merely to show how my sympathy with you is likely to grow much livelier, rather than to fade — and not for the sake of regrets.

As for the other side, and Mother, and our all possibly meeting, I can't say anything. More than ever at this moment do I feel that if that were true all would be solved and justified. And it comes strangely over me in bidding you good-by how a life is but a day and expresses mainly but a single note. It is so much like the act of bidding an ordinary good-night.

Good-night, my sacred old Father! If I don't see you again — farewell! a blessed farewell. Your William.[1]

Usually this feeling is not so profound, as shown in these examples, and may be just sufficient to use as a tool and a play interest. But even then the life may be

---

[1] "Letters of William James", p. 218. *The Atlantic Monthly Press.*

so schematized that it plays the main rôle.   Document
No. 14 is a single item taken from an autobiography
of over three hundred closely written pages in which
practically the only type of wish expressed is the desire for response from men, but this wish is never very
strong.

14. At Wichita I went to school till I was about sixteen.
Between ten and sixteen I had lots of little sweethearts.   I
have never been able to be happy without an atmosphere of
love or at least flirtation.   To such a degree is this true that
I fear this story will be little else than the record of my loves
and flirtations, happy and unhappy.   I liked to kiss little
boys from the start, but never cared to kiss the girls.   I
have had many women pals all through my life, but I never
cared to kiss them, as many girls do.   I suppose I am what
my friend the newspaper man calls a man's woman.   Certainly I am miserable unless there is a man around, and I
generally want several.   Until recently I have always been
in love with two at the same time.   But somehow since I
met Harry it is different.   My love for the other sex was
always of an innocent kind.   I loved men as the birds love
sunshine.   It is not a passion, but a necessity, like the air.
I am light-hearted and buoyant by nature, and never thought
of doing wrong.   And yet the ugly side of this passion has
always been forced upon me.[1]

In many girls the awakening of love and its fixation
on an object is slow or incomplete.   The girl in the
following example is cold as a stone toward everything
but herself.   Her affection is turned inward.   She is
the type called narcissistic, in love with herself, like
the mythical Narcissus.   Probably the appearance
of a child will extrovert her feeling to some extent.

---

[1] Hutchins Hapgood : "The Marionette" (Manuscript).

15. I have a sister of sixteen, very beautiful and proud of herself. She is of the type who care only for themselves. She would drown her parents, brothers and sisters in a spoon of water if she could only gain something by it, and without suffering the slightest remorse. Besides, she is very obstinate and must have her own way regardless of anything. . . . But my father and mother and the rest of the family wished her to possess the ordinary school education, so that her ignorance might not be an impediment in her future life, so we put our efforts together and sent her to business school, and thank God she managed somehow to finish the course.

Well, she is now working for the past six months. She has a very good position with a large firm and earns $20 a week. Out of this, mother does not get even a cent, though she sleeps and boards at home. Moreover, she borrows money from mother whenever she can but she never repays it. As if this were not enough trouble, she acts very improperly toward the whole family. She possesses absolutely no sense of shame nor sense of pity and behaves like a wild person in the house; she scolds and shouts and is especially cruel to our younger sisters and brothers.[1]

And in certain characters, almost invariably men, the desire for response is barely sufficient to keep them in contact with or on the fringe of humanity.

16. Many a man leads in London a most solitary, unsociable life, who yet would find it hard to live far away from the thronged city. Such men are like Mr. Galton's oxen, unsociable but gregarious; and they illustrate the fact that sociability, although it has the gregarious instinct at its foundation, is a more complex, more highly developed, tendency. As an element of this more complex tendency to sociability, the instinct largely determines the form of the recreations of even the cultured classes, and is the root of

[1] *Forward*, December 17, 1920.

no small part of the pleasure we find in attendance at the
theatre, at concerts, lectures, and all such entertainments.[1]

Frequently in marriage the wife provides the main
fund of response and the husband is assimilated to the
child.   In No. 17 the wife has had a love adventure,
is living with another man, but is planning to visit
her husband clandestinely and look after him a bit.

17. My Own Dear Dean: So you would like to know if
I am happy.   Well, dear, that is one thing that will never be
in my life again.   It has gone from me forever.   I don't
want you to think that Clarence is not good to me, for he
could not be better — I have a nice home that he has bought,
and chickens and a lovely garden, and if Marjorie was his
very own he could not be better to her.   But he is terribly
jealous, and it makes it very hard for me, for, God knows, I
never give him cause.   Oh, Dean, dear, wait until you see
how I have changed.   If I could only live my life over it
would be so different. . . .
Now, dear, please don't feel that you have no interest in
life, for you have our dear little girl, and just as soon as she
is big enough to be a comfort to you — well, she is yours.
Dean, if you only knew how badly I want to see you.
Now, listen — Clarence leaves here August 31 for Vancouver
and will be there until September 6. . . .   So, if you could
send me my fare one way, why, then he could not refuse to
let me go. . . .   Let me know what you are planning, for
I want to see you and cook you some good old meals again.
. . .   Yours only, Patsy.[2]

In No. 18 a conventional woman permits herself to
have a single new experience in the field of response, as
compensation for a married relation which lacks everything but security, and then returns to her security.

---

[1] E. L. Thorndike: "The Original Nature of Man", p. 87.
[2] *Chicago American*, May 13, 1915.

18. American woman, forty-five years old, married. Husband is a prosperous real estate broker, a member of many clubs, a church warden, director of several corporations, a typical business man of the type termed "successful", a good citizen "without one redeeming vice."

She is a beautiful woman, albeit tired and faded. Her hair is prematurely white, her youthful face with deep-set brown eyes has a wistful contradictory appearance. Has many sides to her nature, can play ball with her boys as well as she can preside at a meeting. Is a good companion, has many friends, and leads a busy life as head of a prosperous household. Has five children, four boys and one girl. One would not guess that she is an unsatisfied woman; her friends all think her life ideal and, in a sense, she does not deny it. This in substance is her view of married life though not literally word for word:

"I suppose there can never be a school for marriage — how could there be? — yet how sad it is that every one must begin at the same place to work out the same problem. I had a good father and mother. They did not understand me but that was probably more my fault than theirs; I never confided in my mother overmuch. My father considered my mental progress at all times and I owe him much for the manner in which he made me think for myself, strengthened my views, and guided my education. When I left finishing school I played in society for two years and many of the men I met interested me, though none compelled me. I had never been given any clear conception of what marriage should be in the ideal sense. I knew vaguely that the man I married must be in my own class, good and honorable, and rich enough to maintain a dignified household. I had more of a vision of love at sixteen than at twenty-six, the year I married, though I was sure I loved my husband and I do — that is he is as much a part of my life as my religion or my household conventions. He is wholly a product of civilization and I discovered too late there is an element of the savage in most women. They wish to be captured, possessed — not in the sense the ^suffragists talk about; it is really a sense of self-abasement, for it is the adoration of an ideal. They wish to love a man in the open — a fighter, a victor — rather than the men we know who have their hearts in money making and play at being men. Perhaps it cannot be remedied, it is only a bit of wildness that will never be tamed in women but it makes for unhappiness just the same.

"My sex life had never been dominant. I had a commonplace adolescence with physical longings and sensations which were not explained to me and which did me no harm. My relation with my husband was perfectly orthodox, and vaguely I longed for something different. My husband was shocked at any demonstration on my part. If I was impulsive and threw myself in his arms he straightened his tie before he kissed me. Once at our cottage in the mountains I suggested that we spend the night in the woods. I saw a possibility of our getting nearer each other physically and spiritually if we could get out in the wilderness away from the restraints and niceties of our luxurious household. That was the first time I ever felt like a traitor. He told me quite sternly to go to bed, I was not a wild Indian and could not act like one. I went to the nursery for the night and snuggled close to my little boy and was glad he was young and slender and hoped he would never grow fat and complacent. I had noticed for the first time that my husband was growing stout, like any other church-warden.

"Since that time I have never been wholly happy. It was not the foolish incident, it was the fundamental principle, and underlying our civilization. Our babies came rather closely together and I was glad that the mother element in me needed to be uppermost. My husband was perfectly content with life, I satisfied him at dinner parties, I could dress well and talk well, managed the household money to advantage and was at hand — tame, quite tame, when he wished to kiss me. I do not mean to sound sarcastic and bitter. It is not what my husband is which troubles me, but what he is not; I think I speak for many women. I am more mated to the vision of what my children's father might have been than to the good kind man whom I teach them to love and respect.

"Perhaps you have guessed I am coming to a confession: I met the man in England two summers ago, but he is an American and is in this country now, a friend of ours whom we both see quite often. Something in both of us flared the very night we met. He and Lawrence (my husband) get along famously; they both believe in many of the same ideals and discuss kindred subjects, but my brain and his supplement each other in a way which is hard to explain. I did not mean to love him. It is an upper strata of myself; I love Lawrence; I mean I belong to him, am part of his very being and he of mine, but I am myself when I am with this other man and I refuse to think what a different self it might have been had I known him before. The very morning after I faced the awful fact that I was thinking of a man other than my husband, Lawrence put a bouquet at my plate at the breakfast table. It was a red geranium, a tiny pink rose, and some leaves of striped grass. Poor Lawrence.

Our adventure in love came rapidly. He understood me perfectly and I knew that he cared. We have never told Lawrence for we do not intend to do anything more that is wrong. He has spent several evenings at the house when Lawrence was away. There was no deception about this — it just happened and we have talked and kissed and faced life in the open. We decided quite calmly, and without passion, that we would have each other entirely just once. I wanted the complete vision of what my love could mean. If it is wrong I cannot think so; at any rate I would not give up the memory of that time. It was only once and it was a year ago. We both knew there could be no continued sex relation. When I have an opportunity I kiss him and he me. Lawrence never kisses my lips, so they belong to him. He has helped me to be more patient, and understanding of my life as it has been and must be. I have my children and must live out the life for their sakes and for Lawrence who loves me, tamed and domesticated.

"If life could be — what it would mean to give him a child, but life in its entirety cannot be — for me. Probably that is the creed of many women." [1]

It is unnecessary to particularize as to the place of response in art. The love and sex themes are based on response, and they outweigh the other themes altogether. Religion appeals to fear, fear of death and extinction, and promises everlasting security, or threatens everlasting pain, but in the New Testament the element of response, connected with the concrete personalities of Jesus and Mary, predominates. Any hymn book will contain many versified love letters addressed to Jesus. There are on record, also many alleged conversations of nuns with Jesus which are indistinguishable in form from those of human courtship.

19. Angela da Foligno says that Christ told her he loved her better than any woman in the vale of Spoleto. The words of this passage are fatuous almost beyond belief: "Then He began to say to me the words that follow, to provoke me to love Him: 'O my sweet daughter! O my daughter, my temple! O my daughter, my delight! Love me, because thou art much loved by me.' And often did He say to me: 'O my daughter, My sweet Spouse!' And he added in an underbreath, 'I love thee more than any other woman in the valley of Spoleto.'" To amuse and to delight Gertrude of Eisleben, He sang duets with her "in a tender and harmonious voice." The same saint writes of their "incredible intimacy"; and here, as in later passages of Angela da Foligno, the reader is revolted by their sensuality.

[1] Edith L. Smith, in collaboration with Hugh Cabot: "A Study in Sexual Morality", *Social Hygiene*, Vol. 2, p. 532.

. . . In the diary of Marie de l'Incarnation there is such an entry as "*entretien familier avec J.-C.*"; and during such interviews she makes use of a sort of pious baby talk, like a saintly Tillie Slowboy.[1]

In general the desire for response is the most social of the wishes. It contains both a sexual and a gregarious element. It makes selfish claims, but on the other hand it is the main source of altruism. The devotion to child and family and devotion to causes, principles, and ideals may be the same attitute in different fields of application. It is true that devotion and self-sacrifice may originate from any of the other wishes also — desire for new experience, recognition, or security — or may be connected with all of them at once. Pasteur's devotion to science seems to be mainly the desire for new experience, — scientific curiosity; the campaigns of a Napoleon represent recognition (ambition) and the self-sacrifice of such characters as Maria Spiridonova, Florence Nightingale, Jane Addams is a sublimation of response. The women who demanded Juvenile Courts were stirred by the same feeling as the mother in document No. 11, whereas the usual legal procedure is based on the wish to have security for life and property.

4. THE DESIRE FOR RECOGNITION. This wish is expressed in the general struggle of men for position in their social group, in devices for securing a recognized, enviable, and advantageous social status. Among girls dress is now perhaps the favorite means of securing distinction and showing class. A Bohemian immigrant girl expressed her philosophy in a word: "After all, life is mostly what you wear." Veblen's volume,

[1] Burr: "Religious Confession and Confessants", p. 356.

"Theory of the Leisure Class", points out that the status of men is established partly through the show of wealth made by their wives. Distinction is sought also in connection with skillful and hazardous activities, as in sports, war, and exploration. Playwriters and sculptors consciously strive for public favor and "fame." In the "achievement" of Pasteur (case 6) and of similar scientific work there is not only the pleasure of the "pursuit" itself, but the pleasure of public recognition. Boasting, bullying, cruelty, tyranny, "the will to power" have in them a sadistic element allied to the emotion of anger and are efforts to compel a recognition of the personality. The frailty of women, their illness, and even feigned illness, is often used as a power-device, as well as a device to provoke response. On the other hand, humility, self-sacrifice, saintliness, and martyrdom may lead to distinction. The showy motives connected with the appeal for recognition we define as "vanity"; the creative activities we call "ambition."

The importance of recognition and status for the individual and for society is very great. The individual not only wants them but he needs them for the development of his personality. The lack of them and the fear of never obtaining them are probably the main source of those psychopathic disturbances which the Freudians treat as sexual in origin.

On the other hand society alone is able to confer status on the individual and in seeking to obtain it he makes himself responsible to society and is forced to regulate the expression of his wishes. His dependence on public opinion is perhaps the strongest factor impelling him to conform to the highest demands which society makes upon him.

20. The chief difference between the down-and-out man
and the down-and-out girl is this. The d.-a.-o. man sleeps
on a park bench and looks like a bum. The d.-a.-o. girl
sleeps in an unpaid-for furnished room and looks very respectable. The man spends what little change he has — if
he has any — for food and sleeps on a bench. The girl spends
what little change she has — if she has any — for a room
and goes without food.

Not because she has more pride than the man has. She
hasn't. But because cops haul in girls who would sleep on
benches, and well-meaning organizations "rescue" girls who
look down and out. A pretty face and worn-out soles are a
signal for those who would save girls from the perilous path,
whereas an anæmic face in a stylish coat and a pair of pol-
ished French heels can go far unmolested. . . .

You will argue that any woman with an empty stomach
and a fur coat ought to sell the coat for a shabby one and
spend the money for food. That is because you have never
been a lady bum. A fur coat gets her places that a full
stomach never would. It is her entrée into hotel washrooms
when she is dirty from job hunting. It gets her into depart-
ment-store rest rooms when she is sore of foot. And in the
last stages it gets her help from a certain class of people who
would be glad to help her if she had suddenly lost her purse,
but who never would if she had never had a purse.

And then, most important of all, it helps her to hang on
to her last scraps of self-respect.[1]

21. Alice . . . wants to be somebody, to do great things,
to be superior. In her good moods, she is overwhelmed
with dreams of accomplishment. She pines to use good
English, to be a real lady. There is pathos in her inquiry as
to what you say when a boy introduces you to his mother
and how to behave in a stylish hotel dining room. Such
questions have an importance that is almost greater than

[1] "The Lady Bum", by One of Them. *New York Times, Book Review
and Magazine*, January 1, 1922.

the problem of how to keep straight sexually. Winning of social approval is an ever-present, burning desire, but she has no patterns, no habits, no control over the daily details of the process whereby this is gained. When one tries to place her in a good environment with girls of a better class, she reacts with a deepened sense of inferiority, expressed in more open, boastful wildness. She invents adventures with men to dazzle these virtuous, superior maidens. The craving for pleasures and something to make her forget increases.[1]

22. One of the most tragic lives we have ever known — now ended, and perhaps happily, with the death of the girl at twenty years of age — was that ensuing from unusually mixed parentage. An intelligent, English-speaking Chinaman married an American woman of no mean ability. One of their children was a girl, who developed splendidly both physically and mentally. She was an exceptionally bright girl, who at fourteen had already commenced a delinquent career which only ended with her death. . . . The fact that she was different, so obviously different, from other girls attending the public and private schools to which she went, and that there were many little whisperings about her, served greatly to accentuate her inner distress. Her capabilities and ambitions were great, but how was she to satisfy them? As a matter of fact, neither the mother nor I could ever find out that any great social discomforts came to this girl; the struggle was all within. She behaved most extravagantly as a direct reaction to her own feelings, of the depth of which she had rarely given any intimation at home. With us she essayed to remember and to reveal all that had gone on in her mind for years back: How could her mother have married this man? Was she really this woman's child? To what could she attain with this sort of stigma upon her? Did she not properly belong to a free-living stratum of society?

[1] Jessie Taft: "Mental Hygiene Problems of Normal Adolescence", *Mental Hygiene*, Vol. 5, p. 746.

This girl wandered and wavered. She tried religion, and she tried running away from home and living with other people; she assumed a Japanese alias and tried to make a new circle of acquaintances for herself.[1]

In many cases, both in boys and girls, particularly at the period of adolescence, the energy takes the form of daydreaming, that is, planning activity, and also of "pathological lying", or pretended activity. The wishes are thus realized in an artistic schematization in which the dreamer is the chief actor. The following, from the diary of a sixteen-year-old girl is in form a consistent expression of the desire for recognition, but very probably the form disguises a sexual longing, and the daydream is thus an example of the sublimation of the desire for response, as frequently in poetry and literature.

23. I am between heaven and earth. I float, as it were, on a dream-cloud which carries me up at times into a glorious atmosphere, and again nearer the mucky earth, but always on, always on. I see not man, I see not the children of man, the big ME lies in my head, in my hand, in my heart. I place myself upon the throne of Kings, and tramp the dusty road, care-free. I sing to myself and call me pretty names; I place myself upon the stage, and all mankind I call upon for applause, and applause roars to me as the thunder from the heavens. I reason that mine is not inevitable stage-madness which comes to all females of my pitiful age; mine is a predestined prophecy, mine is a holy design, my outcoming is a thing to be made way for.

I bathe myself in perfumed waters, and my body becomes white and slender. I clothe myself in loosened gowns, silks as soft as thistledown, and I am transported to scenes of glory. The even stretch of green, bedecked with flowers

---

[1] William Healy: "Mental Conflicts and Misconduct", p. 217.

to match the color of my pale gold gown, is mine to dance and skip upon. A lightness and a grace comes into my limbs. What joy is mine! I leap and spring and dart in rhythm with nature, and music leaps from my steps and movements and before my eyes are men. Men and women and children with heads bent forward, with eyes aglow with wonder, and with praise and love for this essence of grace and beauty which is I. What more, what more! I hang upon this idol of a dream, but it is gone. The height of happiness is reached; alas, even in dreams there is an end to happiness, the bubble bursts, and the dust and noise of earth come back to me. I shut my eyes and ears to these and seek consolation among the poor. In dreams I go often among them. With my heaping purse of gold, I give them clothes and beds to sleep upon, I give them food to nourish them and me, to nourish and refresh my fame. But do I give my gold away, and does my purse cave inwards? Ah, no! Come to my aid, my imagination, for thou art very real to me today. An endless store of gold is mine in banks of state. My name is headed on the lists of all, my money does increase even as I hand it to these poor. The poor bless me, they kneel and kiss my hands. I bid them rise, and the hypocrisy of my godless soul bids them pray and in this find restoration.

I grow weary as I walk, and truth is even harder yet to bear than ever before. I am sad, I have nothing, I am no one. But I speak soothingly to myself, bidding me treat my hungry self to food, and I promise that the night shall be long and the dreams and journeys many.[1]

On the contrary, 24 is in form a desire for response, but the details show that the girl feels keenly the lack of recognition. The response is desired not for itself alone but as a sign and assurance of comparative worth.

[1] Jessie Taft: "Mental Hygiene Problems of Normal Adolescence", *Mental Hygiene,* Vol. 5, p. 750.

24. I am in despair, and I want to pour out my bitter heart. When I have once talked out my heart I feel better afterwards.

Dear editor, why can I not find a boy to love me? I never make a hit with young people. I never have any success with them. I associate with young people, I like them, they like me, but nobody ever runs after me. No boy is crazy about me. All my girl friends are popular with young men. Every single one has a boy or more who is in love with her and follows her steps. I alone have no luck. Do not think, dear editor, that I am burning to marry; it is not yet time for that. But the thought that I am left out makes me very wretched. It distresses me and it hurts me to my soul's marrow to know that no one desires me, that people are indifferent toward me. Oh how happy I should be if somebody would love me, if somebody would come to see me. It must be such a sweet pleasure to feel that some one is interested in you, that some one comes to see you, comes to you especially, on account of yourself. Oh, why can I not have this happiness!

When I go to a party and when I come back I feel so low and so fallen. Young men crowded around my companions like flies around honey. I alone was an exception. I have not a jealous nature, but no other girl in my place would feel otherwise. Can you show me a way to win a boy's heart? What sort of quality must a girl possess in order to attract a young man?

It is true I am no beauty. But what do all the girls do? They fix themselves up. You can buy powder and paint in the drug stores. My companions are not more beautiful than I. I am not sleepy. When I am in the company of young people I am joyous, I make myself attractive, I try my best to attract attention to myself. But that is all thrown to the dogs.

Dear editor, if you only knew with how much care I make my clothes. I go through the great stores to select out the most beautiful materials. I annoy the dressmaker to death until she suits me exactly. If it happens that a hook somewhere on the dress is not in the right place, or a button-hole has a single stitch more or less than it should have, I have the greatest distress, and sharpest heartache.

When I go somewhere to a dance I am full of hopes, my heart is beating with excitement. Before leaving the house I take a last look in the mirror. When I return home I have the blues, I feel cold. My teeth grind together. So much exertion, so much strength lost, all for nothing. A boy has talked to me, another boy has given me a smile, still another boy has made me a little compliment, but I feel that I am not near and dear to any one. I feel that my face has not been stamped on the heart of any one.[1]

From the foregoing description it will be seen that wishes of the same general class — those which tend to arise from the same emotional background — may be totally different in moral quality. The moral good or evil of a wish depends on the social meaning or value of the activity which results from it. Thus the vaga-bond, the adventurer, the spendthrift, the bohemian are dominated by the desire for new experience, but so are the inventor and the scientist; adventures with women and the tendency to domesticity are both ex-pressions of the desire for response; vain ostentation and creative artistic work both are designed to provoke recognition; avarice and business enterprise are ac-tuated by the desire for security.

Moreover, when a concrete wish of any general class arises it may be accompanied and qualified by any or all of the other classes of wishes. Thus when Pasteur undertook the quest described above we do not know what wish was uppermost. Certainly the love of the work was very strong, the ardor of pursuit, the new

[1] *Forward*, September 30, 1921.

experience; the anticipation of the recognition of the public, the scientific fame involved in the achievement was surely present; he invited response from his wife and colleagues, and he possibly had the wish also to put his future professional and material life on a secure basis. The immigrant who comes to America may wish to see the new world (new experience), make a fortune (security), have a higher standing on his return (recognition), and induce a certain person to marry him (response).

The general pattern of behavior which a given individual tends to follow is the basis of our judgment of his character. Our appreciation (positive or negative) of the character of the individual is based on his display of certain wishes as against others and on his modes of seeking their realization. Whether given wishes tend to predominate in this or that person is dependent primarily on what is called temperament, and apparently this is a chemical matter, dependent on the secretions of the glandular systems. Individuals are certainly temperamentally predisposed toward certain classes of the wishes. But we know also, and I shall illustrate presently, that the expression of the wishes is profoundly influenced by the approval of the man's immediate circle and of the general public. The conversions of wild young men to stable ways, from new experience to security, through marriage, religion, and business responsibility, are examples of this. We may therefore define character as an expression of the organization of the wishes resulting from temperament and experience, understanding by "organization" the general pattern which the wishes as a whole tend to assume among themselves.

The significant point about the wishes as related

to the study of behavior is that they are the motor element, the starting point of activity. Any influences which may be brought to bear must be exercised on the wishes.

We may assume also that an individual life cannot be called normal in which all the four types of wishes are not satisfied in some measure and in some form.

CHAPTER II

THE REGULATION OF THE WISHES

ONE of the most important powers gained during the evolution of animal life is the ability to make decisions from within instead of having them imposed from without. Very low forms of life do not make decisions, as we understand this term, but are pushed and pulled by chemical substances, heat, light, etc., much as iron filings are attracted or repelled by a magnet. They do tend to behave properly in given conditions — a group of small crustaceans will flee as in a panic if a bit of strychnia is placed in the basin containing them and will rush toward a drop of beef juice like hogs crowding around swill — but they do this as an expression of organic affinity for the one substance and repugnance for the other, and not as an expression of choice or "free will." There are, so to speak, rules of behavior but these represent a sort of fortunate mechanistic adjustment of the organism to typically recurring situations, and the organism cannot change the rule.

On the other hand, the higher animals, and above all man, have the power of refusing to obey a stimulation which they followed at an earlier time. Response to the earlier stimulation may have had painful consequences and so the rule or habit in this situation is changed. We call this ability the power of inhibition, and it is dependent on the fact that the nervous system carries memories or records of past experiences.

At this point the determination of action no longer comes exclusively from outside sources but is located within the organism itself.

Preliminary to any self-determined act of behavior there is always a stage of examination and deliberation which we may call *the definition of the situation*. And actually not only concrete acts are dependent on the definition of the situation, but gradually a whole life-policy and the personality of the individual himself follow from a series of such definitions.

But the child is always born into a group of people among whom all the general types of situation which may arise have already been defined and corresponding rules of conduct developed, and where he has not the slightest chance of making his definitions and following his wishes without interference. Men have always lived together in groups. Whether mankind has a true herd instinct or whether groups are held together because this has worked out to advantage is of no importance. Certainly the wishes in general are such that they can be satisfied only in a society. But we have only to refer to the criminal code to appreciate the variety of ways in which the wishes of the individual may conflict with the wishes of society. And the criminal code takes no account of the many unsanctioned expressions of the wishes which society attempts to regulate by persuasion and gossip.

There is therefore always a rivalry between the spontaneous definitions of the situation made by the member of an organized society and the definitions which his society has provided for him. The individual tends to a hedonistic selection of activity, pleasure first; and society to a utilitarian selection, safety first. Society wishes its member to be laborious, dependable, regular, sober, orderly, self-sacrificing; while the individual wishes less of this and more of new experience. And organized society seeks also to regulate the conflict and competition inevitable between its members in the pursuit of their wishes. The desire to have wealth, for example, or any other socially sanctioned wish, may not be accomplished at the expense of another member of the society, — by murder, theft, lying, swindling, blackmail, etc.

It is in this connection that a moral code arises, which is a set of rules or behavior norms, regulating the expression of the wishes, and which is built up by successive definitions of the situation. In practice the abuse arises first and the rule is made to prevent its recurrence. Morality is thus the generally accepted definition of the situation, whether expressed in public opinion and the unwritten law, in a formal legal code, or in religious commandments and prohibitions.

The family is the smallest social unit and the primary defining agency. As soon as the child has free motion and begins to pull, tear, pry, meddle, and prowl, the parents begin to define the situation through speech and other signs and pressures: "Be quiet", "Sit up straight", "Blow your nose", "Wash your face", "Mind your mother", "Be kind to sister", etc. This is the real significance of Wordsworth's phrase, "Shades of the prison house begin to close upon the growing child." His wishes and activities begin to be inhibited, and gradually, by definitions within the family, by playmates, in the school, in the Sunday school, in the community, through reading, by formal instruction, by informal signs of approval and disapproval, the growing member learns the code of his society.

In addition to the family we have the community

as a defining agency. At present the community is
so weak and vague that it gives us no idea of the former
power of the local group in regulating behavior.   Originally the community was practically the whole world
of its members.   It was composed of families related
by blood and marriage and was not so large that all
the members could not come together; it was a face-
to-face group.   I asked a Polish peasant what was the
extent of an "*okolica*" or neighborhood — how far it
reached.   "It reaches," he said, "as far as the report
of a man reaches — as far as a man is talked about."
And it was in communities of this kind that the moral
code which we now recognize as valid originated.   The
customs of the community are "folkways", and both
state and church have in their more formal codes mainly
recognized and incorporated these folkways.

The typical community is vanishing and it would
be neither possible nor desirable to restore it in its
old form.   It does not correspond with the present
direction of social evolution and it would now be a
distressing condition in which to live.   But in the im-
mediacy of relationships and the participation of everybody in everything, it represents an element which
we have lost and which we shall probably have to
restore in some form of coöperation in order to secure
a balanced and normal society, — some arrangement
corresponding with human nature.

Very elemental examples of the definition of the situation by the community as a whole, corresponding to
mob action as we know it and to our trial by jury, are
found among European peasants. The three documents
following, all relating to the Russian community or *mir*,
give some idea of the conditions under which a whole
community, a public, formerly defined a situation.

25. We who are unacquainted with peasant speech, manners and method of expressing thought — mimicry — if we should be present at a division of land or some settlement among the peasants, would never understand anything. Hearing fragmentary, disconnected exclamations, endless quarreling, with repetition of some single word; hearing this racket of a seemingly senseless, noisy crowd that counts up or measures off something, we should conclude that they would not get together, or arrive at any result in an age. . . . Yet wait until the end and you will see that the division has been made with mathematical accuracy — that the measure, the quality of the soil, the slope of the field, the distance from the village — everything in short has been taken into account, that the reckoning has been correctly done and, what is most important, that every one of those present who were interested in the division is certain of the correctness of the division or settlement.   The cry, the noise, the racket do not subside until every one is satisfied and no doubter is left.

The same thing is true concerning the discussion of some question by the *mir*.   There are no speeches, no debates, no votes.   They shout, they abuse each other, they seem on the point of coming to blows.   Apparently they riot in the most senseless manner.   Some one preserves silence, silence, and then suddenly puts in a word, one word, or an ejaculation, and by this word, this ejaculation, he turns the whole thing upside down.   In the end, you look into it and find that an admirable decision has been formed and, what is most important, a unanimous decision.[1]

26. As I approached the village, there hung over it such a mixed, varied violent shouting, that no well brought-up parliament would agree to recognize itself, even in the abstract, as analogous to this gathering of peasant deputies. It was clearly a full meeting today. . . .   At other more

[1] A. N. Engelgardt: "Iz Derevni: 12 Pisem" ("From the Country; 12 Letters"), p. 315.

quiet village meetings I had been able to make out very
little, but this was a real lesson to me. I felt only a con-
tinuous, indistinguishable roaring in my ears, sometimes
pierced by a particularly violent phrase that broke out from
the general roar. I saw in front of me the "immediate"
man, in all his beauty. What struck me first of all was his
remarkable frankness; the more "immediate" he is, the
less able is he to mask his thoughts and feelings; once he is
stirred up the emotion seizes him quickly and he flares up
then and there, and does not quiet down till he has poured
out before you all the substance of his soul. He does not
feel embarrassment before anybody; there are no indications here of diplomacy. Further, he opens up his whole
soul, and he will tell everything that he may ever have known
about you, and not only about you, but about your father,
grandfather, and great-grandfather. Here everything is
clear water, as the peasants say, and everything stands out
plainly. If any one, out of smallness of soul, or for some
ulterior motive, thinks to get out of something by keeping
silent, they force him out into clear water without pity.
And there are very few such small-souled persons at important village meetings. I have seen the most peaceable, irresponsible peasants, who at other times would not have thought
of saying a word against any one, absolutely changed at
these meetings, at these moments of general excitement.
They believed in the saying, "On people even death is beautiful", and they got up so much courage that they were able
to answer back the peasants commonly recognized as audacious. At the moment of its height the meeting becomes
simply an open mutual confessional and mutual disclosure,
the display of the widest publicity. At these moments
when, it would seem, the private interests of each reach the
highest tension, public interests and justice in turn reach
the highest degree of control.[1]

---

[1] N. N. Zlatovratsky: "Ocherki Krestyanskoy Obshchiny" ("Sketches
of the Peasant Commune"), p. 127.

27. In front of the volost administration building there stands a crowd of some one hundred and fifty men. This means that a volost meeting has been called to consider the verdict of the Kusmin rural commune "regarding the handing over to the [state] authorities of the peasant Gregori Siedov, caught red-handed and convicted of horse-stealing." Siedov had already been held for judicial inquiry; the evidence against him was irrefutable and he would undoubtedly be sentenced to the penitentiary. In view of this I endeavor to explain that the verdict in regard to his exile is wholly superfluous and will only cause a deal of trouble; and that at the termination of the sentence of imprisonment of Siedov the commune will unfailingly be asked whether it wants him back or prefers that he be exiled. Then, I said, in any event it would be necessary to formulate a verdict in regard to the "non-reception" of Siedov, while at this stage all the trouble was premature and could lead to nothing. But the meeting did not believe my words, did not trust the court and wanted to settle the matter right then and there; the general hatred of horse-thieves was too keen. . . .

The decisive moment has arrived; the head-man "drives" all the judges-elect to one side; the crowd stands with a gloomy air, trying not to look at Siedov and his wife, who are crawling before the *mir* on their knees. "Old men, whoever pities Gregori, will remain in his place, and whoever does not forgive him will step to the right," cries the head man. The crowd wavered and rocked, but remained dead still on the spot; no one dared to be the first to take the fatal step. Gregori feverishly ran over the faces of his judges with his eyes, trying to read in these faces pity for him. His wife wept bitterly, her face close to the ground; beside her, finger in mouth and on the point of screaming, stood a three-year-old youngster (at home Gregori had four more children). . . . But straightway one peasant steps out of the crowd; two years before some one had stolen a horse from him. "Why should we pity him? Did he pity us?" says the old man, and stooping goes over to the right side. "That is true; bad grass must be torn from the field," says another one from the crowd, and follows the old man. The beginning had been made; at first individually and then in whole groups the judges-elect proceeded to go over to the right. The man condemned by public opinion ran his head into the ground, beat his breast with his fists, seized those who passed him by their coat-tails, crying: "Ivan Timofeich! Uncle Leksander! Vasinka, dear kinsman! Wait, kinsmen, let me say a word. . . . Petrushenka." But, without stopping and with stern faces, the members of the *mir* dodged the unfortunates, who were crawling at their feet. . . . At last the wailing of Gregori stopped; around him for the space of three *sazen* the place was empty; there was no one to implore. All the judges-elect, with the exception of one, an uncle of the man to be exiled, had gone over to the right. The woman cried sorrowfully, while Gregori stood motionless on his knees, his head lowered, stupidly looking at the ground.[1]

The essential point in reaching a communal decision, just as in the case of our jury system, is unanimity. In some cases the whole community mobilizes around a stubborn individual to conform him to the general wish.

28. It sometimes happens that all except one may agree but the motion is never carried if that one refuses to agree to it. In such cases all endeavor to talk over and persuade the stiff-necked one. Often they even call to their aid his wife, his children, his relatives, his father-in-law, and his mother, that they may prevail upon him to say yes. Then all assail him, and say to him from time to time: "Come now, God help you, agree with us too, that this may take place as we wish it, that the house may not be cast into disorder, that we may not be talked about by the people, that the neighbors may not hear of it, that the world may not

---

[1] "V Volostnikh Pisaryakh" ("A Village Secretary"), p. 283.

make sport of us !" It seldom occurs in such cases that unanimity is not attained.[1]

A less formal but not less powerful means of defining the situation employed by the community is gossip. The Polish peasant's statement that a community reaches as far as a man is talked about was significant, for the community regulates the behavior of its members largely by talking about them. Gossip has a bad name because it is sometimes malicious and false and designed to improve the status of the gossiper and degrade its object, but gossip is in the main true and is an organizing force. It is a mode of defining the situation in a given case and of attaching praise or blame. It is one of the means by which the status of the individual and of his family is fixed.

The community also, particularly in connection with gossip, knows how to attach opprobrium to persons and actions by using epithets which are at the same time brief and emotional definitions of the situation. "Bastard", "whore", "traitor", "coward", "skunk", "scab", "snob", "kike", etc., are such epithets. In "Faust" the community said of Margaret, "She stinks." The people are here employing a device known in psychology as the "conditioned reflex." If, for example, you place before a child (say six months old) an agreeable object, a kitten, and at the same time pinch the child, and if this is repeated several times, the child will immediately cry at the sight of the kitten without being pinched; or if a dead rat were always served beside a man's plate of soup he would eventually have a disgust for soup when served separately. If the word "stinks" is associated on people's

[1] F. S. Krauss : "Sitte und Brauch der Südslaven", p. 103.

tongues with Margaret, Margaret will never again
smell sweet. Many evil consequences, as the psychoanalysts claim, have resulted from making the
whole of sex life a "dirty" subject, but the device
has worked in a powerful, sometimes a paralyzing way
on the sexual behavior of women.

Winks, shrugs, nudges, laughter, sneers, haughtiness,
coldness, "giving the once over" are also language
defining the situation and painfully felt as unfavorable
recognition. The sneer, for example, is incipient vom-
iting, meaning, "you make me sick."

And eventually the violation of the code even in
an act of no intrinsic importance, as in carrying food
to the mouth with the knife, provokes condemnation
and disgust. The fork is not a better instrument for
conveying food than the knife, at least it has no moral
superiority, but the situation has been defined in favor
of the fork. To smack with the lips in eating is bad
manners with us, but the Indian has more logically
defined the situation in the opposite way; with him
smacking is a compliment to the host.

In this whole connection fear is used by the group
to produce the desired attitudes in its member. Praise
is used also but more sparingly. And the whole body
of habits and emotions is so much a community and
family product that disapproval or separation is almost
unbearable. The following case shows the painful
situation of one who has lost her place in a family and
community.

29. I am a young woman of about twenty; I was born
in America but my parents come from Hungary. They are
very religious. . . . When I was fourteen I became acquainted in school with a gentile boy of German parents.
He was a very fine and decent boy. I liked his company

. . . and we became close friends. Our friendship continued over a period of several years, unknown to my parents. I did not want to tell them, knowing quite well that they would not allow my friendship to a gentile.

When we grew older, our friendship developed into ardent love and one year ago we decided to marry — without my parents' consent, of course. I surmised that after my wedding they would forgive my marrying a non-Jewish young man, but just the opposite turned out. My religious parents were full of scorn when they learned of my secret doings, and not only did they not forgive me but they chased me out of the house and refused to have anything to do with me.

To add to my misfortune, I am now being spurned by my friend, my lover, my everything — my husband. After our marriage he became a different man; he drank and gambled and called me the vilest names. He continually asked why he married a "damned Jewess", as if it were my fault alone. Before our marriage I was the best girl in the world for him and now he would drown me in a spoonful of water to get rid of me. Fortunately I have no child as yet.

My husband's parents hate me even more than my husband and just as I was turned out of the house for marrying a gentile, so he was shown the door by his parents for marrying a Jewess.

Well, a few months ago my husband deserted me and I have no idea of his whereabouts. I was confronted by a terrible situation. Spurned by my own relatives and by my husband's, I feel very lonely, not having some one to tell my troubles to.

Now, I want you to advise me how to find my husband. I do not want to live with him by compulsion, nor do I ask his support, for I earn my living working in a shop. I merely ask his aid in somehow obtaining a divorce, so that I may return to my people, to my God and to my parents. I cannot stand the loneliness and do not want to be hated, denounced and spurned by all. My loneliness will drive me to a premature grave.

Perhaps you can tell me how to get rid of my misfortune. Believe me, I am not to blame for what I have done — it was my ignorance. I never believed that it was such a terrible crime to marry a non-Jew and that my parents would under no circumstances forgive me. I am willing to do anything, to make the greatest sacrifice, if only the terrible ban be taken off me.[1]

In the following the writer is not the father of the girl who has just told her story, but he might well be. His statement shows the power of family and community customs in determining emotional attitudes.

30. [My daughter has married an Italian who is a very good man]. . . . My tragedy is much greater because I am a free thinker. Theoretically, I consider a "goi" [gentile] just as much a man as a Jew. . . . Indeed I ask myself these questions: "What would happen if my daughter married a Jewish fellow who was a good-for-nothing? . . . And what do I care if he is an Italian? But I can not seem to answer these delicate questions. The fact is that I would prefer a refined man; but I would sooner have a common Jew than an educated *goi*. Why this is so, I do not know, but that is how it is, of that there is no doubt. And this shows what a terrible chasm exists between theory and practice! . . ."[2]

The tendency of communities and families to regulate so minutely the behavior of all their members was justified by the fact that in case of poverty, sickness, death, desertion, or ruin the community or family assumed the burden, "submitted to the yoke", as they expressed it. In case No. 31 the former members of a community still support an abandoned child though they are in America and the child in Europe.

[1] *Forward*, March 10, 1920.
[2] *Forward*, January 22, 1921.

31. In the year 1912 in a little [Russian] village a father abandoned his family, a wife and three children. Of the children two were girls and the third was a boy six months old. The mother worried along with the children and finally in despair she changed her religion and married a Christian from a neighboring village. The children she simply abandoned.

Of course the community of the village where this happened took care of the three abandoned children. They gave them out to families to be reared, and the village paid for them by the month. My mother was by no means a rich woman and felt the need of money, so she took the boy, for which the community paid.

For some years everything went well, until the great World War broke out. The village in question was impoverished by the war and was plundered by various bands of pogromists. Great numbers of Jews were killed and the community was destroyed.

My mother no longer received the monthly payment for the child; there was no one to make the payment. But my mother did not have the heart to throw the poor child into the street. They had become attached to each other, the child to my mother whom he called "mamma" and my mother to the child. So my mother kept the child without pay. That is, she and the child hungered and suffered together. Now, dear editor, I come to the point.

The family of the writer of these lines was scattered. My father died at home. I and two sisters are now in America. My mother and the child are still in the old home. Of course we send our mother money for her support and this means that we support not only our mother but also the child of strangers. But it has never occurred to us here in America to reproach our mother because we are compelled to send money for a strange child.

On the contrary, we understand that it is our duty not to behave like murderers toward the innocent, helpless victim

of the present social conditions whom fate has thrown upon
us.   But the following is also true :

We have heard that the child's father is in America, somewhere around New York, and that he is very rich.   So we
think that it is no more than right that the father of the
child shall take the yoke from us who are strangers and support his own child.   I will say that I and my two sisters are
simple working people.   Every cent that we earn is worked
for with our ten fingers.   Therefore, I appeal to the father
of our mother's ward to take over the responsibility for his
child, which is without doubt his duty.[1]

As far as possible the family regulates its affairs within
itself without appealing to the community and thus
subjecting itself to gossip.   Situations arising within
the family where members are not in agreement, where
a conflict of wishes is involved, are defined through argument, ordering and forbidding, remonstrance, re-
proof, entreaty, sulking, tears, and beatings.   But
as a last resort a member of a family may provoke
gossip, appeal to the community.   In case No. 32
the woman defines the situation to her deserting husband publicly.   She does it very tactfully.   She uses
every art, reminder, and appreciation to influence his
return.   She wishes to avoid a public scandal, reminds
him of the noble professions he has always made as
man and father, pictures the children as grieving and
herself as ashamed to let them know, and believes
that he is fundamentally a fine man who has had a
moment of weakness or suffered a temporary madness
— so she says.   In addition the powerful newspaper
through which she seeks publicity will define the situation to the erring husband.   Presumably he will
return.

[1] *Forward*, January 12, 1922.

32. I come to you with the request that you will write a few words to my husband. He has a high opinion of the answers that you give in *Bintel Brief* and I hope that some words from you will have a good effect on him so that we shall be able to avoid a public scandal. In the meantime I am containing my troubles but if matters get worse I shall have to turn to people for help. I will say that my husband and I always lived a good life together. He always condemned in the strongest terms those fathers who leave their children to God's mercy. "Children," he said, "are innocent and we must take care not to make them unhappy" — that was the way he always talked. And now he has himself done what he always condemned and regarded as the greatest meanness.

The last night before he went away my husband kissed our youngest daughter so much that she is now sick from longing for him. The older girl is continually asking, "When will father come?" I am frightfully upset by the unexpected misfortune which has struck me.

Dear editor, I have the greatest confidence in the goodness of my husband. Perhaps he has lost his reason for a time, but he is not corrupt. I am almost sure that when he reads my letter he will come back to his senses and will behave as a man and as a decent person should behave. I beg you to print my letter as soon as possible and help to restore a broken family.[1]

Contrary to this we have the device of public confession, a definition of the situation in terms of self-condemnation. The following is a public apology which gives the injured husband favorable public recognition and seeks a reconciliation.

33. I myself drove out my good and true husband in a shameful manner and placed the guilt at his door, and although he is angry he is decent enough not to say anything

[1] *Forward*, July 9, 1920.

to anybody. He takes the blame on himself. All my friends and acquaintances think that he is really the guilty one.

I have been married for the last eleven years and up to two years ago I thought that somehow I should end my life peacefully, although I have caused many a quarrel. . . . My tongue is sharp and burning. . . . My husband always forgave me. Many times he cried and a week or two would pass by quietly. And then again I could not be quiet. Quite often I would start to fire away at the table and he would get up, leave the house, and go to a restaurant. When he returned he had some more. And according to my behavior my husband began to treat me roughly. . . .

At this time we tried business for ourselves . . . and owing to numerous reasons my husband had everything in my name; I was the owner of everything that we had. After that I began to rule over him still more, and when he saw that he could do nothing with me he stopped speaking to me.

I have tried everything to dirty his name. Oh, now my conscience troubles me when I see three live orphans wandering about. Would it not be better if the community had forbidden me to marry in order to avoid such a family-tragedy.

I am a snake by nature and this is not my fault; that's how I am. My friends meet him and they tell me that he does not say a word about our tragedy. He says: "I am doing the best that I can and when I am able to give a home to my children, then I will worry about them." And I am afraid that some day he will take away the children from me and then I shall be left alone like a stone.[1]

The priests in Poland say that if all the influences of the community are active—the family, the priest, the friends, and neighbors—there are few necessarily bad men. They say also that communities tend to

[1] *Forward*, February 6, 1914.

be all good or all bad, and that this is determined largely by majorities. If a community is good the priest thunders from the chancel against any symptom of badness; if it is already bad he praises and encourages any little manifestation of goodness. In examining the letters between immigrants in America and their home communities I have noticed that the great solicitude of the family and community is that the absent member shall not change. Absence and the resulting outside influence are dreaded as affecting the solidarity of the group. And the typical immigrant letter is an assurance and reminder that the writer, though absent, is still a member of the community. I found the following letter in the home of a peasant family in Poland. It was written from Chicago on "Palmer House" stationery. The writer was a chambermaid in that hotel. She was little instructed, could barely read and write. The letter contained no capitals and no punctuation and was addressed to a girl who could not write at all. This letter was read by all the neighbors. No one would understand keeping a letter private. The introduction, "Praised be Jesus Christ", to which the reader or hearer is expected to reply, "For centuries of centuries, Amen", is a traditional form expressing common membership in a religious-social community. The greetings at the end should be complete enough to recognize every family which ought to be noticed. The sending of money is a practical sign of community membership. The poetry and æsthetic writing is the absent girl's way of participating in the social gatherings of the community, of doing her turn in the festivities where poems are composed and recited. She writes as prettily as she can in order to provoke recognition. For the convenience of Polish immigrants business enterprise even provides printed letters containing appropriate greetings and assurances, leaving blank space for names and informational matter.

34. I am beginning this letter with the words: "Praised be Jesus Christus", and I hope that you will answer: "For centuries of centuries, Amen."
Dearest Olejniczka: I greet you from my heart, and wish you health and happiness. God grant that this little letter reaches you well, and as happy as the birdies in May. This I wish you from my heart, dear Olejniczka.
The rain is falling; it falls beneath my slipping feet.
I do not mind; the post office is near.
When I write my little letter
I will flit with it there,
And then, dearest Olejniczka
My heart will be light, from giving you a pleasure.
In no grove do the birds sing so sweetly
As my heart, dearest Olejniczka, for you.
Go, little letter, across the broad sea, for I cannot come to you. When I arose in the morning, I looked up to the heavens and thought to myself that to you, dearest Olejniczka, a little letter I must send.

Dearest Olejniczka, I left papa, I left sister and brother and you to start out in the wide world, and to-day I am yearning and fading away like the world without the sun.

If I shall ever see you again, then like a little child, of great joy I shall cry. To your feet I shall bow low, and your hands I shall kiss. Then you shall know how I love you, dearest Olejniczka.

I went up on a high hill and looked in that far direction, but I see you not, and I hear you not.

Dear Olejniczka, only a few words will I write. As many sand-grains as there are in the field, as many drops of water in the sea, so many sweet years of life I, Walercia, wish you for the Easter holidays. I wish you all good, a hundred years of life, health and happiness. And loveliness I wish you. I greet you through the white lilies, I think of you every night, dearest Olejniczka.

Are you not in Bielice any more, or what? Answer, as I sent you a letter and there is no answer. Is there no one to write for you?

And now I write you how I am getting along. I am getting on well, very well. I have worked in a factory and I am now working in a hotel. I receive 18 (in our money 36) dollars a month, and that is very good.

If you would like it we could bring Wladzio over some day. We eat here every day what we get only for Easter in our country. We are bringing over Helena and brother now. I had $120 and I sent back $90.

I have no more to write, only we greet you from our heart, dearest Olejniczka. And the Olejniks and their children; and Wladislaw we greet; and the Szases with their children; and the Zwolyneks with their children; and the Grotas with their children, and the Gyrlas with their children; and all our acquaintances we greet. My address: North America [etc.] Good-by. For the present, sweet good-by.

The sets of habits and reactions developed socially, under family, community, and church influence, may become almost as definite as the mechanistic adjustments which I mentioned at the beginning of the chapter. The "folkways" become equivalent in force to the instincts and even displace them. In the following case the girl is completely isolated, and in a very critical situation but resists temptation on the basis of her memories.

35. This happened fourteen years ago. I had been in America but a short time and was a healthy and pretty girl of nineteen.

I had worked in a place seven months and earned the gigantic sum of $4.00 a week. But soon slack set in and I

lost my job. It was summer and in the hot days I continued to look for work. The whole day I used to drag my
tired body from place to place, only to come home in the
evening all fagged out and with no prospect of work.

I was then living with a widow who was even poorer than
myself for she had to provide for her several children. I had
to sleep there for I could not live in the street, but stopped
eating there because she simply had nothing to give me and
I could not afford to pay her. What was I to do? So
twice a day I used to "feed" my stomach on credit, that is,
I would promise to repay it all the foregone breakfasts and
dinners as soon as I got a job.

What I did eat I obtained in the following manner: I
went into a grocery and waited until all the customers were
gone, when I would whisper to the grocer to let me have an
old roll and a piece of herring on the promise of paying for
it when I found work. That's how I managed to live while
starving.

It will be understood that this sort of life did not satisfy
me. I recall with horror the wild thoughts that entered
my mind as I paced the streets in the hot weather, hungry
and thirsty. Temptation was whispering to me that a pretty
and healthy girl like me did not have to wait for honest
labor. . . . That I did not yield to the voice of temptation
was simply a miracle, despite the fact that I am not religious
and do not believe in miracles.

Once I nearly lost control of myself . . . but the memory
of my parents on the other side who were very religious and
respectable people — the love for them — saved me from
taking the false step. It was this way: One afternoon of a
very warm day, being tired of walking around in search of
work, hungry and thirsty, I dropped my hands in despair,
murmuring to myself : "Come what may, I can stand it no
longer. . . . I can't. . . ." And I began to look for some
young man to whom to offer my body. . . .

My heart beat heavily, my hands and feet trembled and
my teeth chattered as I passed by many men without daring

to carry out my decision. Finally, my eyes were set upon a well-dressed young man whom I was going to stop. . . . But at the very last moment the bright faces of my parents appeared before my eyes and I desisted in terror from my plan. I thought it was better to drop in the street than bring disgrace upon my dear parents. I went home afterward.

The point that I want to bring out is this: One evening I went as usual to a grocery to obtain my portion of roll and a piece of herring. The grocer, not a friendly man, at least not a thinking man, drove me out of the store. . . . This experience chased away my hunger and I did not attempt to enter another grocery. Ashamed and embittered, I went home. In the hall of the house I noticed a green slip of paper on the floor. My heart leapt with joy. I picked it up, doubting whether it was really money, for I did not believe that such good fortune could befall me. . . . I examined the paper closely and found it to be a genuine one-dollar bill! I was as overwhelmed with joy as if I had found a whole treasure, as if I had suddenly turned millionaire.

I began to plan a gala meal — bologna and tea . . . but first I decided to go to the candy store for some "lemon and strawberry mixed" soda for three cents. As I walked up the flights of stairs to my room to wash up, I heard a mother's scolding and a child's weeping as it was being whipped by its mother. She was punishing him for losing the dollar on the way to the grocery. The poor boy was crying with his last strength and it could break anybody's heart.

I hesitated no longer and rapped on the door of the flat from which the commotion came. A pale and emaciated woman opened the door for me. "Here is your dollar," I said; "I found it in the hallway." The woman snatched the bill out of my hand without even looking at me, let alone thanking me. . . . And to this very day I don't know whether she acted that way out of embittered feeling or out of ill-manners.

One thing I know: I was more hungry and thirsty that night than at any other time — the bill had so increased my appetite that I could have swallowed that woman and her boy together. . . .

I think I should add that I am now married to a very dear man and have three precious little children, and we make a fine living.[1]

The following passages picture the life of a young American girl of the middle of the last century where the whole community is coöperating with the family to standardize her. Her parents are dead but the influences are complete without them. She is met at every turn with definitions of the situation which in this case are rigid but of the most genial and affectionate character. She does not lose her personality because that is in her nature; she is alert and witty, like her grandmother. If there were no disturbance of the situation she would become such an old woman as her grandmother is. The outside world is, however, beginning to press in. The situation has already been defined to her in terms of "woman's rights."

36. *November 21, 1852.* — I am ten years old today, and I will write a journal and tell who I am and what I am doing. I have lived with my Grandfather and Grandmother Beals ever since I was seven years old, and Anna, too, since she was four. Our brothers, James and John, came too, but they are at East Bloomfield at Mr. Stephen Clark's Academy. Miss Laura Clark of Naples is their teacher.

Anna and I go to school at District No. 11. Mr. James C. Cross is our teacher, and some of the scholars say he is cross by name and cross by nature, but I like him. He gave

---

[1] *Forward*, November 26, 1920.

me a book by the name of "Noble Deeds of American Women", for reward of merit, in my reading class.

Friday. — Grandmother says I will have a great deal to answer for, because Anna looks up to me so and tries to do everything that I do and thinks whatever I say is "gospel truth." The other day the girls at school were disputing with her about something and she said, "It is so, if it ain't so, for Calline said so." I shall have to "toe the mark", as Grandfather says, if she keeps watch of me all the time and walks in my footsteps.

April 1, 1853. — Before I go to school every morning I read three chapters in the Bible. I read three every day and five on Sunday and that takes me through the Bible in a year. Those I read this morning were the first, second, and third chapters of Job. The first was about Eliphaz reproveth Job; second, benefit of God's correction; third, Job justifieth his complaint. I then learned a text to say at school. I went to school at quarter to nine and recited my text and we had prayers and then proceeded with the business of the day. Just before school was out, we recited in "Science of Things Familiar", and in Dictionary, and then we had calisthenics.

July. — Hiram Goodrich, who lives at Mr. Myron H. Clark's, and George and Wirt Wheeler ran away on Sunday to seek their fortunes. When they did not come back every one was frightened and started out to find them. They set out right after Sunday school, taking their pennies which had been given them for the contribution, and were gone several days. They were finally found at Palmyra. When asked why they had run away, one replied that he thought it was about time they saw something of the world. We heard that Mr. Clark had a few moments' private conversation with Hiram in the barn and Mr. Wheeler the same with his boys and we do not think they will go traveling on their own hook again right off. Miss Upham lives right across the street from them and she was telling little Morris Bates that he must fight the good fight of faith and he asked her if that was the fight that Wirt Wheeler fit. She probably had to make her instructions plainer after that.

1854, Sunday. — Mr. Daggett's text this morning was the twenty-second chapter of Revelation, sixteenth verse, "I am the root and offspring of David and the bright and morning star." Mrs. Judge Taylor taught our Sunday-school class today and she said we ought not to read our Sunday-school books on Sunday. I always do. Mine today was entitled, "Cheap Repository Tracts" by Hannah More, and it did not seem unreligious at all.

Tuesday. — Mrs. Judge Taylor sent for me to come over to see her today. I didn't know what she wanted, but when I got there she said she wanted to talk and pray with me on the subject of religion. She took me into one of the wings. I never had been in there before and was frightened at first, but it was nice after I got used to it. After she prayed, she asked me to, but I couldn't think of anything but "Now I lay me down to sleep", and I was afraid she would not like that, so I did n't say anything. When I got home and told Anna, she said, "Caroline, I presume probably Mrs. Taylor wants you to be a missionary, but I shan't let you go." I told her she need n't worry for I would have to stay at home and look after her. After school tonight I went out into Abbie Clark's garden with her and she taught me how to play "mumble te peg." It is fun, but rather dangerous. I am afraid Grandmother won't give me a knife to play with. Abbie Clark has beautiful pansies in her garden and gave me some roots.

Sunday. — I almost forgot that it was Sunday this morning and talked and laughed just as I do week days. Grandmother told me to write down this verse before I went to church so I would remember it: "Keep thy foot when thou goest to the house of God, and be more ready to hear than to offer the sacrifice of fools." I will remember it now, sure. My feet are all right anyway with my new patten leather shoes on, but I shall have to look out for my head. Mr. Thomas Howell read a sermon today as Mr. Daggett is out

of town. Grandmother always comes upstairs to get the
candle and tuck us in before she goes to bed herself, and
some nights we are sound asleep and do not hear her, but
last night we only pretended to be asleep. She kneeled
down by the bed and prayed aloud for us, that we might
be good children and that she might have strength given
her from on high to guide us in the straight and narrow path
which leads to life eternal. Those were her very words.
After she had gone down-stairs we sat up in bed and talked
about it and promised each other to be good, and crossed
our hearts and "hoped to die", if we broke our promise.
Then Anna was afraid we would die, but I told her I didn't
believe we would be as good as that, so we kissed each
other and went to sleep.

Sunday. — Rev. Mr. Tousley preached today to the children and told us how many steps it took to be bad. I think
he said lying was first, then disobedience to parents, breaking the Sabbath, swearing, stealing, drunkenness. I don't
remember just the order they came. It was very interesting,
for he told lots of stories and we sang a great many times.
I should think Eddy Tousley would be an awful good boy
with his father in the house with him all the while, but probably he has to be away part of the time preaching to other
children.

December 20, 1855. — Susan B. Anthony is in town and
spoke in Bemis Hall this afternoon. She made a special
request that all the seminary girls should come to hear her
as well as all the women and girls in town. She had a large
audience and she talked very plainly about our rights and
how we ought to stand up for them, and said the world would
never go right until the women had just as much right to
vote and rule as the men. She asked us all to come up and
sign our names who would promise to do all in our power to
bring about that glad day when equal rights would be the
law of the land. A whole lot of us went up and signed the
paper. When I told Grandmother about it she said she
guessed Susan B. Anthony had forgotten that St. Paul said

the women should keep silence. I told her no, she did n't, for she spoke particularly about St. Paul and said if he had lived in these times, instead of eighteen hundred years ago, he would have been as anxious to have the women at the head of the government as she was. I could not make Grandmother agree with her at all and she said we might better all of us stayed at home. We went to prayer meeting this evening and a woman got up and talked. Her name was Mrs. Sands. We hurried home and told Grandmother and she said she probably meant all right and she hoped we did not laugh.

February 21, 1856. — We had a very nice time at Fannie Gaylord's party and a splendid supper. Lucilla Field laughed herself almost to pieces when she found on going home that she had worn her leggins all the evening. We had a pleasant walk home but did not stay till it was out. Some one asked me if I danced every set and I told them no, I set every dance. I told Grandmother and she was very much pleased. Some one told us that Grandfather and Grandmother first met at a ball in the early settlement of Canandalgua. I asked her if it was so and she said she never danced since she became a professing Christian and that was more than fifty years ago.

May, 1856. — We were invited to Bessie Seymour's party last night and Grandmother said we could go. The girls all told us at school that they were going to wear low neck and short sleeves. We have caps on the sleeves of our best dresses and we tried to get the sleeves out, so we could go bare arms, but we could n't get them out. We had a very nice time, though, at the party. Some of the Academy boys were there and they asked us to dance but of course we could n't do that. We promenaded around the rooms and went out to supper with them. Eugene Stone and Tom Eddy asked to go home with us but Grandmother sent our two girls for us, Bridget Flynn and Hannah White, so they could n't. We were quite disappointed, but perhaps she won't send for us next time.

Thursday, 1857. — We have four sperm candles in four silver candlesticks and when we have company we light them. Johnie Thompson, son of the minister, Rev. M. L. R. P., has come to the academy to school and he is very full of fun and got acquainted with all the girls very quick. He told us this afternoon to have "the other candle lit" for he was coming down to see us this evening. Will Schley heard him say it and he said he was coming too. *Later.* — The boys came and we had a very pleasant evening but when the 9 o'clock bell rang we heard Grandfather winding up the clock and scraping up the ashes on the hearth to cover the fire so it would last till morning and we all understood the signal and they bade us good night. "We won't go home till morning" is a song that will never be sung in this house.

August 30, 1858. — Some one told us that when Bob and Henry Antes were small boys they thought they would like to try, just for once, to see how it would seem to be bad, so in spite of all of Mr. Tousley's sermons they went out behind the barn one day and in a whisper Bob said, "I swear", and Henry said, "So do I." Then they came into the house looking guilty and quite surprised, I suppose, that they were not struck dead just as Ananias and Sapphira were for lying.

1860, Sunday. — Frankie Richardson asked me to go with her to teach a class in the colored Sunday School on Chapel Street this afternoon. I asked Grandmother if I could go and she said she never noticed that I was particularly interested in the colored race and she said she thought I only wanted an excuse to get out for a walk Sunday afternoon. However, she said I could go just this once. When we got up as far as the Academy, Mr. Noah T. Clarke's brother, who is one of the teachers, came out and Frank said he led the singing at the Sunday school and she said she would give me an introduction to him, so he walked up with us and home again. Grandmother said that when she saw him opening the gate for me, she understood my zeal in missionary work. "The dear little lady", as we often call her, has always been noted for her keen discernment and wonderful sagacity and

loses none of it as she advances in years. Some one asked
Anna the other day if her Grandmother retained all her
faculties and Anna said, "Yes, indeed, to an alarming degree."
Grandmother knows that we think she is a perfect angel
even if she does seem rather strict sometimes. Whether we
are seven or seventeen we are children to her just the same,
and the Bible says, "Children obey your parents in the Lord
for this is right." We are glad that we never will seem old
to her. I had the same company home from church in the
evening. His home is in Naples.

Christmas, 1860. — I asked Grandmother if Mr. Clarke
could take Sunday night supper with us and she said she
was afraid he did not know the catechism. I asked him
Friday night and he said he would learn it on Saturday so
that he could answer every third question anyway. So he
did and got along very well. I think he deserves a pretty
good supper.[1]

At the best no society has ever succeeded in regulating the behavior of all its members satisfactorily all the
time. There are crimes of passion, of avarice, of re-
venge, even in face-to-face communities where the
control is most perfect. In the Hebrew code there
were ten offenses for which the punishment was death
by stoning. One of the examples cited above from
the Russian *mir* was concerned with horse stealing.
And the sexual passions have never been completely
contained within the framework of marriage. But
communities have been so powerful that all members
have acknowledged the code and have been ready to
repent and be forgiven. And forgiveness has been
one of the functions of the community, sometimes

[1] Caroline C. Richards: "Village Life in America", pp. 21–138, *passim.*
New York, Henry Holt and Company. Reprinted by permission. Quoted
by R. E. Park and E. W. Burgess: "Introduction to the Science of Soci-
ology", p. 305.

more particularly the function of the God of the community. A dying reprobate (the anecdote is attached to Rabelais) has been represented as saying, "*Dieu me pardonnera. C'est son métier.*" The community usually wishes to forgive and restore the offending member. It wants no breach in its solidarity and morale. And as long as the offender wishes to be forgiven and restored the code is working. The code is failing only if the sinner does not recognize it and does not repent. And when crime and prostitution appear as professions they are the last and most radical expressions of loss of family and community organization.

CHAPTER III

THE INDIVIDUALIZATION OF BEHAVIOR

FROM the foregoing it appears that the face-to-face group (family-community) is a powerful habit-forming mechanism. The group has to provide a system of behavior for many persons at once, a code which applies to everybody and lasts longer than any individual or generation. Consequently the group has two interests in the individual, ⊕ to suppress wishes and activities which are in conflict with the existing organization, or which seem the starting point of social disharmony, and to encourage wishes and actions which are required by the existing social system. And if the group performs this task successfully, as it does among savages, among Mohammedans, and as it did until recently among European peasants, no appreciable change in the moral code or in the state of culture is observable from generation to generation. In small and isolated communities there is little tendency to change or progress because the new experience of the individual is sacrificed for the sake of the security of the group.

But by a process, an evolution, connected with mechanical inventions, facilitated communication, the diffusion of print, the growth of cities, business organization, the capitalistic system, specialized occupations, scientific research, doctrines of freedom, the evolutionary view of life, etc., the family and community influences have been weakened and the world in general has been profoundly changed in content, ideals, and organization.

Young people leave home for larger opportunities, to seek new experience, and from necessity. Detachment from family and community, wandering, travel, "vagabondage" have assumed the character of normality. Relationships are casualized and specialized. Men meet professionally, as promoters of enterprises, not as members of families, communities, churches. Girls leave home to work in factories, stores, offices, and studios. Even when families are not separated they leave home for their work.

Every new invention, every chance acquaintanceship, every new environment, has the possibility of redefining the situation and of introducing change, disorganization or different type of organization into the life of the individual or even of the whole world. Thus, the invention of the check led to forgery; the sulphur match to arson; at present the automobile is perhaps connected with more seductions than happen otherwise in cities altogether; an assassination precipitated the World War; motion pictures and the *Saturday Evening Post* have stabilized and unstabilized many existences, considered merely as opportunity for new types of career. The costly and luxurious articles of women's wear organize the lives of many girls (as designers, artists, and buyers) and disorganize the lives of many who crave these pretty things.

In the small and spatially isolated communities of the past, where the influences were strong and steady, the members became more or less habituated to and reconciled with a life of repressed wishes. The repression was demanded of all, the arrangement was equitable, and while certain new experiences were prohibited, and pleasure not countenanced as an end in itself, there remained satisfactions, not the least of which was the suppression of the wishes of others. On the other hand the modern world presents itself as a spectacle in which the observer is never sufficiently participating. The modern revolt and unrest are due to the contrast between the paucity of fulfillment of the wishes of the individual and the fullness, or apparent fullness, of life around him. All age levels have been affected by the feeling that much, too much, is being missed in life. This unrest is felt most by those who have heretofore been most excluded from general participation in life, — the mature woman and the young girl. Sometimes it expresses itself in despair and depression, sometimes in breaking all bounds. Immigrants form a particular class in this respect. They sometimes repudiate the old system completely in their haste to get into the new. There are cases where the behavior of immigrants, expressing natural but random and unregulated impulses, has been called insane by our courts.

Case No. 37 represents despair, case No. 38 revolt, Nos. 39 and 40 extraordinarily wild behavior.

37. There is a saying about the peacock, "When she looks at her feathers she laughs, and when she looks at her feet she cries." I am in the same situation.

My husband's career, upon which I spent the best years of my life, is established favorably; our children are a joy to me as a mother; nor can I complain about our material circumstances. But I am dissatisfied with myself. My love for my children, be it ever so great, cannot destroy myself. A human being is not created like a bee which dies after accomplishing its only task.

Desires, long latent, have been aroused in me and become more aggressive the more obstacles they encounter. . . . I now have the desire to go about and see and hear everything. I wish to take part in everything — to dance, skate, play the piano, sing, go to the theatre, opera, lectures and generally mingle in society. As you see, I am no idler whose purpose is to chase all sorts of foolish things, as a result of loose ways. This is not the case.

My present unrest is a natural result following a long period of hunger and thirst for non-satisfied desires in every field of human experience. It is the dread of losing that which never can be recovered — youth and time which do not stand still — an impulse to catch up with the things I have missed. . . . If it were not for my maternal feeling I would go away into the wide world.[1]

38. I had been looking for Margaret, for I knew she was a striking instance of the "unadjusted" who had within a year come with a kind of æsthetic logic to Greenwich Village. She needed something very badly. What I heard about her which excited me was that she was twenty years old, unmarried, had never lived with a man or had any of that experience, had worked for a year on a socialist newspaper, and a socialist magazine, was a heavy drinker and a frequenter of Hell Hole, that she came from a middle class family but preferred the society of the outcasts to any other. Greenwich Village is not composed of outcasts, but it does not reject them, and it enables a man or woman who desires to know the outcast to satisfy the desire without feeling cut off from humanity. Hell Hole is a saloon in the back room of which pickpockets, grafters, philosophers, poets, revolutionists, stool-pigeons, and the riff-raff of humanity meet. Margaret loves this place and the people in it — so they told me — and there she did and said extreme things in which there was a bitter fling at decent society.

So that night, when she came with Christine, I invited

[1] *Forward*, March 11, 1921.

her to go with me to Hell Hole to have a drink. She drank whiskey after whiskey and showed no effect. As soon as we were seated in the back room alone she started to tell me about herself. I forget what unessential thing I said to get her started. She knew by instinct what I desired and she told me her story with utter frankness, and with a simple, unaggressive self-respect.

"I belong to what is called a respectable, middle-class family. My father is a prominent newspaper man. Whenever I was ill, as a child, he gave me whiskey instead of medicine. This began at the age of four. One of my childish amusements was to mix cordials and water to entertain my little friends with. We lived in the city, and I had from four years of age the run of the streets. At six or eight I knew everything — about sex, about hard street life. I knew it wrong, of course, for I saw it but did not feel it. I felt wrong about it all, and feared it, wasn't a part of it, except as an observer. I saw no beauty or friendliness in sex feeling. I think it was this that kept me away later from physical intimacy with men; it couldn't appeal to me after my early life in the street. I know it doesn't always happen so, but it did with me.

"When I got to be thirteen years old my father reversed his attitude towards me; before then, all freedom; after that, all restraint. I was completely shut in. Soon after that I became religious and joined the church. I had a long pious correspondence with another girl and used to brood all the time about God and about my transcendental duties. This lasted till I was sixteen, and then life, ordinary external life, came back with a rush and I couldn't stand my exclusive inner world and the outward restraint any longer, and I wanted to go away from home. So I worked hard in the High School and got a $300 scholarship in Latin and Greek. With this I went to a Western College and staid there two years, working my own way and paying my expenses. I read a lot at this time, and liked revolutionary literature; read socialism, and poetry that was full of revolt. I took to anything which expressed a reaction against the conditions of my life at home.

"I stood well in my studies, and suppose I might have completed the college course, except that I got into trouble with the authorities, for very slight reasons, as it seems to me. I smoked cigarettes, a habit I had formed as a child, and that of course was forbidden. It was also forbidden to enter the neighboring cemetery, I don't know why. One day I smoked a cigarette in the graveyard — a double offense — and then, in the playfulness of my spirit, I wrote a poem about it and published it in the college paper. In this paper I had already satirized the Y. W. C. A. A few other acts of that nature made me an undesirable member of the college and my connection with it ceased.

"After an unhappy time at home — my father and I could not get on together; ever since my early childhood he had been trying to 'reform' me — I got a job on the socialist *Call*, a New York daily newspaper, at $—— a week. It was hard work all day, but I liked it and I didn't drink — I didn't want to — and lived on the money without borrowing. Later I went on the *Masses*, and there I was well off. [Then I went to Washington to picket for the suffragists and got a jail sentence, and when I returned the *Masses* had been suspended.] It was at that time that I began to go with the Hudson Dusters [a gang of criminals] and to drink heavily. Greenwich Village seemed to think it was too good for me, or I too bad for it. Most of the women were afraid to associate with me. Only the Hudson Dusters, or people like them, seemed really human to me. I went, in a kind of despair, to the water-front, and staid three days and nights in the back room of a low saloon, where there were several old prostitutes. And I liked them. They seemed human, more so than other people. And in this place were working men. One man, with a wife and children, noticed I was going there and didn't seem to belong to them, and he asked me to go home with him and live with his family; and he meant it, and meant it decently.

"I want to know the down and outs," said Margaret with quiet, almost fanatical intenseness. "I find kindness in the lowest places, and more than kindness sometimes — something, I don't know what it is, that I want."[1]

39. There came a day when my wife heard that there was an Atlantic City not far from Philadelphia. So I granted her wish and rented a nice room for her in a hotel there and sent her with the two children to that seashore. . . .

The next summer I did not make out so well and could not afford to send my wife to the country, but she absolutely demanded to be sent even if I had to "hang and bring." . . . My protestations and explanations were of no avail. She went to Atlantic City and hired a room in the same hotel. . . .

I took my wife's behavior to heart and became ill. Some of my friends advised me to teach her a lesson and desert her, so that she would mend her ways in the future. They assured me that they would take care of my family, to keep them from starving. I was persuaded by them and left Philadelphia for a distant town.

My wife in Atlantic City, seeing that I sent her no money, returned home. Upon learning what had happened, she promptly sold the furniture, which had cost $800, for almost nothing and went to New York. My friends notified me of all that had occurred in my absence, whereupon I came back.

I advertised in the papers and found my wife. My first question was about the children and she replied she did not know where they were. Upon further questioning she answered that she had brought the children with her from Philadelphia but as she could do nothing with them in her way she simply left them in the street.

After great efforts made through my lawyer, I succeeded in obtaining the release of my children from the Gerry Society, after paying for their two months' keep there. . . .

Since this unhappy occurrence, my wife has many times wrecked our home, selling the household goods while I was

[1] Hutchins Hapgood: "At Christine's" (Manuscript).

at work and leaving me alone with the children. Whenever she feels like satisfying her cravings, or whenever she cannot afford to buy herself enough pretty clothes and hats, she deserts me. One time she was gone 9 months and never saw the children during this period. . . .

I tried to make up with her every time and give her another chance. But her cordiality lasted only until she again took a craving for some rag, when she would again leave home. She was even mean enough once to leave me with a five months' old baby who needed nursing and the only way out seemed to be the river for me and the baby. . . .

I assure you that everything I have written is the truth. If you do not believe me, you may convince yourself at the Desertion Bureau where my case has been recorded several times.[1]

40. . . . She was one of the thousands of girls who are drawn to the great city from small towns. She perished because of her thirst for adventure. . . . While stopping at the Hotel Buckingham she went out one evening and never returned. A chauffeur told the police that he met the girl on the evening of her death and that she had been on a tour of the cafés and cabarets with him and that at 2 o'clock in the morning Miss Dixon became ill. She was taken to the Harlem Hospital, where her case was diagnosed as morphine poisoning. . . .

She came of a fine Virginia family and was educated at a fashionable boarding school. Four years ago she was married to a Yale graduate. [A friend] who had known her all her life said, "She had just gone mad with love of pleasure, though at heart she was a thoroughbred and exceedingly fine. She decided to make her own living and took a small part in a couple of shows. The discipline and routine were too much for her and she gave it up and went back to [her husband] from time to time. But always the lure of New York seemed to hold her in a spell."[2]

[1] *Forward*, December 8, 1920.
[2] Newspaper item.

The world has become large, alluring, and confusing. Social evolution has been so rapid that no agency has been developed in the larger community of the state for regulating behavior which would replace the failing influence of the community and correspond completely with present activities. There is no universally accepted body of doctrines or practices. The churchman, for example, and the scientist, educator, or radical leader are so far apart that they cannot talk together. They are, as the Greeks expressed it, in different "universes of discourse."

41. Dr. Austin O'Malley writes rather passionately about the control of births, in the Catholic weekly, "America." Says Dr. O'Malley: "The most helpless idiot is as far above a non-existent child as St. Bridget is above a committee on birth control." Let us pause over the idiot and the non-existent child. Must we say that all potential children should be born? Are we to take a firm stand against celibacy, which denies to so many possible children the right to be baptized? And will Dr. O'Malley tell us which is the greater virtue, to bear children that they may be baptized, or to have no children for the glory of one's own soul? This solicitude over the non-existent child has certain drawbacks. How large a family, in fact, does Dr. O'Malley desire a woman to bear? May she stop after the fourteenth infant, or must she say to herself: "There are still non-existent children, some of them helpless idiots; perhaps I will bear them that they may be baptized."[1]

Or, if we should submit any series of behavior problems to a set of men selected as most competent to give an opinion we should find no such unanimity as prevailed in a village community. One set of opinions would be rigoristic and hold that conformity with

[1] Editorial in *The New Republic*, June 19, 1915.

the existing code is advisable under all circumstances; another pragmatic, holding that the code may sometimes be violated. For example, in 1919, the United States Interdepartmental Social Hygiene Board authorized the Psychological Laboratory of the Johns Hopkins University to make an investigation of the "informational and educative effect upon the public of certain motion-picture films", and in this connection a questionnaire was sent to "medical men and women who have had most to do with problems in sex education and the actual treatment of venereal infections." From the manuscript of this investigation I give below some of the replies received to question 13.

42. Question 13. Do you consider that absolute continence is always to be insisted upon? Or may it be taught that under certain conditions intercourse in the unmarried is harmless or beneficial?

Dr. A. I know of no harm from absolute continence. Intercourse in the unmarried cannot be justified on any grounds of health or morals.

Dr. B. No. For some absolute continence would be easy, for others, impossible. It is an individual problem to be decided by the individual, with or without advice.

Under certain conditions in the unmarried, male or female, intercourse is harmless or beneficial; under other conditions it is harmful and injurious (irrespective of venereal disease).

Dr. C. I think it is harmless and beneficial. But our standards are against it. And who could possibly conscientiously teach such a thing, no matter what he thought?

Dr. D. Certainly not. It is probably well to teach young people that continence before marriage is in general very desirable, as contrasted with the results of incontinence.

Dr. E. It is best to teach conformity to custom.

Dr. F. Absolute continence should always be insisted upon.

Dr. G. I know of no condition where one is justified in advising the unmarried that intercourse is harmless or beneficial.

Dr. H. Absolute continence.

Dr. I. No. [Continence is not always to be insisted upon.]

Dr. J. The first should not be insisted on any more than the latter should be recommended. . . .

Dr. K. The latter may be taught.

Dr. L. Not convinced either way.

Dr. M. Absolute continence should be preached as a doctrine to the unmarried, and let the individual adjust himself to this stern law according to his lights.[1]

Fifty-one replies were received to this question. Twenty-four were, in substance, "not permissible"; fifteen, "permissible"; four, "in doubt"; eight were indefinite, as, for example: "Adults will probably decide this for themselves."

As another example of a general defining agency, the legal system of the state does not pretend to be more than a partial set of negative definitions. An English jurist has thus described the scope of the law: "If A is drowning and if B is present, and if B by reaching out his hand can save A, and if B does not do this, and if A drowns, then B has committed no offense." All that the law requires of B is that he shall not push A into the water. The law is not only far from being a system capable of regulating the total life of men, but it does not even regulate the activities it is designed to regulate.

[1] These materials, edited by John B. Watson and K. S. Lashley, have been printed in part in *Mental Hygiene*, Vol. 4, pp. 769–847.

43. A misdemeanor may be much more heinous than a felony. The adulterator of drugs or the employer of child labor may well be regarded as vastly more reprehensible than the tramp who steals part of the family wash. So far as that goes there is an alarming multitude of acts and omissions not forbidden by statute or classified as crimes which are to all intents . . . fully as criminal as those designated as such by law. . . . For example, to push a blind man over the edge of the cliff so that he is killed . . . is murder, but to permit him to walk over it is no crime at all. It is a crime to defame the character of a woman if you write on a slip of paper, but no crime at all in the state of New York if you rise in a crowded hall and ruin her forever by word of mouth. It is a crime to steal a banana off a fruit stand, but no crime at all to borrow ten thousand dollars from a man whose entire fortune it is, although you have no expectation of returning it. . . . It is a crime to ruin a girl of 17 years and 11 months, but not to ruin a girl of 18. . . . Lying is not a crime, but lying under oath is a crime, provided it relates to a *material* matter, and what is a material matter jurists do not agree on. . . . Many criminals, even guilty of homicide, are as white as snow in comparison with others who have never transgressed the literal wording of the penal statute. "We used to have so and so for our lawyer," remarked the president of a street-railway corporation. "He was always telling us what we could n't do. Now we have Blank and pay him $100,000 a year to tell us how we can do the same things."[1]

The definition of the situation is equivalent to the determination of the vague. In the Russian *mir* and the American rural community of fifty years ago nothing was left vague, all was defined. But in the general world movement to which I have referred, connected with free communication in space and free

[1] A. Train: "The Prisoner at the Bar", p. 6.

communication of thought, not only particular situations but the most general situations have become vague. Some situations were once defined and have become vague again; some have arisen and have never been defined. Whether this country shall participate in world politics, whether America is a refuge for the oppressed of other nationalities, whether the English should occupy India or the Belgians Africa, whether there shall be Sunday amusements, whether the history of the world is the unfolding of the will of God, whether men may drink wine, whether evolution may be taught in schools, whether marriage is indissoluble, whether sex life outside of marriage is permissible, whether children should be taught the facts of sex, whether the number of children born may be voluntarily limited, — these questions have become vague. There are rival definitions of the situation, and none of them is binding.

In addition to the vagueness about these general questions there is an indeterminateness about particular acts and individual life-policies. It appears that the behavior of the young girl is influenced partly by the traditional code, partly by undesigned definitions of the situation derived from those incidents in the passing show of the greater world which suggest to her pleasure and recognition. If any standard prevails or characterizes a distinguished social set this is in itself a definition of the situation. Thus in a city the shop windows, the costumes worn on the streets, the newspaper advertisements of ladies' wear, the news items concerning objects of luxury define a proper girl as one neatly, fashionably, beautifully, and expensively gowned, and the behavior of the girl is an adaptation to this standard.

44. Supreme Court Justice Tierney remarked in the course of a trial between two women over the purchase of silk lingerie and paradise feathers yesterday, "The workings of the feminine mind are beyond me." . . .

The articles which Mrs. Small admits buying and the prices asked by Mme. Nicole are as follows:

Six suits of silk underwear, $780; six suits linen underwear, $780; six pairs silk stockings, $180; paradise feathers for fan, $1,480; handle for fan, $720.[1]

45. . . . My sweetheart remarked that she would like to have a great deal of money. When I asked her what she would do with it, she replied that she would buy herself a lot of beautiful dresses. When I said that it was all right to have them but it ought to be all right without them too, she protested that she loved fine clothes and this to such extent, that —

Here she made a remark which I am ashamed to let pass my lips. I would sooner have welcomed an open grave than to have heard those words. She said that she would sell her body for a time in order to procure nice clothes for herself.

And since that day I go around like a mad person. I neither eat nor sleep. In short, I am no more a man.

She afterward excused herself, claiming that it was said in a joke, and that as long as one talks without actually doing it there is no harm in it. But this is not reassuring to me. I have a premonition that she would go further than mere talk after marriage, for if she carries such notions in her head now, what might happen after we are married.[2]

Intermediate between the home and work (or the school) there are certain organized influences for giving pleasure and information — the motion picture, the newspaper, the light periodical — which define the situation in equivocal terms. They enter the home and are dependent upon its approval, and are there-

---

[1] *N. Y. World*, February 4, 1922.
[2] *Forward*, May 4, 1920.

fore obliged to present life in episodes which depict
the triumph of virtue. But if they limited themselves
to this they would be dull. The spectacle therefore
contains a large and alluring element of sin over which
virtue eventually triumphs. The moral element is
preserved nominally but the real interest and substance
is something else.

46. A young girl may be taught at home and church that
chastity is a virtue, but the newspapers and the movies feature women in trouble along this line, now painting them
as heroines, now sobbing over their mystery and pathos.
Apparently *they* get all the attention and attention is the
life blood of youth. The funny papers ridicule marriage,
old maids and bashful men. The movies, magazines, street
conversation and contemporary life are filled with the description of lapses that somehow turn out safely and even
luxuriously. If the modern young girl practises virtue she
may not believe in it. The preliminaries to wrong-doing
are apparently the accepted manners of the time. When
the girl herself lapses it is frequently because of lack of a
uniform, authoritative definition of the social code.[1]

Among well-to-do girls a new type has been differ-
entiated, characterized by youth, seeming innocence,
sexual sophistication and a relatively complete de-
pudorization.

47. The modern age of girls and young men is intensely
immoral, and immoral seemingly without the pressure of
circumstances. At whose door we may lay the fault, we
cannot tell. Is it the result of what we call "the eman-
cipation of woman", with its concomitant freedom from
chaperonage, increased intimacy between the sexes in adolescence, and a more tolerant viewpoint toward all things

[1] Miriam Van Waters: "The True Value of Correctional Education."
Paper read at the 51st American Prison Conference, November 1, 1921.

unclean in life? This seems the only logical forbear of the present state. And are the girls causing it now, or the men? Each sex will lay the blame on the heads, or passions, of the other, and perhaps both sexes are equally at fault.

Whosesoever the fault may be (and that is not such an important question, since both sexes are equally immoral), the whole character of social relations among younger people is lamentable. The modern dances are disgusting — the "toddle" and its variations and vibrations, the "shimmy" and its brazen pandering to the animal senses, and the worst offspring of jazz, the "camel-walk." There is but one idea predominant in these dances — one that we will leave unnamed.

It is not only in dancing that this immorality appears. The modern social bud drinks, not too much often, but enough; smokes considerably, swears unguardedly, and tells "dirty" stories. All in all, she is a most frivolous, passionate, sensation-seeking little thing.[1]

48. "Flappers" usually are girls who believe personality is physical, who consider all advice as abstract, who love continual change, who converse in generalities and who are in many higher institutions of learning.

To present a picture of the normal girl as she exists to-day is a daring venture. She has no average, she has no group tie. She is a stranger to herself — sometimes especially to members of her own family — and cannot be compared with her kind of a previous age.

We are tempted to think of her as living in a spirit of masquerade, so rapidly and completely can she assume different and difficult rôles of accomplishment.

She tantalizes us by the simpleness of her artfulness and yet unrealness. We find her light-hearted, which is the privilege of youth. She believes with Stevenson that to have missed the joy is to have missed it all. We find her harboring secrets and imbedded emotions which are her hidden

---

[1] Editorial in the Brown University *Daily Herald* quoted in the *New York World*, February 3, 1921.

treasure in the mysterious discovery of herself as a private individual. If we do not understand these symptoms we call it temperament and try to dispose of the girl as difficult or as needing discipline.[1]

Formerly the fortunes of the individual were bound up with those of his family and to some degree with those of the community. He had his security, recognition, response, and new experience in the main as group member. He could not rise or fall greatly above or below the group level. Even the drunkard and the "black sheep" had respect in proportion to the standing of his family. And correspondingly, if a family member lost his "honor", the standing of the whole family was lowered.

Individualism, on the other hand, means the personal schematization of life, — making one's own definitions of the situation and determining one's own behavior norms. Actually there never has been and never will be anything like complete individualization, because no one lives or can live without regard to a public. Anything else would be insanity. But in their occupational pursuits men have already a degree of individualization, decide things alone and in their own way. They take risks, schematize their enterprises, succeed or fail, rise higher and fall lower. A large element of individualism has entered into the marriage relation also. Married women are now entering the occupations freely and from choice, and carrying on amateur interests which formerly were not thought of as going with marriage. And this is evidently a good thing, and stabilizes marriage. Marriage alone is not a life, particularly since the decline

[1] Mary Ide Bentley, Address at Berkeley, California. *New York Sun*, February 7, 1922.

of the community type of organization. The cry of despair in document No. 37 is from a woman who limited her life to marriage, probably by her own choice, and is now apparently too old to have other interests. But on the other hand document No. 49 is a definition of marriage as exclusively a device for the realization of personal wishes and the avoidance of responsibility. This may be compared with No. 71 (p. 122) where a girl organizes her life similarly without marriage.

49. Girls, get married! Even if your marriage turns out badly, you are better off than if you had stayed single. I know half a dozen women whose first marriages were failures. They got rid of their first husbands easily and have made much better marriages than they could have made if they had stayed single. Their new husbands idolize them. One of my women acquaintances who has been married four times is the most petted wife I know.

My own marriage has turned out well. Everything seemed against it. I was well known in my profession, and when I married I was making as much money as my husband. We were of different religions. He drank.

But he had one big quality. He was generous. Since our marriage he has refused to let me work. Girls, be sure the man you pick is generous. Look out for a tightwad. If a man is liberal with his money he is sure to be easy to get along with. Liberal men in money matters do not annoy their wives in the other concerns of life. . . .

But even if my marriage had turned out badly, I would have been better off than if I had neglected the opportunity to become married. I met new friends through my husband. If I had divorced him at any time, I know many of his men friends would have courted me. There is something about the magic letters "Mrs." that gives a woman an added attraction in the eyes of men. There is a middle-aged widow in our apartment house that has more men taking her to theatres and dances than all the flappers and unmarried young women. . . .

I often wonder what men get married for. They take heavy financial responsibilities. They mortgage their free time to one woman. What a wife's clothes cost them would enable them to enjoy expensive amusements, extensive travel and better surroundings generally. Then, too, a bachelor, no matter what his age or social position, gets more attention socially than a married man. Children, too, give less pleasure and service to a father than a mother.

But for women, marriage is undoubtedly a success. It raises their position in the community. In most cases, it releases them from the danger of daily necessary work and responsibility. It brings them more attention from other men. Even when incompatibility intervenes, alimony provides separate support without work. In such cases, it also provides a more strategic position for a new and better marriage.[1]

In the same connection, the following cases show the growing tendency toward individualized definitions of sexual relations outside of marriage. In case No. 50 an immigrant girl explicitly organizes her life on the basis of prostitution instead of work. In No. 51 the girls commercialize a series of betrothals. In No. 52 the girl has worked out her own philosophy of love and calls herself a missionary prostitute.

50. [When I left Europe] my little sister's last words were, "Here, in hell, I will dream through the nights that far, far, across the ocean, my loving brother lives happily." And my last words were, "I shall forget my right hand if I ever forget you."

I suffered not a little in the golden land. . . . Five years passed. I loyally served the God of gold, saved some money

[1] *New York American,* September 27, 1920.

and sent for my sister. For three years I believed myself the happiest of men. . . . My sister bloomed like a rose in May and she was kind and motherly to me. We were tied by a bond of the highest love and on my part that love had until now remained the same. But listen what a terrible thing occurred.

About a year ago I noticed a marked change in my sister — both physically and spiritually. She grew pale, her eyes lost their fire and her attitude toward me changed also. She began to neglect her work (I taught her a good trade), until half a year ago she entirely gave up the work. This angered me very much and I began to shadow her in order to discover the mystery in her life, for she had recently avoided talking to me, particularly of her life. I concluded that she kept company with a boy and that caused her trouble.

But I soon noticed that she was wearing such expensive things that a boy could not afford to buy them. She had a couple of diamond rings and plenty of other jewelry. I investigated until I discovered, oh, horrible! that my sister was a prostitute. . . .

You can understand that I want to drag her out of the mire, but . . . she tells me that I do not understand life. She cannot conceive why it should be considered indecent to sell one's body in this manner. When I point out to her the end that awaits her she says in the first place it is not more harmful than working by steam for twelve to fourteen hours; in the second place, even if it were so, she enjoys life more. One must take as much as possible out of life. When I call her attention to the horrible degradation she replies that in the shop, too, we are humiliated by the foreman, and so on. . . .

I know that if I could convince her that I am right, she would be willing to emerge from the swamp, but I am unfortunately too inadequate in words, she being a good speaker, and I am usually defeated.[1]

[1] *Forward*, January 1, 1920.

51. I read in the "Bintel" the letter of a young man who complained that his fiancée extorted presents from him and that when, as a result of unemployment, he was unable to buy her everything she demanded, she began to make trouble for him — that she was evidently playing to have him desert her and leave her the property she had extorted.

Well, I am a woman myself, and can bear testimony that there are unfortunately such corrupted characters among my sex, who rob young men in this disgraceful manner. With these girls it is a business to "trim" innocent and sincere young men and then leave them. To them it is both business and pleasure. It gives them great joy to catch a victim in their outspread net and press as much of his hard-earned money out of him as possible.

I know a girl who . . . extracted from her naïve victim everything she laid her eyes on. When he stopped buying her so many things she began to treat him so shamefully that the poor boy was compelled to run away to another town, leaving all his gifts with the girl. The poor fellow was not aware that his so-called fiancée merely tricked him into buying her all kinds of jewelry and finery. He was afraid she would sue him for breach of promise and this fear caused him to leave town.

And don't think for a moment that that girl is ashamed of her deed. Not at all. She even boasts of her cleverness in turning the heads of young men and their pockets inside out. She expects to be admired for that. . . .

I attempted to explain to her that she is a common swindler and thief, but she replied that not only is it not wrong but a philanthropical act. Her argument was that there are many men who betray innocent girls and it is therefore no more than right that girls should betray men also.[1]

52. [After the marriage of a brilliant man who had flirted with her but never mentioned marriage] she went on the stage, and was immoral in an unhappy sort of way. She

---

[1] *Forward,* December 15, 1920.

met a young artist whose struggles for success aroused her pity and motherly instinct. With the memory of her faithless lover uppermost she plunged into a passionate realization of sex, more to drown her feelings than anything else. She roused the best in this boy, made a man of him, and steadied him. With her sexual tempests there came an after-calm when she forbade any familiarity. This was not studied but an instinct. She hated men, yet they fascinated her, and she them.

She studied stenography and worked as private secretary in a theatrical company. She tried to face life with work as her only outlet, but the restlessness of her grief made her crave excitement. She made friends easily, but her sexual appeal made it difficult for her to fit into a commonplace social atmosphere. She married the artist to the girl he loved, after a terrible struggle to make him realize it was not herself he loved. Later he came and thanked her. "The quiet women make the best wives," he said, "but my wife would not have loved me if you had not made me into a man. She cannot, however, give me what I get from you. I wish I could come to you once in a while?"

She said yes, and he came. That was five years ago and that is why she calls herself a prostitute. Her women friends have no idea she is not the quiet, dignified woman she appears to be, and men, many of them married men, want her for their own. She has no use for the man about town; only the man with brains or talent fascinates her at all. She says, "I suppose every one would think me a sinner; I am. I deliberately let a married man stay with me for a time. It is an art. I have learned to know their troubles. They tell me they are unhappy with their wives, wish to go away, are desperate with the monotony of existence. It is generally that they are not sexually mated, or the wife has no sex attraction. Of course she loves him, and he her. I give them what they need. It is weary for the brain to understand men, it is harder on me mentally than physically. I control them only because I have self-

restraint. I send them away soon. They are furious;
they storm and rage and threaten they will go to some other
woman. What do I care? They know it and I send them
back to their wives. They will go to her; they would not
go to any other woman. That is where I do good. This
sex business is a strange thing. I am a missionary prostitute. I only do this once in a while, when I think a man
needs me and he is one who will come under my influence.
I know I have managed to avert the downfall of several
households. If the wives knew? Never mind; they don't.
I am not coarse; I can be a comrade to a man and doubt if
I harm him. I make him sin in the general acceptance of
the term, the common interpretation of God's commandments. How do we know God did n't mean us to use all the
powers he gave us? [1]

In the two cases following, adjustment to life is
highly individualized but moral and social. The one
is a response adjustment, recognizing freedom for new
experience, particularly for creative work, and in the
other marriage is based on the inherent values of the
relationship, and on nothing else.

53. Being firmly of the opinion that nine out of ten of
the alliances I saw about me were merely sordid endurance
tests, overgrown with a fungus of familiarity and contempt,
convinced that too often the most sacred relationship wears
off like a piece of high sheen satin damask, and in a few
months becomes a breakfast cloth, stale with soft-boiled egg
stains, I made certain resolutions concerning what my marriage should not be.

First of all, I am anxious to emphasize that my marriage
was neither the result of a fad or an ism, but simply the
working out of a problem according to the highly specialized
needs of two professional people.

[1] Edith L. Smith, in Collaboration with Hugh Cabot: "A Study in
Sexual Morality", *Social Hygiene*, Vol. 2, p. 537.

We decided to live separately, maintaining our individual studio-apartments and meeting as per inclination and not duty. We decided that seven breakfasts a week opposite one another might prove irksome. Our average is two. We decided that the antediluvian custom of a woman casting aside the name that had become as much a part of her personality as the color of her eyes had neither rhyme or reason. I was born Fannie Hurst and expect to die Fannie Hurst. We decided that in the event of offspring the child should take the paternal name until reaching the age of discretion, when the final decision would lie with him.

My husband telephones me for a dinner appointment exactly the same as scores of other friends. I have the same regard for his plans. We decided that, since nature so often springs a trap as her means to inveigle two people into matrimony, we would try our marriage for a year and at the end of that period go quietly apart, should the venture prove itself a liability instead of an asset. . . .

On these premises, in our case at least, after a five-year acid test, the dust is still on the butterfly wings of our adventure. The dew is on the rose.[1]

54. I am a college graduate, 27, married five years and the mother of a three-year-old boy. I have been married happily, and have been faithful to my husband.

At six I had decided upon my husband. Jack was his name; he was a beautiful boy, fair, blue eyes, delicate and poetic looking. He was mentally my superior, he loved poetry and wrote good verses. He read a great deal and talked well. He loved me and I loved him, yet there was no demonstration of it in embraces. We played together constantly, and we spoke of the time when we might marry. His great desire was to have a colored child with light hair and blue eyes for a daughter, and we had agreed upon it. All of our plans were spoken about before our parents, there was no effort made to hide our attachment. I was by nature

[1] *New York World*, May 4, 1920.

rough and a great fighter, Jack was calm and serious, and at times I fought his battles for him. I was maternal towards him. His mother died during our friendship, and I tried to take her place. It was a pure love, nothing cheap or silly. He was killed in the Iroquois Fire and my life was dreary for a long time. I remember the hopeless feeling I experienced when I heard the news. I did not weep, I turned to my mother and said, "I don't want to live any longer."

We had always been allowed to sit across from each other at school, and after Jack's death, I was granted permission to keep his seat vacant for the rest of the year, and I kept a plant on the desk which I tended daily as a memorial to my friend.

. . . In college, a coeducational school, I was not allowed to remain ignorant long. I was young and healthy and a real *Bachfisch* in my enthusiastic belief in goodness. I was fortunate in having a level-headed senior for my best friend. She saw an upper classman [girl] falling in love with me, and she came to me with the news. Then she saw how innocent I was and how ignorant, and my sex education was begun. She told me of marriage, of mistresses, of homosexuality. I was sick with so much body thrown at me at once, and to add to the unpleasantness some one introduced me to Whitman's poetry. I got the idea that sex meant pain for women, and I determined never to marry.

But the next year I felt very differently about sex. I was used to the knowledge and I went with a crowd of girls who were wise, and I had a crush. I had never been stirred before, but I was by her. She told me her ambitions, and I told her mine; it was the first time I had ever been a person to any one, and I was her loyal and loving friend. I kissed her intimately once and thought that I had discovered something new and original. We read Maupassant together and she told me the way a boy had made love to her. Everything was changed, love was fun, I was wild to taste it. I cultivated beaux, I let them kiss me and embrace me, and when they asked me to live with them, I was not offended but pleased. I learned my capacity, how far I could go without losing my head, how much I could drink, smoke, and I talked as freely as a person could. I discussed these adventures with the other girls, and we compared notes on kisses and phrases, and technique. We were healthy animals and we were demanding our rights to spring's awakening. I never felt cheapened, nor repentant, and I played square with the men. I always told them I was not out to pin them down to marriage, but that this intimacy was pleasant and I wanted it as much as they did. We indulged in sex talk, birth control, leutic infection, mistresses; we were told of the sins of our beaux, and I met one boy's mistress, an old university girl. This was life. I could have had complete relations with two of these boys if there had been no social stigma attached, and enjoyed it for a time. But instead I consoled myself with thinking that I still had time to give up my virginity, and that when I did I wanted as much as I could get for it in the way of passionate love. Perhaps the thing that saved me from falling in love was a sense of humor. That part of me always watched the rest of me pretend to be swooning, and I never really closed my eyes. But there was a lot of unhealthy sex going around because of the artificial cut off. We thought too much about it; we all tasted homosexuality in some degree. We never found anything that could be a full stop because there was no gratification.

During this period of stress and heat I met a man, fine, clean, mature and not seemingly bothered with sex at all. I kissed him intimately too, but it was very different. He had great respect for me, and he believed in me. I respected him, admired his artistic soul and his keen mind. There was no sex talk with him, it was music and world-views and philosophy. He never made any rash statements, nor false steps. He could sense a situation without touching it, and I felt drawn to him. I knew he had never been with a woman and he told me once that he could never express

more than he felt for a person, and could sustain. After
five years of friendship we married. There was no great
flair to it; it was an inner necessity that drove us to it;
we could no longer escape each other. We tried to figure it
out, but the riddle always said marry. Sexually I had more
experience than he, I was his first mistress, his wife, his
best friend, and his mother, and no matter what our moods
were, in one of these capacities I was needed by him. Our
adjustment was difficult; he had lived alone for thirty years.
I was used to having my own way, and he was a very sensitive man, nervous, sure of his opinion, and we quarreled for
a while, but never very bitterly. Sexually we were both
afraid of offending the other and so that was slow. But in
four months we had found our heads again and were well
adjusted. He was, and is, the best friend I ever had. I
love him more as I know him longer. We can share everything, we are utterly honest and frank with each other, we
enjoy our sex life tremendously as well as our friendship.
But it was difficult for us to abandon ourselves. To allow
any one to know you better than you know yourself is a
huge and serious thing and calls for time and love and humor.

I have never known any one as fine as my husband. He
is generous, honest, keen, artistic, big, liberal, everything
that I most want in a person. I have never been tired of
him. I feel confident that he loves me more now than ever
before and that he thinks me very fine, a good sport. We
have been thrown together a great deal through poverty, and
I feel that we are alone in the world and facing it together,
a not too friendly world at that. Yet with all this love and
closeness, I don't feel that I possess my husband, nor that
he does me. I am still the same old girl, the same personality, and my first duty is to develop my own gifts. I have
no feeling of permanency with him because we are legally
married, but at present a separation is unthinkable. I am
worth more to myself with him, and life is infinitely sweeter
and richer within the home than any other place.

But if I had married the average American husband who

plays the business game as a religion, then I should long ago have been unfaithful to him. I could never disclose myself and be happy with a man who had any interest more important to him than our relationship.

As long as our relationship continues as it is I think we will both be faithful to each other. But I need to have freedom to move about now with all this. And perhaps part of my happiness consists in the fact that I do have freedom. I have had intimate friendships with other men since I am married, kissed them, been kissed, been told that they would like to have me with them. But none of this seems to touch my relation with my husband. I want, and I need to be, intimate on my own hook in my own way with other people. I don't honestly know whether I would take a lover or not. If my husband gave me the assurance that he would take me back, on the old basis, I think I would try it to see if it's as great as it's said to be. But if I had to give up my husband, I would not. I need him as I need my eyes and hands. He is the overtone in the harmony, and I am that for him. I like to experiment, but from past experience I believe the cost would be greater than the gain. I am free at home as I am not anywhere else. I love it, I express myself freely and completely emotionally, and the only reason I could have for being unfaithful would be experimentation. And if I were unfaithful I should have to tell my husband the whole affair; I could not enjoy it otherwise. I have no feeling against it, and no urge towards it. I can honestly say that I am a happy woman, that I have every opportunity to develop my potentialities in my present relation, that I am free as any one can be, that my husband is superior, as a mate for me, to any one I have ever seen. I regret nothing of the past; it could have been improved tremendously, but it was pleasant and human.[1]

[1] Autobiography (Manuscript).

CHAPTER IV

THE DEMORALIZATION OF GIRLS

THE rôle which a girl is expected to play in life is first of all indicated to her by her family in a series of æsthetic-moral definitions of the situation. Civilized societies, more especially, have endowed the young girl with a character of social sacredness. She has been the subject of a far-going idealization. "Virginity" and "purity" have almost a magical value. This attitude has a useful side, though it has been overdone. The girl as child does not know she has any particular value until she learns it from others, but if she is regarded with adoration she correspondingly respects herself and tends to become what is expected of her. And so she has in fact a greater value. She makes a better marriage and reflects recognition on her family.

But we must understand that this sublimation of life is an investment. It requires that incessant attention and effort illustrated in document No. 36 (p. 62) and goes on best when life is economically secure. And there are families and whole strata of society where life affords no investments. There is little to gain and little to lose. Social workers report that sometimes overburdened mothers with large families complain that they have no "graveyard luck" — all the children live. In cases of great neglect the girl cannot be said to fall, because she has never risen. She is not immoral, because this implies the loss of morality, but a-moral — never having had a moral code.

55. Nine of the fifteen families [of the working class in Rome] are formed on a non-legitimate basis. . . . In fourteen of the fifteen families there is habitual obscenity. . . . The children hear and repeat the obscenity and are laughed at. Each member lives on the average on 25 lire a month. . . . Criminals and prostitutes frequent the homes and have liaisons with the girls. Mothers, going to work, leave the children with a prostitute. . . . The finer sentiments are notably lacking. Brothers and sisters quarrel and fight. . . . Fights are habitual in eight of the fifteen families. . . . The sentiment of modesty and delicacy does not develop in the young. The regard for the child is expressed in the remark of a father (about children who were not fed and picked up scraps on the street) : "Let them have food when they make their own living."[1]

56. Any person who has dwelt among the denizens of the slums cannot fail to have brought home to him the existence of a stratum of society of no inconsiderable magnitude in which children part with their innocence long before puberty, in which personal chastity is virtually unknown, and in which "to have a baby by your father" is laughed at as a comic mishap.[2]

57. The experiences of Commenge in Paris are instructive on this point. "For many young girls," he writes, "modesty has no existence; they experience no emotion in showing themselves completely undressed, they abandon themselves to any chance individual whom they will never see again. They attach no importance to their virginity; they are deflowered under the strangest conditions, without the least thought or care about the act they are accomplishing. No sentiment, no calculation, pushes them into a man's arms. They let themselves go without reflexion and without motive, in an almost animal manner, from indifference and without pleasure." He was acquainted with forty-

[1] Résumé from A. Niceforo: "Les Classes Pauvres", pp. 257–274.
[2] Sidney and Beatrice Webb: " The Prevention of Destitution", p. 306.

five girls between the ages of twelve and seventeen who were deflowered by chance strangers whom they never met again; they lost their virginity, in Dumas's phrase, as they lost their milk-teeth, and could give no plausible account of the loss. . . . A girl of fourteen, living comfortably with her parents, sacrificed her virginity at a fair in return for a glass of beer, and henceforth begun to associate with prostitutes. Another girl of the same age, at a local fête, wishing to go round on the hobby horse, spontaneously offered herself to the man directing the machinery for the pleasure of a ride. . . . In the United States, Dr. W. T. Travis Gibb, examining physician to the New York Society for the Prevention of Cruelty to Children, bears similar testimony to the fact that in a fairly large proportion of "rape" cases the child is the willing victim. "It is horribly pathetic," he says, "to learn how far a nickel or a quarter will go towards purchasing the virtue of these children."[1]

58. In round numbers nine tenths of the delinquent girls and three fourths of the delinquent boys come from the homes of the poor. Sixty-nine per cent of the girls and 38 per cent of the boys come from the lowest class, the "very poor", the class in which there exists not merely destitution, but destitution accompanied by degradation, or destitution caused by degradation. . . .

In Table 19 it appears that 31 per cent of the delinquent boys and 47 per cent of the delinquent girls before their appearance in court had lost one or both parents by death, desertion, imprisonment, or similar misfortune, and that they had not had the benefit of the wholesome discipline which normal family life affords. . . .

These children come in many instances from homes in which they have been accustomed from their earliest infancy to drunkenness, immorality, obscene and vulgar language, filthy and degraded conditions of living. . . .

Among the 157 girls in the State Training School from

[1] Havelock Ellis: "Studies in the Psychology of Sex", Vol. 6. p. 275.

Chicago, for whom family schedules were obtained, 31 were
the daughters of drunken fathers, 10 at least had drunken
mothers, 27 had fathers who were of vicious habits, 16 had
immoral, vicious, or criminal mothers, while 12 belonged to
families in which other members than the parents were
vicious or criminal.   In at least 21 cases the father had
shirked all responsibility and had deserted the family.

There were also among these girls 11 who were known to
be illegitimate children or children who had been abandoned,
and there were 10 who had been victims of gross cruelty.
Forty-one had been in houses of prostitution or had been
promiscuously immoral, one having been "a common street
walker" at the age of eleven.   Four had sisters who had
become immoral and had been committed to such institutions as the Chicago Refuge for Girls or the house of correction, while in seven cases two sisters had been sent to Geneva ;
nine had brothers who had been in such institutions as the
parental school, the John Worthy School, the Bridewell,
the state reformatory at Pontiac, or the state penitentiary
at Joliet.

The worst cases of all are those of the delinquent girls
who come from depraved homes where the mother is a delinquent woman, or from homes still more tragic where the
father has himself abused the person of the child.   As a result of the interviews with the girls in the State Training
School at Geneva, it appeared that in 47 cases the girl alleged that she had been so violated by some member of her
family.   In 19 cases the father, in 5 the uncle, in 8 the brother
or older cousin had wronged the child for whom the community demanded their special protection.   In addition to
these cases discovered at Geneva, the court records show
that in at least 78 other cases the girl who was brought in as
delinquent had been wronged in this way — in 43 of these
cases by her own father.   In families of this degraded type
it is found, too, not only that the girl is victimized by her
father but that she is often led to her undoing by her mother
or by the woman who has undertaken to fill a mother's place.

It was found, for example, that in 189 cases where the girl was charged with immorality, the mother or the woman guardian — an aunt, a grandmother, or an older sister with whom the girl lived — was implicated in the offense if not responsible for it. . . .

Attention should be called to the fact that degraded and drunken habits of life are not the peculiar product of large cities. The personal interviews with the girls at Geneva who came from the smaller cities and rural communities of the state, together with the statements in the school records regarding the circumstances responsible for their commitment, show a degradation in family life which parallels that found in the homes of many of the Chicago children. Out of 153 of these country girls, 86 were the children of fathers with intemperate habits, and 13 had intemperate mothers. In 31 cases the girl's delinquency had been caused by her father or some other relative.[1]

59. Helen comes from a large family, there being eight children. Her father is a miner and unable to support the older girls. She was told at the age of fourteen that she was old enough to support herself and to get out. She came to Chillicothe because of the draftees from Western Pennsylvania, some of whom had been her acquaintances. She came to Chillicothe with $30.00 given her by a man in Ellsworth, but we could never learn his name.

The girl was found living in a dirty basement room with "Mag" Strawser, a character of local repute, and spent every evening either at the movies or at the public dance halls with soldiers. She was taken home from the movies and an effort was made to place her in a decent room, but twice she ran away and back to the same environment. The Juvenile Judge wrote to the father, asking him to send money for her return home, but he responded by saying that he did n't want the girl home as she must make her own living. As he could n't send her money she was sent back

---

[1] Sophonisba P. Breckenridge and Edith Abbott: "The Delinquent Child and the Home", pp. 74, 105.

with money furnished by Protective Bureau.   Three months later she was picked up in the park with soldiers.   At the time she was dressed like a trapeze performer, in pink satin trimmed with eider down, grotesque in the extreme.   She escaped from the Detention Home and three days later was picked up in the woods back of the Base Hospital with five soldiers.   Upon examination, was found to have gonorrhea. . . .   In a few weeks she had developed from the little red hood and mittens with the stout shoes of the foreigner into a painted-cheeked brow-blacked prostitute.   She had her name and address written on slips of paper that she passed out to soldiers on the streets.   She was never able to give the names of soldiers with whom she cohabited, but upon first acquaintance would lend her bracelet or ring without hesitation.[1]

60. Evelyn claims to know absolutely nothing of her family or relations.   Was found in a room in a hotel, where she had registered as the wife of a soldier.   Seemed entirely friendless and alone.   Had scarcely any clothing, and there was no evidence of refinement to be found about her.   She is small, slight and anæmic, has an active syphilis as well as an acute gonorrhea.   At first she seemed to be entirely hardened, not caring what any one thought of her or what became of her.   Later however she broke down and was just a poor broken-hearted child.   Admits to many dreadful experiences for her tender years.   Claims for the past year has been on the vaudeville stage and has had illicit relations with a number of members of the company.   Left the troop at Wilkesbarre, Pennsylvania.   Here she picked up with a soldier who brought her to Columbus, Ohio, and she has been picking up soldiers on the streets and going out with them in taxis.

The only person who could be reached having an acquaintance with the girl is Mrs. Harding at Columbus.   She wrote us that her daughter Gladys had become acquainted

---

[1] Records of the Girls' Protective Bureau.

with her while on a visit to Wheeling where the girl was working as a little household drudge in a private home. When
the girl came to Columbus she came to the Harding home
and was treated as one of the family until she became incorrigible, when she went to the working girls' home.

Evelyn believes herself to be an illegitimate child. From
her earliest recollection she was in a Catholic institution.
Was placed out when she was nine years old and from that
time has been in many cities, in private homes, in institutions and out again. Has had no supervision of any kind.
Has sought companionship and friendliness of any one that
would show her any affection. Did not seem to feel that
she had done anything very wrong. It seems to be a case
of society's neglect to an orphan. She was taken to the
Isolation Hospital for treatment for syphilis infection and
escaped within 24 hours.[1]

61. Frances was 12 years old when in July, 1912, a probation officer of the Juvenile Court reported that she remained out late nights, sometimes all night, refused to obey
father or mother, would go into a room and lock the door,
compelling parents to force an entrance, etc. When 14
years old she was brought into court on the complaint of
her mother that she kept bad company and was known in
the neighborhood as a depraved child, being accused by
one neighbor of stealing a bracelet. She had been on probation and the reports had been fairly encouraging. Every
little while there were reports of disobedience with threats
of sending her to an institution, followed by improved conduct for a while. For a short time Frances had tried boarding outside her home.

At the hearing in court her mother testified: "She did
not want to go to work and also stayed away from home
nights, would not tell where. . . . When I looked for her
I almost got a licken from the old man. He says I did not
have to look for her when she was no good. He licked me

---

[1] Records of the Girls' Protective Bureau.

many times on account of her; does not want me to go to look for her." The officer stated: "The father is a hard drinker and very quarrelsome. Sets very bad example for the children. The other children [4 younger ones at home] seem to get along and mind the mother, but this girl and an older married sister were the wayward ones." Frances said her father sometimes struck her with a strap when he got drunk. Her mother drank but was never intoxicated. She was sent to the House of Good Shepherd where she remained a full year and "made good." There was no complaint against her there. Her mother then applied for her release on the ground that she had rheumatism and a new baby 6 months old.

An investigation of the home was made. The neighbors reported the "family are quarreling, parents continually drunk, use vile language, and while well fed and kept, the environment is such that just as soon as the girls become self-supporting they leave home. Mr. Sikora is abusive to his wife, insanely jealous, charges his wife with immorality constantly." Probation officer was called to house to put down a disturbance one night at 9 P.M. The mother, when questioned, admitted that an older daughter, now 18 years old, had had a "wild" career and then married. The next daughter left home because of complaints of her staying out late nights. She had been in the House of the Good Shepherd, was not 17 years old and her mother knew nothing of her whereabouts.[1]

62. Catherine was sent to the industrial class at Geneva when only nine years old, apparently for immorality. She said her mother was a very "nice woman" but her father was a "poor sort of father." He drank, beat her mother and was in jail "a lot of times." Two years after she entered the school her mother took sick. Catherine was allowed to return to her until she died three months later. The father disappeared and Catherine returned to Geneva. Catherine

[1] Records of the Juvenile Court of Cook County, Illinois.

had an uncle in Wisconsin whom she had not seen for 4 years and a brother, who considered Catherine "wild" and was willing she should stay in Geneva.

The Genevan authorities reported that Catherine was hard to control at first but after she had been made to see that the whole world was not against her, she settled down, became very obedient and was one of their best girls. She had nothing vicious about her, was easily influenced for good and showed she had a great deal of good in her and much energy, which if properly directed would make her develop into a good woman.

When Catherine was fourteen years old her brother had her released from Geneva on parole to him. He took her to live with him in Rockford, Ill., where he had the reputation of being a very industrious man. He got Catherine a job, topping stockings in a factory for $7.00 a week and took all her earnings. Catherine worked steadily and well for six months.

Catherine got acquainted with her brother's sister-in-law, Jennie Sopeka, a girl ten years older, with an exceedingly bad reputation. Ever since she came from New York six years before she had led a disgracefully immoral life, was known to have a venereal disease, which was thought to be affecting her mind. Catherine said she knew nothing of this girl when she came to see her and proposed they go to Chicago "to have a nice time and nice clothes." But Catherine left Rockford with Jennie at once. They came to Chicago and registered at the Imperial Hotel. For a week some man supported them. They then became acquainted with two junior medical students. . . . These boys called on them at the hotel and after a two weeks' acquaintance took them and another girl to their rooms. All lived together for about two weeks. The police then raided the apartment, arrested the boys and Jennie and the other girl. Catherine happened to be out when the raid was made, but the following day she called at the police station to know what had become of her friends and she was detained there. The boys were charged with rape, as Catherine was under the age of consent. Jennie, who was going under one of her many aliases, was fined $50.00 and sent to the House of Correction. She was later accused of pandering.

Every one felt sorry for Catherine. The Court said: "It seems as if she had never had a chance, but it would be dangerous to give her one now." The Probation officer also felt sympathetic, though she thought Catherine had had a chance in Rockford and had not tried quite hard enough. Her brother refused to take her back into his home and the Court was in a quandary what to do with her. At first she said she would do housework, especially taking care of children, as she was very fond of babies and would like to be a nurse. Later, however, she decided she would not do housework and asked to be sent back to Geneva. This the Court would not do, and Catherine was sent to the House of Good Shepherd.[1]

[63.] Carrie is a colored girl, 23 years of age at the time of her commitment. She was sentenced to Bedford for possessing heroin. She was born on Long Island — the illegitimate child of a notorious thief and prostitute known only as "Jennie." She was adopted when fifteen months old and went to public school until she was fifteen, in spite of which at the time of her commitment she could read and spell only with great difficulty. Foster mother was a very poor housekeeper, went out to work, and the rooms she occupied were unspeakably filthy. Carrie had served five previous terms in the New York City Workhouse and 30 days in White Plains jail. She was first sentenced to the House of The Good Shepherd, but returned to the Court on account of her color. She was then sent to Inwood House and returned for the same reason. She had been committed to the Workhouse Hospital for treatment for the drug habit. She had practiced prostitution since she was fifteen years of age, during which time she lived for considerable periods with

[1] Records of the Juvenile Court of Cook County, Illinois.

two consorts, by one of whom she had a child, born in the
New York City Workhouse. She had used drugs steadily
for eight years, beginning with opium and more recently
using cocaine and heroin. Her foster mother states that
she was always a difficult child and very stubborn. When
she was as young as nine years old the neighbors complained
of her immoral conduct with young boys on roofs and cellars.
She seemed to have no feeling of shame.

Physical examination showed Carrie's condition to be
fair. The mental examination showed her to be a trifle
over nine years by the Stanford-Binet tests. Her attitude
was that she preferred the life of prostitution and planned
to return to it upon her release. It was felt that she would be
a bad influence in the Reformatory and that in view of her
sociological as well as her mental history she should be given
permanent custodial care.[1]

I was present in a Juvenile Court when a young girl
who showed charm and dignity was brought in for
stealing from department stores an astonishing number
of pretty things — a mirror, beads, a ring, a powder
box, etc. — all on the same afternoon. And she did
not forget to include a doll for her baby sister. The
inquiry brought out that she worked in a book bindery
in a suburb of the city. She had not lost a day for
two years, until laid off temporarily. Then she visited
the city. She gave all her pay, which was $9.00 a week,
to her mother. Of this her mother returned ten cents
for the girl's own use. The girl had no other blemish
and her thoughtfulness in stealing the doll for her sister
created some consternation. On the advice of the
court the mother agreed to increase the girl's allowance
to twenty-five cents a week.

On another occasion a father was asked by the court

[1] Case Histories of 21 Women . . . at Bedford Hills (Pamphlet) p. 3.

what he had to suggest in the case of his girl who had left home and was on the streets. He complained that she had not been bringing in all her pay. When told he must not look at the matter in that way, that he had obligations as a parent, he said, "Do what you please with her. She ain't no use to me."

The beginning of delinquency in girls is usually an impulse to get amusement, adventure, pretty clothes, favorable notice, distinction, freedom in the larger world which presents so many allurements and comparisons. The cases which I have examined (about three thousand) show that sexual passion does not play an important rôle, for the girls have usually become "wild" before the development of sexual desire, and their casual sexual relations do not usually awaken sex feeling. Their sex is used as a condition of the realization of other wishes. It is their capital. In the cases cited below Mary (case No. 64) begins by stealing to satisfy her desire for pretty clothes and "good times", then has sexual relations for the same purpose. Katie (No. 65) begins as a vagabond and sells her body just as she does occasional work or borrows money, in order to support herself on her vagabonding tours, sexual intercourse being only a means by which freedom from school work is secured. In the case of Stella (No. 66) the sexual element is part of a joy ride, probably not the first one. Marien (No. 67) treats sexual life as a condition of her "high life", including restaurants, moving pictures, hotels, and showy clothes. Helen (No. 68) said, "I always wanted good clothes." To the young girl of this class sexual intercourse is something submitted to with some reluctance and embarrassment and something she is glad to be over with. Nothing can show better the small importance attached to it than the plain story of the many relations of Annie (No. 69). She objects only to being used by a crowd.

64. When Mary was 14 years old she was arrested on the charge of stealing some jewelry and a dress and waist, altogether worth $100. While employed as domestic she had entered a neighboring flat through the dining-room window and helped herself. When arrested she said her father and mother were dead. But it was found they were both alive. The mother said she was glad the police had gotten hold of Mary, who stole and refused to work. The probation officer stated that the home was very poor, the father would often not work and they had made Mary begin to work when 12 years old and give all her wages to them.

Mary had obtained her present position by going to Gad's Hill Center a month and a half before and representing herself as an orphan. She had tried to throw the neighbor off her track by going to her with a story of a "big noise" she had heard in the flat, but they had searched her and found the stolen things. Her employer also complained that Mary had taken clothing from her and hidden it. Mary was sent to the House of the Good Shepherd, but after her mother's death in April, 1915, she was given some housework to do. On Dec. 17, 1915, she took $1 from her aunt and went away. She was sent to the Home for the Friendless. From there she wrote the probation officer complaining that the girl friends with whom she had been staying refused to let her have her clothes.

On Jan. 4, 1916, work was found for Mary at $7 a week. She worked one half day and then disappeared. She was located Jan. 10 and admitted remaining over night at a hotel four different nights with men. She did n't know their names. . . . "I was drove away from home by my aunt. How could I stay there?"

"Q. to aunt: Did you drive Mary away from your home?

"A. Yes. She took $1 and I did not want her home.

"Officer: I found out something since then. When she came from the House of the Good Shepherd she worked at housework and took two rings there and silk stockings and underwear.

"Q. You hear, Mary? Why did you do that?

"A. Because I did not have no clothes."[1]

65. Katie, 13 years old. August 22, 1913, in court. Picked up by an officer late at night after having wandered about the streets the two nights previous. Begged not to be taken home. . . . The home is poor. The mother sometimes goes out to work, leaving the girl at home alone. Parents are not capable of giving her the protection and supervision she ought to have. Though the mother claimed she had proper care she wanted her sent to an institution for a few months and then to have her home again. Girl sent to St. Hedwig's. She was released in October and behaved well for a few months, helping with the new baby at home.

April 16, 1914, brought to court with another younger girl for having stolen money and a watch from the purse of a woman in the shower-bath room in Eckhard Park.

Katie told the court she did not know why she left home, that she often left home and wandered around — could not control wandering impulse and habit she had fallen into, that when she left she worked in a hat factory half a day, for which she received 75 cents, which she used for meals, and on Feb. 14th she secured work and remained at it until arrested April 1st. Josephine, the younger girl, told the court that Katie asked her to go to a show with her. On the way Katie said her hair was falling down and suggested going into the park to arrange it. They went to the shower-bath rooms and Katie wished to take a bath. They looked into different bathrooms and in one room saw a purse which Katie suggested taking, saying she wanted money for a nickel show. Josephine took the purse and hid it under the bench,

[1] From the Records of the Juvenile Court of Cook County.

THE UNADJUSTED GIRL

but when the owner complained to the matron and threatened the girl with prison, Katie confessed and gave the purse back, putting most of the blame on Josephine. As it was proved that Josephine did not have a proper home atmosphere she was sent to the House of the Good Shepherd, while Catherine, who was a good girl, according to her mother, except for her wandering impulses, and who had never before stolen, was paroled.

May 19, 1914, held at police station. Claims to have known Robert Smith, a colored man 64 years of age, for several years. He lives in 2 rooms. . . . Learning that girls went there she too went and had immoral relations with Mr. Smith at different times. On one occasion he gave her 15 cents and other occasions 25 cents. . . . [She said] "I went away from home that day. My uncle [father] wanted to send me away to school, so I ran away. . . . I stayed [away 3 days and spent the night] in front of our house in the hallway."

Katie was sent to the House of Good Shepherd and released at her parents' request at the end of May, 1915, and behaved until July 31, she was arrested in a rooming house with 2 young men. She had intercourse with one, 21 years old, whom she knew before she was sent away and whom the officer described as a "bum." A social worker testified: "I met the girl at the police station . . . and I suggested that she be sent to the House of Good Shepherd, but she was very much prejudiced by her past years there. . . . I told her that if she met boys on the street she couldn't protect herself. She was very indignant in the police station." At her mother's request she was given another chance but was soon arrested for going with another girl, a saloon keeper and a photographer. When asked by the court what she had to say for herself she replied, "I don't care what you do; I deserve it." But she requested to be sent to Geneva instead of the House of The Good Shepherd — "they all say it is better." She ran away from Geneva after a few weeks but was apprehended through an anonymous telephone mes-

sage from a house on S. Michigan Ave.   After she was sent
back to Geneva she again escaped.[1]

66. Stella was 15 years old when she told this story to
the Juvenile Court: "On the night of June 7, 1916, about
8 o'clock Helen Sikowska and I were standing at the corner.
. . . Mike and Tomczak and another Mike came along in
an automobile and Helen asked them for a ride. We went
quite a ways, and then Tomczak said he wanted to [have
intercourse with] me. He said if we did not do it he would
not take us home. . . . They drove up in front of a saloon
and all three of the fellows went in the saloon and stayed
there about one hour. Helen and I sat in the car and waited
for them. They came out and we started back for home.
We drove for a ways, and when we came to a place where
there was no houses they stopped the machine and said it
was broke. Tomczak went to sleep. Mike, the driver of
the car, got out and took me with him and walked me over
the prairie. There he knocked me down and . . . did
something bad to me. . . . Then they took us back home."[2]

67. Marien was arrested for acting "obstreperous" with
another girl in a railway waiting room. She had no under-
clothing on when arrested [in June]. She was 16 years old,
had left home before Easter and had been going much to
shows and moving picture theaters. She told a police woman
that she had been drugged on the North side and carried to
a room by two men on different nights. . . . Marien said
she had "no fault to find" with her home, her father and
mother were kind to her.

The following letter was received from her while she was
away: "Dear Mother, I am feeling fine. Everything is all
right, don't worry about me. I am leading high life because
I am an actress. I got swell clothes and everything, you
wouldn't know me. I had Clara down town one day I was
out with the manager. She had a nice time. . . . I never
had such nice times in all my life. Everybody says that I

---

[1] Records of the Juvenile Court of Cook County.
[2] Records of the Juvenile Court of Cook County.

am pretty. I paid 65 dollars for my suit and 5 dollars had [hat], 6 dollars shoe 3 gloves 2 dollar underwar 5 dollar corest. Know I have hundred dollars in the bank but I want you to write a letter and say youll forgive me for not telling the truht but I will explain better when I see you and will return home for the sake of the little ones. I will bring a hundred dollars home to you and will come home very time I can its to expensive to liv at a hotel now sent the letter to me this way General Devilery Miss Marion Stephan."

Her father testified: "After Easter got a letter from her something like that one only more in it. She was rich and everything else, which is not so. So she says answer me quick as you can because I to go Milwaukee tomorrow. And I answer it right away to come home as soon as possible. Thought maybe the letter would reach her and heard nothing more until 3 weeks ago and then this letter come and I begging her to come home and be . . . a good girl. She come home and asked if wanted to stay home now and she feel very happy that she is home and thought maybe she would behave. . . . Next day she said she was going for her clothes . . . and I says I go with you. And I could not go and left my boy and girl to go with her Sunday. And she left them in the park and did not come home. Then she was back again Tuesday and in the evening when I come home from work she was not there."[1]

68. "When I saw sweller girls than me picked up in automobiles every night, can you blame me for falling too?"

Pretty Helen McGinnis, the convicted auto vamp of Chicago, asked the question seriously. She has just got an order for a new trial on the charge of luring Martin Metzler to Forest Reserve Park, where he was beaten and robbed. The girl went on:

"I always wanted good clothes, but I never could get them, for our family is large and money is scarce. I wanted good times like the other girls in the office. Every girl

---

[1] Records of the Juvenile Court of Cook County.

seemed to be a boulevard vamp.   "I'd seen other girls do it, and it was easy."[1]

69. Annie was brought into the Juvenile Court when she was 15 years old.   Her story was as follows: She first had relations with a man 7 months before.   He was an usher in the Eagle Theater.   She went many times to this theater and saw him often.   Once she stayed in the theater after the show and they had relations.   He later left town but she had his address.   Then she met a boy who sold papers in her neighborhood.   Another fellow introduced him as "John Johnson" and she knew him under that name, though it was not his right one.   They used to go to the park together and had intercourse once in the hallway of her home.   She was not sure who the next man was but thought his name was "Nick."   She met him in a theater and knew him for two weeks.

Later she met Simon Craw in an ice-cream parlor, flirted with him and they became acquainted.   He asked her to go joy riding.   She said "no", but made a date with him to go to Lawy's Theater.   After the show they went to the ice-cream parlor and had hot chocolate.   She told him she was afraid to go home so late — it was 12 P.M.   He talked to a man and then said a friend had offered to let them have his room in the Triangle Hotel.   She did not want to go at first, but he said if anything came up in court he would marry her.   Simon's friend took them to his room and went after coal.   Meanwhile she and Simon had relations.   The boys went to bed and she sat up all night in a chair, none of them undressing.

A week later, on Sunday evening she met Simon in the ice-cream parlor at 7 P.M.   They stayed until 8 o'clock and then went to Lawy's Theater.   They returned to the ice-cream parlor and Simon introduced a soldier whose name she forgot.   She told them she did not want to go home as it was 11 P.M. and she had promised to be home at 8

[1] *New York American,* January 2, 1922.

P.M. The soldier said he knew that the proprietor of the
Ohio Hotel would let all three of them have one room for
the night. She said: "I don't want to go. I don't
want to be used by everybody." Simon said: "You don't
have to," and they persuaded her to go.[1]

Doctor Katharine B. Davis, formerly superintendent of
the New York State Reformatory for women, at Bedford
Hills, has made a careful analysis of the life-histories
of 647 prostitutes committed to that institution from
New York City which throws light on the conditions
under which girls begin their sexual delinquency.
The study shows that very few prostitutes come from
homes where all the conditions are good, — good family
life, opportunity for education, economic security.
The occupations of the fathers show a low economic
status. Of the 647 girls only 15, or 2.4 per cent, had
fathers belonging to the professional classes, and this
category is stretched to include a veterinary surgeon,
a colored preacher, a trained nurse, a musician, etc.
Thirty-four fathers were farmers or farmhands, 29
shopkeepers, 1 a brewer, 5 sea captains, 1 gambler,
106 cases where there were no records, and the remaining fathers were mainly laborers or artisans, plas-
terer, plumber, peddler, miner, shoemaker, blacksmith,
hod-carrier. Also janitor, porter, cook, waiter, coach-
man, street sweeper, teamster, elevator man, sandwich
man, etc. [2]

As to the schooling of the girls, "fifty individuals, or
7.72 per cent, cannot read or write any language.
Of these 15 are American born. Thirty-two can read

[1] Records of the Juvenile Court of Cook County.
[2] Katharine Bement Davis: "A Study of Prostitutes Committed from
New York City." Supplementary chapter in Kneeland's "Commercialized
Prostitution in New York City", p. 205.

and write a foreign language; 45.3 per cent have never finished the primary grades, while an additional 39.72 per cent never finished the grammar grades. Thirteen individuals had entered but not finished high school; only four individuals had graduated from high school; three had had one year at a normal school, and one out of 647 cases had entered college." In addition, the average wage of the girls who had worked was very low. This point was determined in only 162 cases. "The average minimum," says Doctor Davis, is $4 and the average maximum $8. It will be noted that even the average maximum is below $9, an amount generally conceded to be the minimum on which a girl can live decently in New York City."[1]

In comparison with this the girls reported relatively high wages from prostitution. The average weekly maximum, as reported by 146 girls, was $71.09, and the average weekly minimum, as reported by 95 girls, was $46.02. Thirty-eight girls gave figures of $100 or more, up to $400.[2]

These statements, as Doctor Davis says, are to be taken "with allowances", but other statistics show that the earnings of prostitutes are about four times as great as the same girl could make at work.

An attempt was made also in this investigation to determine the causes leading up to prostitution from the standpoint of the girl. Two hundred and seventy-nine girls gave 671 reasons. That is, some of them gave a number of reasons. Among these reasons 306 were bad family life (in 166 cases no father or mother

---

[1] Katharine Bement Davis: "A Study of Prostitutes Committed from New York City." Supplementary chapter in Kneeland's "Commercialized Prostitution in New York City", p. 177.
[2] Ibid., 221.

or neither); 55, bad married life; 48, desire for pleasure (theater, food, clothes); 38, desire for money; 17, "easy money"; 20, lazy, hated work; 13, dances; 15, love of the life; 9, stage environment; 4, tired of drudgery; 5, idle or lonely; 4, sick, needed the money; 10, no sex instruction; 2, white slave; 3, desertion by lover; 10, lover put girl on street; 10, "ruined anyway"; 7, previous use of drink or drugs; 1, ashamed to go home after first escapade; 75, bad company; 5, couldn't support self; 1, couldn't support self and children; 13, couldn't find work.[1]

In spite of the bad economic conditions apparent here and in any report on prostitution it is remarkable that very few girls ever allege actual want or hunger as a reason for entering prostitution. In Doctor Davis' list only 23 girls named something like this among the 671 reasons. There is no doubt that economic determinism is present, that if they had an abundance of money they would not lead the life, but they are unstabilized as the result of a comparison between what they have and what they want and what others have. The servant class affords the best illustration. Between 37 and 60 per cent of professional prostitutes have been servant girls, according to different reports from different countries. The average is perhaps 50 per cent. Yet this class is well fed and housed, they supply a universal demand and have no economic anxieties. But they are treated as an inferior class, shown no courtesies, come and go by the back door; their work is monotonous and long, and they rebel against what they call "that hard graft", and seek pleasure, response, and recognition in the evening.

---

[1] Katharine Bement Davis. *Op. cit.* pp. 145, 225.

The cases which I have cited do not represent at all, and the report of Doctor Davis represents only slightly, a large and equivocal class of girls who participate in prostitution without becoming definitely identified with it. The present tendency of irregular sex life is definitely toward limited and occasional sexual relations on the part of girls who have more or less regular work, and the line between the professional and the amateur prostitute has become vague.

The usual beginning is in connection with an acquaintanceship, keeping company, which is not necessarily regarded by either side as preliminary to marriage but as a means of having a good time. The charm of the girl is an asset, a lure, which she may use as a means of procuring entertainment, affection, and perhaps gifts. Where marriage was assumed as an object of association, marriage was also assumed as the payment which the girl would ultimately make as her contribution to the expense of the association, but in the more casual associations of the "great society" there has grown up a code that the girl shall pay something as she goes, and she does not pay in cash but in favors. Girls of the class who have "fellows" tend to justify sexual intimacy if they are "going to marry", if the man says he will marry if there are "consequences", if the relation is with only one man, and not for money. These are called "charity girls" by the professional prostitutes. When the girl has had some experience in sexual life she will multiply and commercialize her casual relationships. Girls talk of these matters, say "they all do it", create a more favorable opinion of it, and show the less sophisticated girl how to make easy money.

The shop or office girl who makes sexual excursions

does not usually become a public prostitute. Her work is more attractive, her income better, she has more class, frequently a home, and she may often find marriage among her acquaintances. There are also girls who do not work, who live in comfortable homes, and are yet found on the street; married women who prostitute themselves in order to have luxuries; women who go on the street when work is slack and return to work; others who limit their relations to a small group of men; mistresses who are promiscuous between periods when they are kept by one man; factory girls and other workers who regularly supplement the work of the day by work on the street. There is thus a general tendency to avoid identification with the prostitute class. Illegal sexual relations are becoming more individualized. Even regular prostitution is not and has never been so fixed a status as we should suppose; it is rather a transitory stage from which the girl seeks to emerge by marriage or otherwise. In his profound work on French prostitution Parent-Duchatelet pointed out that "prostitution is for the majority only a transitory stage; it is abandoned usually during the first year. Very few prostitutes continue until extinction."[1] And this is confirmed by other reports.

Document No. 70 represents a type of organization which has arisen in connection with occasional prostitution, and in No. 71 the girl operates independently.

70. Mrs. X seems to take great pride in the fact that her girls are always fresh, young and attractive. She will not have a prostitute in her place who has ever been in houses of ill-fame. . . . These girls, she said, will never do in a

[1] "Histoire de la Prostitution" . . . quoted by Ellis in "Studies in the Psychology of Sex", Vol. 6, p. 261.

quiet place. They love excitement, the music, lights and large business at small prices. They also want to have cadets. Once she took such a girl, but she could not keep her as she longed to return to the excitement of her former life and her cadet. The girls who do come to her are in many instances from surrounding towns or from other States. They stay long enough to earn a few clothes and then return home, where they tell other girls of the easy way they earned their clothes. She has a list of 20 or 22 girls who have been with her at different times. They come and go.

One of the girls now in the flat is called Rosie. This girl lives in Iowa, and was so wild at home that her mother could do nothing with her, so she came to Chicago. Sometimes Rosie and the keeper have a quarrel and the girl returns home. After awhile she writes and says she wants to return to the flat, so Mrs. X sends her a ticket. Rosie is one of a family of three or four boys and three girls. One of these sisters, called Violet, has also been an inmate of the flat and comes occasionally. Rosie's mother says she realizes that Mrs. X can do more with her daughter than she can, so she allows her to come [not knowing what is happening]. The last time Violet was in the flat she stayed 10 days and earned $50.00, then went home again. She is 25 years old. Rosie is younger and a good money maker. During July, Rosie earned $156.00 as her share. During 27 days in August she earned $171.00.

The men who come to this flat are mostly married. Mrs. X says they are "gentlemen" and do not make any trouble. They prefer a place that is quiet and secret. Other customers are buyers from commercial houses, bringing out of town men who are here to purchase goods. In addition to this there are many traveling men who bring friends who gradually become regular customers. . . . The business depends largely on the telephone service. The girls are summoned to go to similar flats about town if they are needed, and in turn Mrs. X secures girls from other flats when her regular inmates are out when a customer calls. For instance, on September 20th the investigator was in the flat when only one girl was at home. In a few moments a telephone call came for the girl Helen to go to a flat near by. On September 30th a phone call came for three girls to go to a restaurant in Madison Street and report in the back room where they had been the previous night.[1]

71. American girl, twenty-one years old, semi-prostitute, typical of a certain class one grows to know. Works as salesgirl in one of the high class shops — a pretty girl, languid manner but businesslike; popular with business associates. Has a very clear skin, grey-blue eyes, perfect features. Father is a contractor, mother a hard-worked woman whose morals, personally, are beyond reproach but who regards her daughter's affairs as only partly her business, preferring to let surmising take the place of knowledge.

She grew up the eldest of seven children, went through grammar school and through one year at the high school, then to work. She was bright and was soon promoted to position of salesgirl, where she worked in an atmosphere of luxury and, with a cleverness very common in this type, aped the manners and dress of the women she served. She had been a shy child and had never confided in her parents about feelings or her comings and goings, and they left her absolutely untaught, except that she attended church regularly (Roman Catholic) and was expected to do as she was told.

Sex had been a closed book to her and, as she was naturally cold and unawakened, she was not tempted as some girls are. She did not care about being loved, but the wish to be admired was strong within her and love of adornment superseded all else, particularly when she realized she was more beautiful than most girls.

The department store is sometimes a school for scandal. Many rich women are known by sight and are talked over, servants' gossip sometimes reaching thus far, the intrigues

[1] "The Social Evil in Chicago" (Report of the Vice Commission of Chicago), p. 80.

between heads of departments and managers are hinted at and the possibility of being as well dressed as some one else becomes a prime consideration.

Freedom from household cares, independence of home obligations, and parental weakness all began to have their effect.

When she was seventeen years old she was first approached by college students who wanted her to go to dinners, dances, to the theatre, and for motor rides. This was innocent enough for a time. She did not dare do anything wrong because of the Church and her traditional standard of virtue. Then she met an artist who asked her to pose for him, and she consented; and after several sittings he asked her to pose in the nude. Five dollars an hour was a temptation, for it meant almost a whole week's work in the store (she got seven there) so she consented, not telling her mother. Then her knowledge of sex began. This man kissed her, glorying in her beauty and promised her everything she wanted if she would be his mistress. Shocked, yet tempted, she hesitated. She was not at all passionate, but he roused in her her dominant emotion — love of power, conquest over men — and she realized in one short week that this was to be her life's exciting game.

Other girls in the shop began to tell her their experiences. The career of a clandestine prostitute seemed rather the common thing. The good girls seemed rather pathetic and poverty struck; most of them were homely anyway; but there was her virtue to consider, the Church, the future. She would want to marry some one who would appreciate her beauty, who would demand that her womanhood be unscathed. She must compromise. She would give the man all that he wanted without losing her virtue technically. No man would have her completely. Then she could play the game. She had never heard of the perversions of sex, but she soon learned them and practised her arts with no sense of shame.

She has no use for the working man — indeed, her life

for the last four years has been a mixture of shop work or posing in the day and luxury at night. It would be impossible for her to live at home in an atmosphere of soapsuds and babies, hard work and poverty.

When forced to think out the situation as it is, she is fair-minded. Virtue to her has become a technicality. She is not harmed and no man is strong enough to overcome her if she herself is frigid. She likes to be kissed and adores to rouse men's passions. She thinks many girls are like her who have never given themselves wholly to men, but most of them are more easily roused. She seldom stays all night with a man. She likes to "keep them guessing." Besides her mother would make trouble if she stayed out all night. If she thinks she is at a dance, she says nothing about her coming in late.

She admits her scorn of her own station in life but says the luxury-loving age is responsible for that, that no girl who loves pretty things (which most women do) is going to be content with shabby clothes and stupid makeshifts if she can be as feminine and as lovely as other women who do not work and yet have their hearts' desires. She does not think she does the men harm; in fact, she is a good companion and coarseness of speech is repugnant to her. She smokes cigarettes but drinks very little. She admits she has no motive in life except to marry, some day, a man who has a good deal of money. She could easily marry a rich man; several have already asked her but she intends to wait a while. She knows the pleasures of the intellect are not for her. She says excitement has been her master and that nothing else in the world matters greatly. Cold and superficial, she admits she is not much of a woman but denies that her conscience is dead, — says it has never been born. The girls who are mistresses to one man have more womanly qualities than she because they are aroused and fully developed.

She has no desire for children, does not care for them, but has no aversion to having one. It would have to be a pretty baby and must be brought up nicely. Clutter, pots and pans and drudgery are as remote from her life as if she had been born a princess.

"Probably I am spoiled," she says, "but there are hundreds of others like me, though most of them are too human to resist sex temptation themselves. There are three types of people responsible for a vast number of girls like me: Mothers who spoil their daughters — anything rather than have them household drudges like themselves; society women who make the poor girl's lot seem harder to her than she can bear; and the men who are glad to use the working girl for everything in life but marriage. Personally I am to blame, of course, but I consider myself swept by the current — glad to drift — yes; but afraid to think where it may end. I have never been in love. Something is still sleeping in me. Perhaps it will come to life some day."[1]

The last document is very significant. The girl's schematization of life is further from the bordel and nearer the strategic form of marriage recommended by the wife in document No. 49 (p. 87).

In none of the documents in this chapter up to this point is an unfortunate love affair or a betrayal with promise of marriage mentioned as the cause of later delinquency. Girls do make these representations, and very often, but they are always to be discounted, and for two reasons. In the first place girlhood and womanhood have been idealized to the degree that this explanation is expected and the girl wishes to give it. Betrayal is the romantic way of falling, the one used in the story books and movies. Many girls have finished stories of this kind which they relate when asked to tell about their lives. In addition, a seduction does usually accompany the first adventure into the world,

[1] Edith L. Smith: "A Study in Sexual Morality", "Social Hygiene", Vol. 2, p. 541.

as we have seen in the documents (Nos. 64–69), but we saw also that sex in these cases was used, as a coin would be used, to secure adventure and pleasure. On the other hand, not a few girls have tragedies in connection with courtship, promises of marriage, pregnancy, and childbirth which demoralize them when they had no previous tendency to demoralization. In a few cases girls yield to their own sexual desire.

72. Ellen is twenty years old. When her mother died six years ago her father immediately remarried and she went to an aunt in Poughkeepsie, but when her aunt found out she had broken connections with her father, she turned her out. . . . The aunt is an old maid living alone in a nice house, with one servant. She stayed with her one year. The aunt made it evident that she disliked Ellen. She did housework in Rochester, and then went to Poughkeepsie and later to Albany. She has worked as a maid, and as a salesgirl in a department store, but would not give the name nor any information regarding her employer.

Nine months ago she attended a Knights of Columbus banquet with a girl friend, where she was introduced to a man who began to call upon her shortly afterward and they became intimate. She was invited to his mother's home, together with a great many other friends, who were evidently people of wealth, she says. His mother did not know that she was a working girl, because he furnished her with clothing. She further states that his mother never knew that her son had had immoral relations or that he even expected to marry her. She is sure that the mother would not allow the marriage because Ellen is a Catholic. She says his mother owns a garage which her son manages. He often took her for long rides in the machine to road houses and recently had intercourse with her twice during such trips. On the first such occasion he promised to marry her, bought her a small diamond ring for which he paid $98, and the other day when he proposed a trip to New York, he said he had secured a marriage license. Said they would be married here in New York City and return to Albany to live. When they arrived with their friends, another girl and a man, she states she asked him where they were to be married and he said: "No, we're young yet and don't have to be; let's have a good time first." She said that scared her and she got out of the car near the park on Second Avenue. She hid in the bushes and finally came out, looked around, but did not see them anywhere. She accosted a policeman and said to him, "Arrest me; do anything you like, but I have got to have a place to go to." She said he laughed at her and said she was crazy and wanted to know what was the matter. So she told him a little of her story. He said he would look after her when off his beat, but in the meantime she should stay in a Catholic Church nearby, which she says she did. When the officer came off his beat he came and took her to the police station. She says she would not marry the man now if he could be found and if he were willing. She feels that he has disgraced her before all her friends and consequently she does not want to see any of them.

Her great ambition was to be a trained nurse. She has applied at different hospitals and every one has refused her because she has not enough education. She says that she will do anything or give up anything to realize this ambition. She would be very happy if she could even become a child's nurse and would be willing to live on a very small salary while she is training. She prefers to stay in New York as there is less probability of her seeing the man again. . . . Religion means a great deal to her and would like to see a priest in a day or two.[1]

73. I was born at Marietta, Ohio, December 22, 1902. My father at that time was making pretty good money. He was an oil man. He was discouraged over a loss and was working on a farm. We moved to one farm and lived there two years when the house burned with but little saved. From there we moved on to another farm and lived there

---

[1] Records of the New York Probation Association.

about two years. At a failure of crops we moved again to Tennessee. . . . I worked about three months on a railroad grade, doing men and boys' work. I made $2.50 a day working 10 hours. I was dumping the cars, laying track, carrying water — just anything they needed some one to do, just anything to fill in. There was about 20 of us girls. I saved about $90 out of my wages during those three months beside paying my board at home and buying my clothes. Father borrowed this $90 when we got to Morgantown, saying his money was all gone and saying that he would have to have some money to keep the family until the household goods came. [I had planned to use my money to pay my school expenses, but father said he couldn't afford to send me to school, so I went to work in a restaurant, but father wanted me to work in a private family and I went to the home of Mrs. Jernigan.]

Most of the management of the house was left for me to do, as the woman was away from home most of the time. She wanted to be going out all the time; she never stayed at home. Just so long as the work was taken care of she didn't care. There were four children. I had to do all the work and take care of the children. She was gone most of the time. It was the 26th of January, 1919. For the last two or three weeks before that I noticed he was getting familiar. I didn't seem to realize anything of it at the time. He treated me just like one of the family until the 26th. Mr. Jernigan was not able to go to Sunday School. He was sick so he told his wife and that was the excuse she made to the Sunday School superintendent and to his pupils. Before she went she asked me to see that he got his medicine because he might doze off and not take it on time, but to be sure he got it on time. He was sitting in the living room before the fire, in a big lounging chair when I brought his medicine to him first. I got him his medicine and I started to go away and he asked me why I was in such a big hurry for. I told him that if I was to get the work done and dinner ready on time as Mrs. Jernigan was going out that afternoon, and if I didn't keep busy I wouldn't get it accomplished. He says, "Oh, hang the work! You don't have to be working all the time." I told him that that was what I was there for and that that was what they were paying me for and it was not for him to detain me and cause Mrs. Jernigan inconvenience as well as myself. He says, "All right, you don't like Daddy Joe any more." That was what they called him, Daddy Joe. I tried to reason with him that I cared for him just as much as I ever did but that I must get my work done. He said I could at least sit down on the edge of his chair awhile and I thought I would as I would get away quicker rather than by arguing with him. He started to caress and make over me and I tried to get away, saying that that wouldn't do that he was to go on asleep or amuse himself, that I must get my work done. But he refused to let me go. He kept making over me until he got my passions aroused and until he had no control over himself at all, and though a sick man, he picked me up and carried me upstairs and there he ruined me. I didn't realize the harm he was doing me. . . . I didn't feel that I wanted to work there any more. I was ashamed to meet the look of Mrs. Jernigan. It seemed that I couldn't get interested in my work and in about a week I asked for about a couple of weeks' vacation. I went to a friend of mine at Flemington. I stayed there the two weeks and a few days over, but I telephoned Mrs. Jernigan that if she could get some one for my place to do so, that I didn't know exactly when I would be back, I was going to stay a few days longer. But when I got back she had not succeeded in getting any one. Mr. Jernigan came to see me where I was at the time and promised that he wouldn't repeat his actions as before if I would go back. He said Mrs. Jernigan would think of me just as my parents, and I was just as anxious to conceal my wrong then as he. So I went back. I was there about two weeks and he didn't keep his promise. I told my parents that I was going to leave there.

I started back in the restaurant life then again. I met a

young man who seemed very interested in me. I was discouraged and disgusted with the way I was living and the restaurant life began to have its effect on me then, and I decided that I would accept his proposal and that we would get married. But one thing happened and then another until we had to postpone it and it was just a plan of his, I found out later. He had coaxed me into improper relationship with him once. Then he started running around town with other girls. When I asked him what he meant by that kind of action he said he had come to the conclusion that I was too young to know what it was to get married, that I had just better drop that idea altogether. I was discouraged and disgusted with myself that I could be led into anything so easily. . . . [I married a man who was very surly and associated with negro women, infected me with gonorrhoea, told the workers in the mine that I had infected him, and finally disappeared.]

I went home and my sister's husband came to live with us and I seemed to know him better than I did before. He had just come back from the Army and he was the only comfort I had, so I talked with him. When a girl gets the blues she falls harder than ever. He had a fight with those at the mines who repeated the story that my husband told. It was about the first of March when we had a physical relation and at that time I was made pregnant.[1]

74. In this case a girl of American parentage was a bright and attractive type. Her mother had been a prostitute for years and had provided a home in which the standards were so degrading that the courts had given the five other daughters to relatives six years previous. The girl in question was sent to live with a widowed uncle and his two daughters, who welcomed her to a home of many comforts and interests, but allowed at the same time much unsupervised recreational time. During afternoons of leisure she found many opportunities to spend hours in the company

[1] From the manuscript of an autobiography and case study by Professor E. B. Reuter.

of a married man in the neighborhood, and a few years later at the age of 16 she gave birth to an illegitimate child.

Her father died when she was two years old. During the next few years the home life was deplorable. The family suffered much through poverty, and the mother was so neglectful of her children that the neighbors brought about her arrest. At an early age this girl had witnessed many immoral scenes, and she said that when she was only 8 years old she remembered seeing her mother in bed with a man. It was also reported that she had locked one of the daughters in a room with a man, receiving payment from him for this opportunity.

When this young girl went to live with her uncle and two older cousins in her tenth year, she found an excellent home. The family attended church regularly, and she took an active part in the services. It was noted that after she started an intimacy with the father of her child she failed to speak at the prayer meeting. At school she was considered one of the most promising girls in her class and much above the average in her school work. She reached the sophomore year and left because of her pregnancy. She was associated with a group of good friends and was much enjoyed by her cousins. They had little time to give her, as one attended college and the other held a responsible position in a business house. After school hours she had the afternoon to herself. She was not allowed to go out evenings except when chaperoned by older people. In appearance she was an attractive type, with fresh coloring and a childish, innocent expression. Her uncle stated that she had always been a good girl, was quiet and obedient, and had never showed any tendency to run after the boys. Her child was born at a private maternity home and was healthy and robust and greatly beloved by the mother, who declared that she would never give her up. Later the child was placed out with the mother and both did extremely well.

Her sex history is as follows. She met the father by chance going home from school, when she accidentally ran into him. After this she happened to see him occasionally, and their casual meetings finally terminated in an intimacy. She knew the father three years and had relationships with him in the woods for a year and a half before the birth of her child. The girl said, "When I was 13 there came to me an awful longing for some one to love me and kiss me at night. I thought it was a mother's love I wanted, but when this man talked to me I thought that was what I wanted. I had no wish to do wrong but longed to be loved." For some time this man made love to her and represented himself as her truest friend. He told her that because she was an orphan she needed such a friendship. For many months there was no sexual intimacy between them. Finally he began to ask her questions concerning her menstrual periods and afterwards generally instructed her in sex matters. Following this conversation she frequently had relationships with him and did not learn that he was married until some months later. She declared that she loved and trusted the father of her child, and even after she became pregnant said that she could not regret her sexual relations with him or feel that she had done wrong. Meantime she had been twice assaulted by a man of loose character.

This is her statement regarding her attitude at this time: " He was not wholly to blame, because as soon as a man speaks to me concerning these things I get so aroused that I do not know what I am doing." Both men were arrested, and the judge was unable to establish paternity. He gave the father, so called, a suspended sentence of one year and ordered him to support the child. . . . . It was interesting to note the girl's attitude after confinement. She said, "I wonder if these men who had intercourse with me didn't feel beforehand that it would be an easy thing to do, since my mother had been so bad."[1]

75. At sixteen Patty was a dreadful flirt, a fairly good student, and an adept at every kind of sport. About this time she made friends with a girl whom all the girls knew,

[1] P. G. Kammerer: "The Unmarried Mother", p. 148.

but only slightly. There were rumors about her family which the girls heard long before their elders, but knowing nothing of real facts they kept their surmises to themselves, gossiped and wondered. Patty spent much time at this girl's house and her aunt did not interfere. Soon stories began to be whispered. Boy students went to call on the girls and stayed very late. Patty always stayed with this girl when her parents were away. The servants in the house knew the facts of the case and had been bribed to keep still. All of Patty's friends were desperate but loyal. No one would tell on her. Patty kissed the boys and ran after them. Olive, her friend, did worse things — but what? Led by this wholly bad girl, Patty was living the life of a wilful, passionate, little harlot, her heart wholly rebellious, her keen sex instincts wholly aroused. Class protection saved her for a long time. None of the boys quite dared to seduce her, but as time went on there were plenty of people who believed the worst and finally she let herself go completely. Soon after she became pregnant. Before this her aunt had stopped her friendship with Olive, but when she became quiet, wild-eyed, and shy, no one could believe the awful truth. The news spread like wild-fire and Patty left the town. One of the boys was anxious to marry her but she admitted she was not sure which of three boys was the father of her child and said she would not marry any one. She lived in the country with some good people and motherhood woke all the emotions of her best self. The baby lived only a short time and she came to her home town to visit her aunt, apparently for the purpose of being confirmed in her old church. She was the same fascinating girl with a sudden dignity of womanhood that amazed every one. People talked of her bravery in facing them all and no one would have dared to be anything but nice to her. Even the gossips realized that Patty was something of a person, after all. She went abroad after this, studied, and traveled. She was as talkative as ever and did every wild and impetuous thing which struck her fancy but with a contradictory element of

reserve too elusive to explain. Her chaperone, who knew
nothing of her past, often commented on the fact that Patty
could manage the men, — no one presumed to take liberties
with her.

When twenty-three she lost her heart to a man ten years
her senior, a strong character with a dominant personality.
When he told Patty he loved her, she flung herself in his
arms and told the whole story rapidly, truthfully, without
thought of the consequences. He held her close while she
sobbed and quieted her as no one had ever quieted Patty
before. "Hush, dear," he said. "Of course it was necessary to tell me; we will never speak of it again. I know
how much you need me. You have always needed me. I
think I can make you happy."

Patty ends the story by saying that in this man she found
the refuge which was her salvation. Though intellectually
her superior, her husband is stimulated by her active mind.
Their sex relation is perfect. She has plenty of friends,
both men and women, and he loves and admires her. Their
home is comfortable, secure. They have two lovely children — a boy and a girl.

This woman realizes the faults of her nature. In looking
back she thinks she flew blindly as a bird would fly, yet never
without a subconscious realization of her folly. Her impulses were merely stronger than her control. She thinks
she is probably more dependent upon a sex life than many
women, yet intellectually she has developed wonderfully
and is really a splendid woman, albeit too nervous, over-
sensitive, and frail.[1]

76. American girl, 19 years old, pregnant. Many elements of the feminine mind are demonstrated in her sin-
cerity and truthfulness of understanding. Had no previous
knowledge of sex life; did not know men were like that; did
not know her own nature and the awakening of passion within
herself was overwhelming.

---

[1] Edith L. Smith: "A Study in Sexual Morality", "Social Hygiene",
Vol. 2, p. 535.

Came to Boston a year ago. Lives with another girl, good as far as she knows. They have never talked about men's relation with women. It is hard for her to talk about intimate matters, so she does not know how her friend feels. Is a Roman Catholic, but there is no good of her going to church now. She thinks the man would marry her, but how could she marry a man like that? Does not want him to kiss her now. When it was explained to her that this might be because she was pregnant, she was again interested. Perhaps, because how was it she loved to have him kiss her before? Motherhood is natural to her, but to face society unmarried seems an impossibility. When she speaks of her baby, her face lights with a look which is not sentimentalism. "Oh I could love it if I could only let it be born." None of her family could ever know she was like "that." "That" means that she could have a child when it is not right to have one. She had not a clear memory of her temptation and actual sex experience. "I was as much to blame as he was, for he did not make me, but I did not realize quite what I was doing, I felt numb. I had so much feeling I had none."

This girl is difficult to describe. Unusual because with only a little help she could understand herself, probably with the whole of her nature, which few women do. Has the rare gift of seeing things as they are when she wishes to see them differently. Never had much education, went through grammar school, could have gone to high school but wanted to go to work. Works in a restaurant. Earns five dollars a week with meals and tips. Lives with another girl and together they pay $3 a week for their room. Met this man on the street. "All the girls do that." He did not mean to harm her, she thinks; there was no talk of wrong doing at first; just good friends. "He is a strong man, makes me do things, yet asks me about everything we do. I cannot quite explain it." (The truthful feminine mind again, the civilized desire to be a comrade warring against the primitive woman who wishes to be captured. Women of this type are particularly sensitive, apparently, particularly to be desired by the masculine mind.)

This girl is wholly natural. She came to me in an impulsive way. "I know a girl who knows a girl who knew you. I must tell some one so I came to you. I am in trouble." Religion is remote to her as a personal experience. "That is a different part of myself — the part I dream with. I hate myself now. I do not feel like myself, but yet I feel differently. I can never be the same again."

Many girls of this kind, unmarried and pregnant, do not realize motherhood. It is a misery remote from their consciousness, not a part of their being. With this girl it is. She is 100 per cent feminine, it seems to me, yet with a spirit which is brave and fine. If her maternal instinct dominates, the child will be born. If consciousness to outside influence gets the better, she will have an abortion. I should say it was an even chance, but no one will decide it for her. She is glad of advice, humble in the asking, and sincere, but weighs it all, and another's mind but shows her her own opinion more clearly. Married the man; perfectly happy.[1]

77. Prostitute, twenty-four years old, of English parentage. Lived in this country since she was ten years old. Typical English type, high cheek bones, clear skin, bold grey eyes; womanly in bearing, with a contradictory dignity and boldness of speech and manner. Went to school through grammar grade, began to work at fifteen. Had nothing in common with her family, had no sex training, did not talk to her mother about things she felt deeply. She said, "I was fond of my mother, but we were not intimate; one does not talk to one's mother." Worked at housework, then restaurant work, left home and boarded alone. Was wild and irresponsible, did not understand life, wanted fun and novelty. When eighteen met a business man with plenty of money who was kind to her. There was no talk of marriage.

[1] Edith L. Smith: "A Study in Sexual Morality", "Social Hygiene", Vol. 2, p. 540.

Went with him for three months before sex relation was established. Finally became pregnant. Her family found her and issued a complaint against her as a stubborn child. Her baby was born in a hospital and afterwards she continued to live an irresponsible life but without immorality. "There was only one man in the world for me," she said, "no one seemed to understand that." She was misunderstood and was ultimately sentenced to prison, her child cared for by the State.

She is reticent about the father of her child. She swore upon the witness stand she did not know the father of her child, to protect him. He never knew that she was pregnant. In prison she learned much evil. Her life with this one man had been almost innocent, a first realization of sex. She knew nothing about prostitutes, of perverts, of "French immorality", all of which she learned from other girls and women in prison. She was told a girl was a fool to work hard for nothing when she could have everything for the price of a spirit of adventure. Her love of her child was real and earnest. When she came from prison she went to work in a family with her child. She became of age while here. All the furies of her nature were aroused by her dealings with social workers who judged her wrongly. Her antagonism was interpreted as hardness. "They thought I was a jail-bird or something like that. They took the baby away and put it in a place where I could not see it; even the family where I had worked did not know where it was."

About this time she met some of her prison acquaintances. They made fun of her attempt at virtue. "Why wouldn't I listen to them? They were all the companions I had had for ten months. The State drove me on the street because I wouldn't be meek and was saucy to them. I meant to support my baby and they took it away. I'm not a proper person to bring up a child. I'm not, but they ('they' is most of the world) made me what I am."

She is now a regular prostitute. She lives in a tiny apartment of one room, bath, and kitchenette, a cheerless place with a telephone which looks business-like. She helps in the office of the place and cares for some other apartments, and earns enough to pay her rent and a little more. The rest she earns immorally.

"I was innocent," she said, "until I was 18. I went on the streets for excitement and fun. People said and thought all sorts of things about me which were not true, — my family, the court people, and all. My mother would never have known about the baby if the State hadn't blabbed. Why do they have to tell a person's private affairs and sins? My mother had enough trouble without having mine thrust on her. I ought to bear my own troubles without breaking her heart. Social workers think they're such saints.

"Nowadays girls go wrong younger. Today there are girls on the Common at night, thirteen and fourteen, who know everything bad there is to know. I am not a café girl. You would be disgusted with the café girls. If the city really wants to stop this sort of thing why don't they shut up the cafés? Some of those girls are awful; some of them are desperate. On the street few girls speak to men. It is the other way round. If a girl is alone on the streets at night the men know what she is there for. There is more money in New York than Boston. I'm not a real sporting girl. They have to be bad, that is willing to do anything a man wants. They get $25, whatever they want, if they are attractive enough, but a girl has to be bad all through to satisfy such men. I usually get $10, sometimes $5 if the man is nice but poor. No girl need go with men that make it worse. It's bad enough. I never go with a man who has been drinking much and only with a certain kind of men." As far as could be learned this type bears a resemblance to the kind of man who is the father of her child. She says she still loves him. She has seen him sometimes on the street. It is a temptation but she keeps away. "It makes me tremble and feel sick; besides I wouldn't give him the satisfaction of knowing they took the child away. Oh, how I hate them all. It's a fierce life. There are two kinds of pros-

titutes, the ones who would get out of the life any minute
if they could earn a decent living any other way, and the
ones who were born to the life. Silly fools! they wouldn't
be satisfied with anything else. (The feeble-minded?)
Why do I live so if I hate it? What else can I do? I have
no education; any work I can get is hard work and I am not
strong. I worked for a family all summer as a second girl.
My back ached all the time. A maid goes in the back door
and out of the back door. In this life she can be comfortable,
get plenty to eat, plenty of good clothes, and she is as good
as the men with whom she goes.

"I generally get home by eleven or twelve o'clock, sometimes I stay all night. I never have visitors here; I never go
with but one man in a night. No one here knows me. What
people don't know won't hurt them. I generally go to a hotel.
Most decent men would rather go to a hotel and pay the
extra price for a room. Such hotels are not apt to be raided.
I don't long for the life at all. I cared for that one man. I
mean to save money and I am a little ahead. We don't
hate the men half as much as we hate ourselves. They could
stop before it was too late if any one would really sympathize
with their love of freedom and understand them. Social
workers say, "I want to help you"; they just preach. Many
of them are women of education. They expect a girl to
know all that they know with their years of experience
when she is just ignorant. What can she know of herself
and men and the world? Things are all wrong between
men and women — I don't know why. People with education ought to think about it. More than half the men we
girls meet are married men. The women get tired of their
husbands; the husbands get tired of them. Sometimes the
wives are sick, sometimes they don't understand a man's
nature; they are cold and unsympathetic and drive them
to girls like us.

"I pretend as far as I can. One might as well do it in
the same spirit as any other distasteful work. It may wear
out one's soul but it doesn't wear out one's body as much as

house work or factory or store work. I haven't been to church in seven years. I can't believe much in God. It's hard to see the justice in anything and the so-called good people think they are so perfect."

This woman with all her hardness and bitterness cries when she speaks of her child. When I came away she acted the hostess very prettily, picked up my books for me, and showed a gentle side of her nature. "No, I haven't minded talking of myself," she said. "Please come again. I have no real friends — you will always find me here alone, and sad." [1]

Pregnancy and illegal motherhood are among the most tragic of all situations and tend to deprive the girl of her sense of worth, to isolate her socially, and to handicap her economically. But when the girl is not already prepared for demoralization the recuperation in these cases is greater than we should expect. It is a disaster like other disasters, such as sickness and loss of fortune, and a reconstruction of life may follow, perhaps on a lower level. The attitude toward an otherwise orderly girl who has had a sexual experience or borne a child is not so severe as formerly. Frequently the girl marries, often she marries the father of the child. In his study of five hundred unmarried mothers Kammerer says :

"It appears that 48, or 9.6 per cent, of the women in this study married the father of their illegitimate child either before or after confinement; 37 or 7.4 per cent married a man not the father of their child. Figures in regard to the unmarried mother are probably considerably lower than they would have been had it been possible to observe the situation longer. Accord-

[1] Edith L. Smith, "A Study in Sexual Morality", "Social Hygiene", Vol. 2, p. 538.

ing to the German experience over 30 per cent of the mothers of illegitimate children marry before their child reaches the age of three years." [1]   And since it has been calculated by Adele Schreiber [2] that 50 per cent of all German women are unmarried between the ages of 20 and 30 it appears that the chance to marry on the part of the unmarried mother is very good. (In Germany, however, it is half-customary among peasants and the lower city classes to begin sexual relations before marriage and to marry when pregnancy follows.)   At any rate it appears that prostitution is not recruited largely from the victims of love affairs.

The most sensational aspect of the girl's delinquency is connected with white slavery and the character called "pimp", "cadet", or "souteneur." If a young and simple girl is abducted or captured in the most brutal and audacious way she may nevertheless become broken and submissive, as an animal is broken and trained. She will then be put on the street to "hustle", or in a house, and her earnings collected. She is held first by fear and then acquires habits and works with the system, like a trained animal. Frequently there is marriage or pretense of marriage and the girl finds that the next step is to go on the street. This is the typical procedure of the white slaver. In addition he purchases girls who are already "broken in" and transfers girls who are already prostitutes from place to place, as notably from Galicia or Hungary to South America.

The other side of the matter, the relation of the girl to the pimp, is connected with her desire for response.

[1] P. G. Kammerer: "The Unmarried Mother", p. 302.
[2] "*Mutterschaft*", p. 459.

When for any reason a girl is "ruined", on the street, used as a convenience by everybody, she is in a condition of great and unnatural isolation and loneliness and craves a relationship which is personal and intimate. Her attachment to the pimp is simply an underworld love affair. He is her man. She is jealous and he is jealous. She works and brings her earnings as if she were earning in another business. Sometimes her pimp will not allow her to enter the room until she has put $10 under the door. If he abuses her, particularly if he is jealous, she rather welcomes this as a sign of his attachment. That the girl supports a pimp to protect her and keep her out of trouble with the police is not the main element. In European cities where girls are registered by the police and protected as far as possible from this exploitation, they nevertheless support pimps, and in some cities the number doing this is as much as 90 per cent of the registered prostitutes.

It frequently happens also that a girl is drawn or drifts out of her family and community into a bad gang, as in case No. 78, becomes identified with them by assimilation, and cannot free herself. She may then be kept by one of the men or sold into a house. Cases No. 79 and No. 80 are typical of the psychology of the girl in this relation.

78. I am a girl 18 years old and am from a Polish village. Now I am an orphan. I was two years old when my mother died. Several years later my father left for America and left me with my grandfather. After spending several years in America, my father brought me here to New York. I was then 15 years old. I soon went to work and earned $5 a week. My father took the money from me and supported me. And now my troubles begin. After I was here several

months, I became acquainted with a boy and through him I became acquainted with several other boys. I was yet young and did not very well understand that the boys accompanied me for their pleasure and not out of friendship. When my father found it out, he began to argue with me in a good way; but as he could not persuade me in a good way, for I did not then understand that it was dear friendship of a father to his child, he began to beat me. After my father gave me a good beating, I became mad; left the house and entered on a wrong path.

My father remained alone and dejected and was forced to marry. I now have a stepmother and I am staying away and I feel that I am falling. I feel that my body is fading along with my soul. When I look at my companions, who shun me, who do not want to know me on account of my immoral life, I envy them. I now realize how bad and wrong my life is; and I see my future in dark colors.

Now when I want to disengage myself from the charlatans and licentious scoundrels in man's image, I cannot do it. My heart is bound to them. I am attracted to them as to a magnet. When I do not see them for a day, I am almost crazy.

I do not know what to do. The question is; how can I wean myself from the boys, my murderers. . . . Perhaps it would have been well for me to leave New York altogether and go to some other city? [1]

79. Five pimps were playing cards in a restaurant on Seventh Avenue. The day was very hot. During the afternoon the girl who is "hustling" for one of them came into the restaurant wearing a heavy velvet suit. The wife of the proprietor asked, "What are you doing, wearing a suit like that in this kind of weather?" She replied that though she was bringing home eight, ten, and twelve dollars every night, she could not afford a new dress. "He needs it for gambling," she said, pointing to her pimp. Leaving the table in anger he deliberately slapped her in the face. "Didn't

[1] *Forward,* November 18, 1913.

you pay $32 for that suit?" he said. "What more do you want?"[1]

80. I met [a police officer] in June 1917. . . . I fell in love with him right away, to tell the truth. I had been having trouble with my husband and had tried to divorce him, but couldn't. Anyhow, we were separated. When I was with my husband I was a good girl, and didn't go out with other men. . . . I won't say that he asked me to go into the life I began to lead. That was my own choice. I wasn't any innocent child. But he told me he could "help" me a lot in the life. He told me, first, to keep within the bounds of his inspection district, and to walk Broadway between 42d Street and 109th, but never to go beyond those lines, or else he couldn't protect me. . . . After I had taken a man home, and then the man had left the apartment, Ginton would come in and get some money. How much? Oh — 25 per cent, sometimes, or 50 per cent, or maybe even 100 per cent. He was always saying, "Honey, I need money. I have to have $25", or sometimes he would ask for $10 or $20 — never less than $10. Oh, I couldn't begin to figure how much I gave him. But I didn't mind that. I loved him, and I always had plenty of money for myself, anyhow. . . . I don't mind the money, but I do mind his saying he doesn't know me. I'd have given him anything I had — I would even now, I think. See this ring? Well, that's worth $3000. He asked me for it once, and I was going to give it to him, except the other girls wouldn't let me. I've bought him lots of clothes — and you might ask him about the belt with the gold buckle I gave him for a present. Oh — he knows me, all right.

After seeing my folks and talking to them and having them treat me nicely, I made up my mind that when I got back to New York I was going to give up the life I had been leading and get a job and go straight. So I got a place in a

[1] George J. Kneeland: "Commercialized Prostitution in New York City", p. 90.

hairdresser's shop at 85th Street and Broadway that paid
me $25 a week.

He didn't like that, and told me so. I guess it was because he wasn't getting any more money from me. Anyhow,
I hadn't been at work long before he came into the hairdresser's and said to the boss, "You'd better get rid of that
girl; she's a prostitute." So I was discharged.

I made another try and got a job in a millinery shop on
Broadway, near 95th Street. The same thing happened.
He told the people I was working for that I was a street
woman, so they had to let me go. He had me discharged
from a third job in a store in the same neighborhood. It was
impossible for me to get any kind of straight work because
of him. I had to go back to the street.[1]

Italians and Jews have been noticeably identified
with white slavery. The Italian methods are particularly atrocious, showing the same desperation as
their black-hand operations. At the same time Italian
girls and Irish are the most intractable among the
nationalities. The Jewish operations tend to the
form of business organization.

81. I come to this country when I fourteen years old with
my mother and father and brothers and sisters. My father
go back to Italy three years ago when sick. I work as
operator and earn $3 a week. Then I get $6 and for two
years I make $9. I walk with my friend Florence who live
in same street and we meet Frank Marino drinking soda.
He ask me if I have a drink and I say "No", and he say,
"Come on, don't be bashful, take a drink." After we take
a drink he say, "I take you girls to moving picures." I
say, "No, I can't." He say, "Oh, come on; I own a moving picture place; it do you no harm to go." We went into
a place after a while. When we come out, he say, "You
come again to-morrow; I take you again." I say, "No, I

[1] *New York World*, March 5, 1920.

can't go, my mother would not like." He walk home with me and I say to him, "If you want to know me, come in; here's the house; I live here." He say, "No, you meet me on Wednesday and I take you to moving pictures." I told him "No." He say, "Yes, you come."

Florence say, "You go; maybe he's your luck; you get married. He seem like a nice fellow." So I say, "You go with me and I go. I afraid to go alone." Wednesday we go again and I not tell my mother. Saturday I go with him again and Florence too. He introduce her so she had man, called Jim, to take her. When we come out he say, "I take you now to see my mother and sisters on Charles Street." I not want to go; I was afraid, but he say, "Florence and Jim go too; my mother and sisters want to see you."

So we go and he want me to go upstairs and I say, "No, I afraid." He say, "Oh, you have a bad mind; you think bad. My mother is upstairs waiting for you; come on." I step into the hall and he shut the door and Florence outside. Then he say, "Come upstairs; don't have such a bad mind," and I say, "Why not Florence come too?" and he say, "Oh, Jim got a key, he come." We get upstairs, he push me in a room and lock the door. He say, "Now I got you here I do what I want," and I say "No", and I try to get out and I can't. Then he takes out a pistol and hold it right up against my ear. He know I was a good girl, and I say, "Are you going to marry me? If you don't, I kill myself. I will jump out the window."

I go home to my mother and I tell her. She faint. I most crazy and she too. She says, "He must marry you and your brother must not know or he kill him." We are a respectable family and my father he has property. I see Frank after this and tell him he must marry me now that he knows I a good girl, and he say he would and on next Tuesday we go to City Hall. He takes out license and we was married by some man there. Then he takes me to a furnished room. All the time we was in this room he just bring me things to eat like crackers, cheese and a little wine. He twice try to make me go on the streets and the first time he beat me and pull my hair and knock me around; he show me a pistol till I faint on the floor and then he throw water over me and tell me not to be so foolish.

One day he take me out with his cousin Jim and his wife Rosie. She's bad; she goes on the streets. She say, "Why don't you do what he wants you? Look at me! I have good clothes," and she showed me a diamond pin. "I get that by doing bad business." I say, "I go to my mother if he not want to take care of me, or I go to work, and Frank go to work and we have rooms. We buy a little furniture. We not need things so fine." And my husband, he say, "What you look like with this kind of clothes." I say, "My mother buy me this suit, it good enough."

One day he comes in, he bring me a little short dress and red garters and big red bows for my hair. He say, "You put on." I say, "No, I not put on. I shamed." Then he slap me and beat me and put pistol to my face and I go way from him and I go down to Carmine Street to Mary, who is a good woman and some relation to him, and I tell her about it. She say, "My God! Is he so bad?" She send for him and say, "What you mean when you get a good girl? What for you want to put her in this bad life?" And he say, "Oh, I don't want to; I just crazy," and he say, "Come home, I not ask you any more."

We go home and his cousin Jim is there and we have coffee to drink and he put something in the coffee. And by and by my head go round and I stupid and he say, "Come out in the air", and I go out and get on the car and we go some place on the Battery in a house and he leave me there. Pretty soon a man come and he say, "Why you not undressed?" and I say, "I not undress. I not bad girl. I married. I not want to be bad." And he say, "Then you get out of my house. I not want to get into trouble," and I go back. I afraid to go home because I get married without my brother seeing the man I marry.

Then Frank say, "I got work in a barber-shop, come."
We go down to Houston and Mott Street and there he get
ticket and money and then we go to Gran Central, and get
on train. This was Wednesday of the next week when we
married. It was six o'clock and we rode and it gets to be
nine o'clock and I say, "Where we go? How long it takes?"
He say, "We going to Chicago!" Then I cry, "Now I
know you put me in the bad life." He say, "You make
noise on train, I kill you." We get to Chicago and he take
me to a house where a man live, his name is Nino Sacco.
There he show me razors and pistols and say, "You do not
do what I tell you, you be dead." One day I get out, but
that man Sacco, he come after me and take me back. Another
time I get out of the house, but every time they catch me
and take me back. Then I get sick and cannot do business,
and they say, "She no good", and my husband he write to
my brother and say, "You want your sister back, you be on
Bleecker Street in drug store, and I give you back your sister.
You bring $100 and I give you your sister."

Then he bring me to New York. He say to me, "You put
police on me you be dead girl. I not 'feard for myself, I
can get free. I know how. I have had other girls; but
you try and I kill you." Then we met my brother. He
gave Frank $100 and he took me home. I wait two days,
then I tell police. Frank he get arrested and then we found
he had another wife. I was only one month in Chicago, but
my life is spoiled and my family ruined and I sick and can't
work. [Marino and Sacco were sentenced to five years in
prison.][1]

82. I am a girl from Galicia. I am neither old nor young.
I am working in a shop like other girls. I have saved up
several hundred dollars. Naturally, a young man began
to court me and it is indeed this that we girls are seeking.
I became acquainted with him through a Russian [Jewish]
matchmaker who for a short while boarded with a country-
man of mine. He is really handsome and, as the girls call

---

[1] Maud Miner: "The Slavery of Prostitution", p. 105.

it, "appetizing." But he is poor, and this is no disgrace. He became dearer to me every day. One day he told me he was in want owing to a strike, so I helped him out. I was never stingy with him and besides money also bought him a suit of clothes and an overcoat. . . Who else did I work for if not him? In short we became happily engaged.

Some time after, we hired a hall in Clinton Street and we were on our way to the bank to draw some money for the wedding expenses and also to enter the savings in both our names. On the way we passed some of his countrymen who were musicians, and we needed music, so we stopped in. He introduced me as his bride. I offered to have them play at our wedding. Incidentally, I inquired about my fiancé and they gave good opinions of him. Only a musician's boy pitifully gazed at me and remarked, when my fiancé was not near us: "Are there not enough people from the old country to ask for their opinion?" I understood the hint and asked him for an address, which he gave me. Meanwhile, we were late for the bank, and fortunately, too. I could hardly wait for evening when I rushed over to his country-man and inquired about him. They were surprised at my questions and told me he had a wife and three children in — Street. As I later found out she was the same woman whom he introduced me to as his boarding mistress. . . . I can-not describe my feelings at that time. I became a mere toy in the mouths of my countrymen. But what more could I do than arrest him? But his wife and children came to court and had him released.

I found out of the existence of a gang of wild beasts, robbers who prey upon our lives and money. I then adver-tised in a Jewish newspaper, warning my sisters against such a "fortune" as befell me. I was not ashamed and told of my misfortune wherever I came and gave warnings. The East Side has become full of such "grooms", "matchmakers", "mistresses", "sisters", and "brothers." Inquire of their countrymen. There are plenty of their kind.

A girl from my country has also married one of the band,

the one who was my former matchmaker. To the warnings that he had a wife and child in Europe, she replied, "Well, if she comes she will be welcome." And good countrymen did indeed send for her and she came with a four-year-old boy. Her predicament is horrible to describe. She is poor and lonely and my countrywoman did not welcome her as she boasted, and her husband said: "Whoever sent for you may support you."[1]

White slavery has never been a quantitatively important factor as the beginning of delinquency and together with the cadet system it is passing out, partly as the result of public indignation and severe penalties, and partly as the result of the changing attitude of the women concerned, who have become "wise" and are going more "on their own." Many of them scorn the pimp. The change is a part of the general individualization.

[1] *Forward,* June 7, 1906.

CHAPTER V

SOCIAL AGENCIES

I⊤ is true in general that if you have a good family you do not have a bad individual. The well-organized family, with property and standing, is in a position both to regulate and gratify the wishes of its members. The boy of good family has no occasion to steal or the girl to practice prostitution. Therefore, when a member of a family shows a tendency to demoralization, good people, benevolent institutions, and the State naturally try to strengthen the family, to save the whole situation of which the boy or girl is a part; and when a family is about to be wrecked they try to strengthen it both for its own sake and for the security of the children.

If we examine the following document, which is a specification of the type of family situation described more generally in document No. 58 (p. 100) above, we realize the difficulty of the task of a social agency which attempts to rehabilitate a broken family and to save the children from demoralization by visiting, giving food or money, taking the parents into court, and coming to the rescue in times of crisis. The case represents the patient and heroic work of a charity organization during nearly twenty years. The record extends from the time the oldest child was three months old to a period following her marriage. It is a very long record, and I am able to give only a portion of it. This is an immigrant family, but in the largest cities as many as 80 per cent of delinquent children are foreign born or native born of foreign parents.[1]

83. Joseph Meyer, a German Pole born of peasant parents, came to this country at the age of twenty-three.

Mrs. Meyer, an illiterate woman, had been in America six years at the time of her marriage. She had for two years prior to her marriage done housework. . . . The first application for assistance occurred in 1898 when Mrs. Meyer came to the Relief and Aid Society of Chicago, asking rent. Mr. Meyer had been out of work for three months; there was one child [Mary] 13 months old. . . . [This was two years after the marriage. There is no further report until the family applied to United Charities in 1908. Meantime other children were born, Tillie in 1899, Theodore in 1903, Bruno in 1908].

January 30, 1908, Mrs. Meyer came to office of United Charities. Husband had not worked for four years; mentally slightly abnormal. She had recently begged, but usually had been working very hard. Mary picking coal from the tracks. . . . [Helped by United Charities and County Agent.]

January 3, 1909. Visited man at home, says he had to care for children while wife went out to work. Told him he must get work at once as doctor says he is able to work. Family receiving help for a year and a half. Woman working as janitress in United Charities office.

November 1, 1910. Miss Campbell, whose mother has employed Mrs. Meyer for years, in office to ask if man cannot be sent to Bridewell. Says woman has come to work with arms black and blue from beatings. . . . Mrs. Meyer says man has not worked for more than two months at a time in the 19 years of his married life; says he taunts her with the fact that she must work while he stays at home.

November 3, 1910. . . . Man given 60 days in Bridewell.

[1] See Breckenridge and Abbott: "The Delinquent Child and Home", p. 59.

January 13, 1911. Visitor heard . . . that man had taken carbolic acid New Year's eve. Asked woman about this; at first she did not want to tell, but finally acknowledged it; says he took 20 cents worth of poison while she was at work. The children yelled when he fell and the landlord came in. . . . Woman says man sleeps during the day and will not sleep at night, annoying her considerably, thus causing her to lose considerable sleep. Quarrels with her and uses vile language in the presence of the children.

January 16, 1911. Man in office asking to be arrested, said he is unable to live with woman any longer. [Jealous of unmarried man who calls.] Also stated that woman took some clothes from office of United Charities, where she is janitress. Mrs. Meyer acknowledged doing this and said man told her to take anything she could lay her hands on, as she did not receive enough salary for the amount of work she did. . . . While woman was away at work, man burned all the bedding, lace curtains, new veil Mary had received at Christmas, insurance policies, all the woman's clothes he could get hold of and some of the children's clothes; also broke a clock and bit up woman's wedding ring. . . .

January 20, 1911. Visited a neighbor who said at the time the man was in the Bridewell the woman had some man staying with her. . . .

Visited. Mary ironing; does not go to school; said father has not returned; said father has very often abused mother for many years and mother would not tell any one; also says the man who has been coming to the house bought her mother a comb for Christmas, worth about $1.00, which her father also burned.

February 8, 1911. Mary in office to say her mother was sick; told same story as mother regarding Tony R., says he is a brother of Mrs. Meyer's brother's wife. [March 7, 1911. Man given a year in Bridewell. August 25, Mrs. Meyer gave birth to a boy. Mary working in the Mary Crane Nursery at $3.00 a week.]

October 21, 1911. Miss C. 'phones to advise office about

Mary. Says that many small articles have been disappearing since Mary arrived. Finally they deliberately put temptation in her way by leaving money in the nursery room, which disappeared within a half hour and nobody but Mary had entered the room. Mary steadfastly denies everything, and they feel absolutely baffled by the mother; they had found her to be untruthful several times which has complicated matters since she has been working at the nursery. . . . Later visited and told mother. . . . She cried and said that Mary did not bring anything home, and said she had warned her before she started to work that she was not to touch anything; said she never brought home any candy or anything which would lead her to suspect her of wrong doing. Mother went to work; Mary stayed home.

February 8, 1912, woman in office; said man had come home the day before at noon . . . and the children let him in. When she came home he knelt before her and kissed her hands and begged her to allow him to remain. Because he humbled himself to kneel before her she weakened and told him if he worked he could stay. . . .

March 14, 1912, Mary in office first thing in the morning to say that her father tore good overcoat into strips last night and burned it in the stove; that early this morning when they were all asleep in the house, he tore the curtains down and cut them, cut some of woman's clothing into strips, poured kerosene over feather beds, slashed the leather seats of the four dining-room chairs and did other damage of this sort. [Threatened to buy pistol and kill Mrs. Meyer.] . . . Mrs. Meyer frightened and nervous and broken-hearted over the loss. . . . [Later Mary 'phones that her father has come home and is sitting quietly in the kitchen.] Visited. Mr. Meyer announced that he had nothing to say for himself except that "the woman got the best of it and had everything her way." He stated that he knew the patrol was coming for him that day and wished to "fix" things for his wife, that he "had not done much but had done something." His attitude in the matter was one of spite and the attitude of his wife toward him unusually fine. Despite all that had happened she was rather gentle and almost pathetic in her statement of the case. . . .

March 15, 1912, case tried in court. Man had no excuse to give and did not attempt to defend himself before Judge other than to make the statement that "there was a God in Heaven." Was given $100 costs; sent to House of Correction. . . .

May 3, 1912. Took Mary to Dr. Healy . . . he could find nothing wrong with the child. . . . While she is slow she is normal. . . . He finds no evidence of kleptomania; he fears that too much temptation was put in the child's way. [Found new rooms for the family so that man might not find them when released.]

December 12, 1912, a neighbor 'phones, saying Mr. Meyer home, and as Mrs. Meyer wanted to put him out again he beat her unmercifully [with a poker].

December 24, 1912, woman says man was arrested. . . .

February 14, 1913, visited Detention Court. Man was sent to Kankakee [insane asylum]. After sentence was pronounced woman and Mary were hysterical; said they had never wanted him to go and they would not leave the court unless he was released. Woman's cousin told Mr. Moore that Mary is not working . . . and that she is making her mother's life miserable. Mary . . . begins to show something of her father's temperament. . . . The child's confidence has never been gained. She has always taken her father's side, and her mother is worried over her as she feels she is untrustworthy, is rouging her cheeks and not coming home directly from her work. She is a woman whose enjoyment of household possessions is undiminished by the miseries of her domestic experience, as is a natural coquetry which she has always possessed. We believe that this is an innocent attribute and that all her husband's accusations of infidelity are the suspicions inevitably resulting from sexual obsession in a man otherwise unoccupied for 20 years. He has, undoubtedly, a diseased mind.

April 3, 1913, woman says that Mary did not go to work today as the paint made her sick. Asked that we call up the firm and verify this. Mary had been to Miss Farrell to get suit which had been promised her, but failed to see Miss Farrell and insisted upon getting a coat for which she agreed to pay $8 on the installment plan. An agent came to the house to collect for this and Mary behaved so badly, screaming and crying, that woman finally paid him $2. Mary now has the suit from Miss Farrell and woman wishes to return the coat, but she refuses to do so. [Mary discharged from present position because it was proved she stole from one of the girls. Mary refused to take housework offered her.]

June 9, 1913, woman in office in great distress; says Mary has not worked at all at the hat factory [as she had pretended]. . . . Has been going with a girl who worked there. The girls say the employer is an evil man and showed them a check book and said they could draw what they liked. . . . Mary [refused to let him kiss her but] stole this check book and on the 29th forged a check for $12 which she brought her mother saying it was her pay. On the 2nd she forged another check for $11; $6 of this she gave to her mother and $5 she spent at Riverview Park. . . .

July 29, 1913. . . . Probation officer says Mary lost her job on the 25th, that one of the girls had loaned Mary a ring and when the time came for Mary to restore it, Mary could not find it. . . . [A report from Kankakee that Meyer had escaped was followed by a letter saying] "he escaped one evening but returned of his own free will at bedtime and has since been residing in the Institution." . . .

January 17, 1914, Mary brought home $6 on the 14th but insisted upon $4 being returned to her, and with this she bought a very elaborate hat of black velvet and gold lace. Talked with Mary. She was very defiant and said that she would spend her money on clothing until she had something to wear. Was not satisfied with the coat that United Charities had given her from second-hand store. Said she would keep her money until she could buy a new-style coat. Told

her that if she did so the United Charities would not help
with food.

January 22, 1914, Mrs. Meyer in tears. The forelady at
the shop where Mary works telephoned that Mary had got-
ten married in court today. . . . Mary gave the date of
her birth as December 18, 1895 [instead of 1896] and signed
the affidavit herself. . . .

January 30, 1914, visited. Asked Mrs. Meyer to take a
position. . . . Suggested Mary could stay and take care of the
children. . . . Mary was at first very unwilling to consent
to the plan. While the visitor was there Mr. Andersen [her
husband] came in. He agreed to the plan at least temporarily.

February 4, 1914, Mrs. Meyer in office. Says the work
is too hard at the present situation and she is not earning
enough to feed the children. Mary has had to give her
money and she is ashamed and sorry. She feels too nervous
to work and wants United Charities to get Mr. Meyer out of
asylum to support her. Jennie, her niece, took her to visit
him and she found him nicely dressed and sober, doing team-
ing work. He promised never to drink and to support the
family.

A letter written by the United Charities June 16, 1914,
states "We have found her this spring in a peculiar mental
condition due, we think, to sheer discouragement and a feeling of having been defeated in life. All of her home furnishings are dilapidated and of long usage, because of her in-
ability to replace them. She has been a woman who always
took a peculiar delight in her home and longed to have it
furnished daintily so that it did not compare so poorly with
the homes where she has worked. We feel now that if we
might help her replenish her linen and some of her household
supplies we might be able to tide over their period of discouragement and help her to feel that life was again worth
living. . . ."

August 19, 1914, Mrs. Meyer and Mary in office. [Mary
very well dressed and living in her own apartment.] Mary
says she has been helping her mother continually with food

and clothing. Her husband makes $19 a week but she has to pay $17 rent and $5 a week for her furniture. She also has to save money because she is now several months pregnant. Her husband wishes her to have a doctor. She is planning to have a midwife because it is cheaper. Advised her not do this. . . . During a period of unemployment for her husband she refused to seek aid at her mother's suggestion as she felt too proud. . . .

November 13, 1915. Tillie still earns $4.00 a week. . . . Must buy new dress [refuses to wear dresses given by charity as being old-fashioned — same as Mary]. For lack of satisfactory dress she has not gone to church for 3 weeks. Mrs. Meyer fears she will slip away from church unless allowed clothes she wants. Her [Mrs. Meyer's] ideas become more and more erratic. She said she wishes she were dead, had only trouble.

For the past year the church [Irish, not Polish, for the latter always demanded money instead of giving assistance] has had a decided influence over Mrs. Meyer. Her children attend the parochial school and the priest has taken a very active interest in their welfare. . . . The family lives in a less congested district and although Mrs. Meyer is still very nervous and frequently complains, the whole complexion of the family has changed. She is very interested in a mothers' cooking class started last winter . . . and is also being taught to write by her 12-year-old son. . . . If the man remains in Kankakee and the children keep well we feel sure the family will eventually become self-supporting. It is surely the highest point as far as the standard of living is concerned. . . . The present system of County relief cannot but have a debasing effect upon the family, particularly upon the children, who frequently must accompany the mother in order to bring home the dole of inadequate rations. . . . Mary is a good housewife and a sensible mother. She is contented and happy and her ideals are considerably higher, due directly to her husband." [1]

[1] Records of the United Charities of Chicago.

In this case the social agency, the charity organization, takes the part formerly played by the large family (kinship group) and the community. The man in the case, the cause of the disorganization, is treated as insane. Pretty certainly he would not have been insane in Europe, in his original community. He would have been difficult, but the pressure of the large family and the community would have kept him within certain bounds. His violent behavior is also due in part to the fact that his wife does not behave as a member of a community or family. She resorts to American institutions, hales him into court and lands him in jail. She must do this because she has no family and community back of her, but she breaks the family solidarity. This and the fact that she practices American freedom in associating with another man and receiving presents from him make him "insane." The wife in the European community would not have taken such liberties; community gossip would have restrained her.

On the other hand the woman never lost her ideal of a home, and the coöperation of the charity organization enabled her to endure. The removal of the man was a positive benefit. Further, the Irish Catholic Church came into the case at a certain point and played the part of a religious community. Its intervention gave aid, status, and recognition, particularly to the girls. (The Polish Catholic Church in America always exacts payment, and in general Polish organizations here interest themselves only in those members who are worth while; the derelicts it leaves to American institutions.)

Another saving element in the situation is that Mary was treated as a member of a family, not as a transgressor against the State. She stole repeatedly and forged checks, but she was never taken into court for it. It was fortunately "overlooked", as parents overlook such defections. Mary was not betrayed sexually; she did not seem to be so disposed. Perhaps she was lucky in this. Certainly she was fortunate in her marriage, and through it became stabilized and an element of strength in the larger family. Her sister Tillie has a better chance than Mary had. But at the same time a review of the whole case leaves the feeling that Mary's future was never secure from the date of her birth to the date of her marriage. There were not sufficient formative influences to assure a social organization of her wishes.

The efforts of the federal government during the war to control the behavior of girls who were either wild already or went wild during the excitement resulted in many cases in the attempt to stabilize the girl by improvising good family and community influences for her. The work was in charge of the Girls' Protective Bureau. The methods used were in the main similar to those of a juvenile court. Families of good standing made it a part of patriotism to take girls into their homes and made extraordinary efforts to influence them. The workers of the Bureau acted both as parents and as community. The result was often very good. Where the girl was not bad but had, for example, run away from a country home to see a boy from her neighborhood, she was eventually returned home without demoralization. But the records show in general that the influence of an extemporized family and community is not usually sufficient to give a new scheme of life to a difficult girl. She does not belong really to the new family and community,

as in the case of the girl born there. She is placed
under discipline. She is not a daughter of the family,
to be married like a daughter of a family. She has
not a life-long train of memories, making her a part
of the situation. She usually appreciates her new
security for a time, but presently the desire for new
experience, recognition and response return and if
possible she runs away. Case No. 84 is typical of the
result when a girl of bad habits is placed with a family of good standing which is sentimental about her,
patronizes her, treats her half as servant, half as
family-member, excludes her as far as possible from
the world and exhorts her. On the other hand this
girl was not very bad. She needed simply a situation in which she could live, with some response and
recognition.

84. Marie Morse, age 16, who first came to our notice on
June 15th when one of our protective officers found her at
11 P. M. in front of the Northwestern Station in the company
of two sailors.

Marie had then been living with her father for three
weeks. It was found that he, in his effort to be what he
considered good to her, had given her her own way until she
did nothing but "run the streets" from morning until late
at night and quite refused to obey him. . . .

Marie claims that her mother "picked up with men" in
Riverview, so she could do likewise. The mother does not
deny having once spoken to a man she did not know, but explains it by saying that Marie was teasing for a ride in Forest
Park and she could not afford to give it to her, so a gentle-
man volunteered to give them both two rides. Marie stated
that her mother had a colored woman living with them, and
that she (Marie) was forced to sleep with this colored woman.
The mother does not deny this, but said that her church
teaches her that color makes no difference, and that Marie

only slept once with this woman, and that was when Marie chose to do so. . . .

Visited Mr. Morse. He showed visitor every corner of their rooms, which were in good order and clean. He does all the work of the home. Marie refuses to do anything, even very personal things. Mr. Morse's young married niece (aged 26) came in to cook his Sunday dinner for him. She stated, when Mr. Morse left the room, that Marie had absolutely no moral standard at all and when she and other relatives would advise her, she would say "That's nothing — mother does it." She states that Marie has told them absolutely dreadful things and thinks nothing of it; thinks it is all right to "pick up" with and go with any man. . . .

Found a place for Marie with Mrs. R. M. Harriman, Winnetka. Marie will care for two children, under three years of age, will receive $3.00 a week, room and board. She will have her own bathroom and very pleasant surroundings. Mrs. Harriman is a woman of quality who will be able to give Marie personal and home standards.

Mr. Harriman 'phoned. Wants to know a little about Marie, as they already like her but she seems so lonesome; wanted to go to movie and they told her that there were none out there. Marie asked to let her "beau", a chauffeur, know where she is and Mr. Harriman told her that his daughter of seventeen is not yet old enough to entertain, so he surely would not let Marie have men call on her. Marie said she was a Roman Catholic, and as the Catholic Church is but three blocks from the house, he told Marie he expected her to go every Sunday. There is a splendid girl working next door and he had Marie meet her, as he knows she will not let Marie do anything she should not do. Mrs. Harriman will be very glad to see visitor if she will 'phone first. Mrs. Harriman took Marie out on Monday and bought her some good sensible clothes.

Marie goes to church with Julia, the Catholic maid next door. They often spend the evenings in one another's yards. This is Marie's only friend and Mrs. Harriman states that she is often quite lonesome. They are interesting her in books and she has nearly finished one. They felt this would keep her mind off her old friends. Mrs. Harriman states that she often keeps her busy unnecessarily "rubbing up the silver or dusting books" just so she won't become so lonesome and sit looking off into space as she did do much during her first week there.

Mrs. Harriman states that her duties are not heavy. All the washing, including Marie's, is sent to the laundry and Mrs. Harriman uses the vacuum cleaner herself on the rugs once a week. When Marie was told to put her laundry in, it was found that she had none — wore no underwear but skirt and corset cover. They were too large, so Mrs. Harriman showed Marie how to fix them and let her do this evenings. Mrs. Harriman told how Marie's eyes beamed when she heard Mr. Harriman talk of a drive they had to Great Lakes, and later in the evening she asked Mrs. Harriman about it.

Marie wanted to bring a chauffeur friend up to the house, but they forbade it telling her she was too young to have company. Mrs. Harriman feels that when her daughter returns from her summer visit with relatives and Marie sees how she is expected to do, Marie will be better satisfied with the program they have mapped out for her. . . .

Mrs. Harriman took visitor in the house to talk with Marie. The girl certainly looks well. She is somewhat stouter and tanned and her cheeks are rosy. She has improved immensely — looks well kept, neat, clean and happy. She showed visitor her room and bath, which are very nice, bright and sunny, well ventilated, clean, and the furniture and carpet were good pieces and in good condition. She stated that Mrs. Harriman was going to put nice curtains and pictures up for her. Marie said that Julia, the girl next door, did not have nearly so nice or large a room and no bath at all. She showed visitor the dresses she was given and said the yellow one which she wears on Sunday "looks fine when it is fresh." Marie expects to finish reading "Pollyanna" tonight, and Mr. Harriman already has another book for her. She liked "Pollyanna" very much. Mr. Harriman also told her there were books of travel there which would teach her as much as if she went three years longer to school, and Marie seems anxious to begin reading them. . . .

August 12, went to Winnetka. Mrs. Harriman says they sent Marie to the Kings' to ride to Lake Geneva. Mrs. Harriman explained that there are times when friends go on trips with them and when they cannot therefore take Marie as they do not have room enough.

Started out with Marie. We walked down to the bank. On the way Marie stated that she had now worked three weeks and that she had no money except the $1.25 balance paid by Mrs. Johnson this morning and 30 cents. Expressed surprise that she had not at least $5.00 saved. Told her we would deposit this $1.00 in the bank, that hereafter she would deposit $2.00 each week and buy one thrift stamp, and the remaining 75 cents was more than enough to spend. Visitor signed bank slip so that Marie cannot draw without visitor's signature. Marie was going to buy thrift stamp and visitor explained that she could wait for that until next week as we were going to the doctor down in Chicago and she would need lunch money. Explained also that she should not expect the Harrimans to continue to give her carfare and R. R. fare, etc., that while they did so through kindness, they were under no obligation to do so. . . . Told her she was no longer a child now and must mold her own character and plan for her future, to support herself, to buy her own clothing, to save something for times of illness or possible accident.

Reached Chicago. Went to Childs for luncheon. Gave Marie bill of fare and advised her to choose good, plain, nutritious food according to what she could afford to spend. She chose well, her luncheon costing her 30 cents. When visitor ordered her own dessert, she ordered ice cream for Marie and paid for same. Marie while on the street passed two Catholic Sisters and remarked to visitor that they were from St. Patrick's, where she went to school when living with her mother. . . .

At County Building and explained case. After examination, Dr. Stanton stated that it is not possible to know if Marie has had improper relations recently on account of [seduction seven years ago]. She questioned Marie very closely and Marie stated that all the sailors and soldiers had asked her to have intercourse with them, but that she positively had not done it.

Took Marie to the Northwestern Station. While going over, Marie said, "I wish I could see my friends." Told her we had her up there to get her away from the seemingly bad company she had been in; that she was not to come to Chicago except with visitor and never, even with her father, to be out of Mrs. Harriman's house after 11:30; that she was no longer a child and just must make up her mind to obey the plans of the G. P. B., or it would make it very hard for herself; that she was old enough now to substitute other forms of recreation for the kind she had been indulging in. She could read, write, sew, or rest after her work. Told her visitor would probably call once each month. . . .

Mr. Harriman in office. Saturday Mrs. Harriman gave Marie a pair of shoes. Monday morning, August 19th, she paid her. Marie cleared her room, etc., and at one o'clock told Mrs. Harriman she was going to the bank. Mrs. Harriman told her she was much pleased. Marie left and has not been seen or heard of since.

Mr. Harriman 'phoned. Said Marie told maid next door some time last week that when things had quieted down a little she was going back to her mother, or to her father's relatives, in Hammond. [Marie went to her mother, but both disappeared and were never located.] [1]

In the following case of far-going demoralization the influences are also improvised. The girl's mother was bad and taught her to be bad. An interesting

[1] Records of the Girls' Protective Bureau.

feature in the document is the complete transformation of the girl under the influence of the physician. She had been dirty and disorderly and became clean, orderly, and interested in work. It frequently happens that some particular influence, perhaps the effect of another personality, defines the situation to the demoralized girl, brings a conversion, and she begins to reorganize her life spontaneously. But in this case the life of the girl was so totally unorganized that it is impossible to regard this transformation as anything more than a phase of security between two periods of new experience. Quiescent and orderly periods are in fact the rule in such cases and social workers learn to estimate the length of their duration. The physician himself does not hope that any permanent change of character has been effected. We may suspect also that Helen is mentally inferior, of the moron type, but even so we must speculate as to her character if she had been situated from the beginning like little Calline in document No. 36. A clean and protected moron is not far from corresponding to the ideal woman of the Victorian age.

85. June 12, 1918. Helen Langley. Age 19. Very childlike in appearance and this impression is exaggerated by her yellow bobbed hair, short skirts, etc. Although she has been observed continually in places and always with men, in scarcely any case has the same sailor or civilian been seen with her more than two or three times. She has no fear of the Protective Officers, with whom she is always free in her attitude — runs to greet them, offers them candy, etc. It has been impossible to have any serious conversation with her, as she is irresponsible and heedless.

Visited her brother Mr. Edward Hunt and his wife. They stated that Helen was born at North Chicago, September 17th, 1899. She was irregular in her attendance at school, did not pass the 4th grade and stopped going altogether when she was 12 or 13 years old. She has never been known to read a book or magazine, not even the "funny" page in the paper, and the brother believes she is unable to write anything beyond her signature. Although the family were known as Swedish Lutheran, Helen had no religious training and did not attend church or Sunday School. According to the brother she was depraved from the time she was 12 years old when she began to "go crazy over the boys", to attend dance halls and to go out on motor trips with unknown men. When 14 years old she was attacked by a neighbor in a field near her home and since that time her life has been a series of immoral relations with sailors and civilians. Edward Hunt believes these tendencies are inherited from his mother, who gave birth to an illegitimate child before her marriage and whose immorality afterwards broke up the family repeatedly and turned his father into a drunkard and an idler. . . . From the time Helen was a child her mother encouraged her in every sort of immorality and helped her in deceiving her father or boldly defying him. Mrs. Edward Nelson stated that Helen to her knowledge has brought on several abortions with the assistance of her mother. . . .

On March 23rd, after a three weeks' acquaintance, Helen married George Langley, a sailor rated as a first class fireman. . . . She was four months pregnant at the time. She told her relatives and friends that she was marrying Langley in order to secure the allotment and insurance. She and her husband lived for three weeks with Mr. and Mrs. Ed. Hunt and then took a room with Mrs. De Lacey, 147 Sheridan Road. Shortly after her marriage Helen appealed to the Red Cross and was given $14.00 to pay her rent. This money she spent for a pink sweater and a silk skirt. . . .

Visited Mrs. Anna Langley. Talked with her and her son, Bill. The whole family has been crushed over George's marriage. Their chief concern seems to be the allotment and insurance, which George transferred from his mother to Helen. They want, if possible, to prevent her from receiving the first payment, which is due July 1st. On one occasion Helen tried to represent herself at the Post Office as Mrs. Anna Langley in order to secure the allotment. George Langley is under treatment at the Naval Station for disease contracted from his wife. For this reason and because of her continued loose behavior he is trying to secure a divorce before he is sent to sea early in July. Mrs. Langley and her son stated that Helen has been brought before the police several times to their knowledge and spent one night in the County Jail last January. Bill is willing to make a sworn statement giving the names of two Waukegan men who have admitted to him they have contracted disease from Helen. . . .

Visited Chaplain Moore. He sent for George Langley, who stated that he had been in love with Helen from the moment he saw her, and had begged her repeatedly to marry him, which she refused to do although she was having immoral relations with him. Langley knew that she was diseased and was going about with other men, but felt certain that she would behave if she married him. He has tried to live with her, but she was lazy, dirty and disorderly, went out every night with other men, returning at two or three in the morning. He stated that Mr. Hart, with whom they lived in North Chicago, is willing to testify that she brought sailors to her room many times in the absence of her husband. . . .

Telephoned Miss Judson, Superintendent of the Lake Bluff Orphanage. She stated that a baby boy, about one week old, was found in the woods by some school children on October 27th, 1916, and brought to the Orphanage. The child was tagged "Baby Langley" and was in a most advanced stage of syphilis. It was attended by Dr. Brown, city physician. Miss Judson took all the care of the baby herself, as it required constant attention and was so diseased that she would not endanger the nurses. The baby died on January 1st, 1917.

Visited Helen. She told about the birth of her baby in October, 1916, and of how she disposed of it in the Lake Forest woods. She stated that she has never worked regularly, but has had several factory positions and has done housework for Mrs. Watrous of Waukegan, Mrs. Gerley of Waukegan and for Mrs. Christianson of North Chicago. She stated that she has succeeded eight or ten times in bringing about miscarriage with the use of an instrument which was bought by her mother at Pearce's Drug Store and which her sister-in-law taught her to use. . . .

Observed Helen at the circus in company with a sailor. She went afterwards to an ice cream parlor and a chop suey restaurant, was followed to North Chicago and was observed in the woods at midnight.

Consulted Judge Pearsons of the County and Juvenile Courts and Assistant States Attorney Welch. They agreed that it was imperative to detain Helen at once and decided that an arrest should be made on a charge of disorderly conduct. The examination will be made immediately so that she can be placed under medical treatment for the three weeks awaiting her trial. In the meantime her age can be verified and a decision made as to whether she will be tried on the grounds of feeble-mindedness or delinquency. . . .

Interviewed Mr. Hart, with whom Helen had rooms with her husband for about two months. Mr. Hart says Helen is a "worthless character"; says he is "in wrong" with the neighbors for having her there. Showed me room and bath occupied by Helen. Both rooms contained a lot of dirty clothes. He said she had not washed while she was there. Trunk filled with rumpled clothes, stained and soiled rags, etc., bedding which was new when she came, was soiled and filthy.

Visited County Jail. Asked to see Helen. Was told by Mr. Griffin, the Sheriff, that Helen was removed by Dr. Brown, County Physician, on June 21. Mr. Griffin said that Helen is not in the County Hospital. He would make no further statement and advised that we go to Dr. Brown for information.

Interviewed Dr. Brown in his office. He offered to accompany visitor to place in which Helen is kept on condition that the address shall not be made known to any one in Waukegan. He said that he expected Helen to be cured and in condition to be discharged in a very short time as several slides according to his own analysis have proved negative. . . .

Drove with Dr. Brown to County Hospital. Helen is under care in one of the tuberculosis cottages. The tuberculosis nurse, Miss Gean Crawford, was willing to assume the care on condition that Helen's disease should not be known to the other nurses. Helen has gained several pounds and looks like a new person, is content and happy, sleeps most of the day and said she feels rested for the first time for years. She takes all the care of her own cottage, has become very tidy in her habits, enjoys washing her dishes, etc., and keeping things in order. Helen said that her plan when she is discharged is to find a good place where she can do housework. She intends to have nothing further to do with men, particularly sailors. She loves to do sewing and handwork and showed the most astonishing amount of embroidery which she has done for one of the nurses. She asked for news of her family and said that she has begged to see her mother, but the Doctor and nurse have convinced her that it is best to have no visitors. She is out of doors most of the day, but sees nothing of the other patients.

Helen is now employed in the kitchen at the County Hospital, lives in the servants' quarters and is to be paid $25.00 a month. She has proved so quick, willing and efficient that Dr. Brown would like to employ her permanently, but he realizes that it will be impossible to hold her after she knows that she is well. He would like to keep her at least through August, as she is a great help with the canning. As long as she continues to be content he will not send the final specimen to the State Laboratory.

Visited Dr. Brown. He refused absolutely to permit Helen to be visited by any of the Protective Workers. Said she is doing excellent work, is very content, and begs to remain at the hospital. Although Dr. Brown is unwilling to undertake the responsibility of Court parole, he would like to retain her as a permanent employee, on condition that there is no interference from the Protective Bureau or the courts.

After talking over the matter with the State's Attorney and Dr. G. G. Taylor of the State Board of Health, it was decided that no better plan can be made for Helen than to allow her to remain in the hospital with the hope that Dr. Brown will change his policy as to visits from the Protective Bureau.[1]

The penitentiary and reformatory, to which offenders are condemned by courts of law, have, as is well known, never been generally successful in reorganizing the attitudes of their inmates on a social basis. They represent the legal concept of crime and punishment and the theological concept of sin and atonement. Where society is not able to organize the wishes of one of its members in a social way it may exterminate him or banish him to a society of the bad, which corresponds to the theological purgatory from which there is a chance to return to a society of the good. The punishment is supposed to atone for the offense and effect the reformation.

The following case was handled by a particularly well equipped reformatory for girls above the juvenile court age. Its staff at the time was large and scientifically trained. It was probably more completely equipped for the psychological study of its inmates than any other institution whatever, and its records are more complete than any I have seen elsewhere. But an institution dealing with a large number of girls

[1] Records of the Girls' Protective Bureau.

sentenced by the law courts, many of them hardened and rebellious, has quite as much as it can do barely to maintain order. The situation is the same as in the penitentiaries for men. The present case is not typical; the girl is far from being as demoralized as the average girl in the same institution. I cite it here to indicate what are the attitudes of a girl in this situation, how accessible a girl may be to influences and how unprepared an institution of this type is to employ any organizing influences.

Esther had no previous bad record. She may or may not have had some sex experiences; that is not unusual with girls of this class. It was not shown that she was sexually diseased. Probably she was not but was frightened into thinking so by a doctor who wanted $100.00. Her offense was slight and casual. It might have been passed over with a reprimand, or, as in the juvenile court, with a period of probation; but she was nineteen — above the juvenile court age. The institution recognized, in the statement given first below, that it would not be for her welfare to hold her there, and placed her out on parole.

86. Statement from the Laboratory of Bedford Hills Reformatory for Women:

Esther Lorenz was committed to the institution March 23, 1914, from Special Sessions, N. Y.

Offense: Petit Larceny. She was born in Prag, Bohemia, and educated in Bohemian and German. She has a father and sister living in the old country and an aunt in New Jersey to whom she came three years and a half ago. This aunt and her family are poor and very foreign and unprogressive. Esther worked for them faithfully and gained little knowledge of English or training of any sort while with them. She left them several times and took positions as waitress in private families, still helping them out from her meager earnings. Her last position was as waitress in a small restaurant in New York where she met Lilian Marx. She had been there eight months when the restaurant went out of business and the girls were thrown out of work.

It was soon after this that the girls stole from Macy's store several articles, two pairs of 59-cent stockings, a belt and some cheap manicure articles, apparently on the impulse of the moment, because they saw another girl doing it so easily. In jail they were warned by the other girls not to tell the truth about anything and they were too frightened to think what to tell. Esther's story was in the main true, but Lilian made up in obedience to the other girl's suggestion a conflicting tale. The probation officer felt that she was not getting the truth, and as the two girls were so young and so without protection, she advised their commitment to the institution in order that the institution might investigate their case more thoroughly.

Investigation in the case of Esther revealed nothing further against the girl than the one offense for which she was arrested. We have found her to be intelligent, conscientious, and, far beyond other girls, sensitive to fine distinctions of right and wrong. It was the opinion of the Laboratory that she might get more harm from association with the girls than good from a long term in the Reformatory and that it would be well to parole her as soon as she had had some training and a suitable position was in view. . . .

She will not write to her aunt because . . . the aunt said she did not know any such girl. Will not write to her father because she does not want him to know anything about the matter. She had heard that we sometimes send girls back to their own country, and she would be glad to go except that she would have to make some excuse to her father for being sent back. When I asked her if she would tell him the truth she said: "Tell him that I was sent home for stealing a pair of stockings?" It seems to strike her as quite ridiculous.

[The following letters (except the last) were written by Esther to her friend Lilian and show her general attitudes. The letters were written mainly in Bohemian during the seven months she was on parole, and were translated for the institution by a Bohemian woman whose rendering is similar to the few letters written in English by Esther. I have adapted the translations only slightly. About half the letters are printed here.]

October 1, 1914. My dearest Friend: I received your letter with which I was very happy. I am glad to hear that you have a nice place. Dear friend, I apologize not to answer you right away. I have lots of work. I have two people and little baby girl. I have so much work; I haven't got even time to wash my face. . . . In the morning I get up at 5 o'clock and I wash porch, then I make breakfast. I had eight to the table and I was the 9th one, so you can immagine what work I had. So then I had to wash dishes, then wash diapers for the baby. I got to clean two ducks and I got to make eight beds as whole first floor and I had to set the table and cooking all alone. No one helps me and everything got to be ready 1 o'clock, so you can imagine how I was dancing in the kitchen. That's the way it goes, every night I go upstairs half past ten or eleven. When I come up I'm like dead; soon as I lay down I sleep. So imagine how I look worse every day. I have $14 month and she promises me more next month — that what she says. I like to know if I see them [money]. She is very snike [snake?] — every evening when she goes to bed she take me around the neck and kiss me but who knows for what she do that. I work very hard, Dear sweetheart, you ask me to come to see you but how can I do that; I haven't got no shoes and no money, I am very poor. If you can you come over on Saturday evening and sleep with me. I got big bed. On Sunday we can look for [an Italian friend, not a bad character] and we go in a place where we can have a good time and lots of kissing. We going to look for some nice man but something better, not only working man; we shouldn't have to go to work. I am angry with my aunt, she don't want to take my lawyer, so they may go on my back ["take the air"] I take him myself when I have that money, don't you think. She told on me that I have different name and that I am Catholic not a Jew, so now Miss R. will be angry with me that I told her lies but she and Miss T. and all the rest may go on my back. I don't worry now they know. How we fool, them. Innocent. Friend, aint they fools, aint they fools! She [probation officer] is a good girl. Sunday School. [Term applied derisively by the girls of the officials, the institution and of themselves.] My dearest Friend, I wrote to T. and the letter come back. He isn't there any more and may be he is in Phila. Wouldn't be that nice if he knows we are paroled; he be happy, don't you think so? Dear Friend, all the time I couldn't come to see you before I have new shoes; and then we go to dance together; they would not know where we were going. If you can, come over. This is such a little country — one house half an hour from the next. Every night when I go to bed I am thinking how I used to have and how I have it now, but when my relatives wouldn't help me out, God knows what he got to do. Your lady ask you how I like my place, so say I couldn't have any better place. My nose is always bleeding; I dont know what to do. My lady told me she send for doctor but I don't want any. So, dear Friend, dont be mad at me I didn't answer right away. For that I wrote you such a letter that is worth something. And write, Esther. And sleep sweet. And sweet dreams. Love to you from your dear friend.

My dearest Friend: . . . I see that you didn't forget me. True friend. When you want me to answer you always right away, every letter, just the same I expect from you that you should answer my letter like a true friend. Don't you think I have a right? Friend, dear, what I'm going anyway to do if I have to suffer always so much with my sickness? I suffer so much, you know. Dear girlie, nobody wouldn't lend you any money. I was asking people and they promised me and later they say again that they hav n't got money themselves. So you see how it is, how the people are false.

Doctor told me that if I let go that further that I would n't have never any children, and you know when we get married we would like to have children, but where I should take $100 when I hav n't got them and for the trial too they ask $100, so answer me if I hav n't got [am not] right. I like to help us out but what can I do without any money. I wrote to the lawyer if he can make trial for you and he answer me that he like to talk to me about — he could n't make any answer — he said that he wrote letter to Bedford, that they should let us free, that we was working hard enough, that we are long enough in places, and so Miss T. wrote me that I should wait and Miss R. wrote me a letter too, that's going to be everything all right, and my lady she received a letter from Miss R. that she come to see me next month and I think that I be free. The lawyer wrote letter to him and they are afraid from him, ha, ha. [frightened into this course]. The lawyer spoke to Judge and Judge he said that we never be free, so lawyer he wrote to me that soon as possible I should come to N. Y., and I should tell him why we want the trial and I tell him that we're not guilty, that we does that from foolishness [thoughtlessness] and we was nervous, and going to tell that we were invited to the wedding and so that happened; that we was like out of mind, that we did n't realize what we were doing. Don't say that we are guilty, otherwise we would n't come out and that would be a shame. We be put in a newspaper when our trial come on and we should n't say "guilty", but if you would n't listen to me, say anything you like. Still I beg on you don't say on me. If they ask you, say that you don't know. Do you understand me? Listen Friend, make yourself stuck up [act proud]. Don't act like a baby — that way you never come out. What should I do next week; I am supposed to come to N. Y. and I hav n't got fare for train; that cost $8. I come there and like to see you but I would n't have much time. The lawyer he going to keep me about one hour and about 4 o'clock I 'm through with my work and then till I get to the station and then take two hours till I get to N. Y. and that be about 7; and I want to be back about ten if be possible. I don't want my lady she should catch on for she never would let me go there. Don't say anything to your lady that I come to N. Y. because you 're be such a one you never can keep quiet, do you understand me? I 'm sometimes so angry at you that I would tear you to pieces cause you never keep your mouth shut. You got too big mouth. I think when you got a sweetheart that your big enough to have more sense. Once in a while you have not got your sense. . . . Sometimes I have a right to tell you that, so don't be angry on me and write me right away, and tell you head you should have a good time, but not yet. Would n't you be glad to see me. Its six months since we did n't see one the other. Maybe we would n't know one the other. I let you know when I come.

November, 1914. Dear Friend : I received your letter and I was very glad to hear from you. I am glad that you don't forget me. I will forgive you this time, but don't do that again. I going to lose my patience. You know what that means. I don't have to wait very long for a letter. Dear friend, I am going to moving pictures every Wednesday and every time when I going out I see the nice young mens. How they love them, the girls, and we can't help that. I met one nice man and he want to go with me for a good time but I realize maybe he some kind of detective, so I told him. "What do you want, I can't understand you." "Oh, you know what I mean," [he said]. I told him, "You big slob, you leave me alone," and he left me. He was very nice, and he was a blond. That was a joke. Dear friend, if you could come with me to moving pictures, there we would meet nice mens. Would n't that be nice? I have my hands so hard like a man from hard work, so you can immagine how hard I am working. So the rest of it I am going to write to you next time. I am writing for a call for a lawyer and he

get one too.   My uncle he pay the lawyer so that going to
be for sure.

With such a Italians [as T.] we wouldn't go any more.
The lawyer want us to have a witness and I told him we had
[the Italian] and now I must tell him we havn't got any.
That's going to be hard again.   I wrote to the Frenchmans
and the letter comes back.   What can I do and I got to give
an answer to the lawyer right away.   Good-by.   Lots of
kisses.   Your friend.

Dear Friend :   Forgive me that I didn't answer your right
away.   Dear Friend I have such a cranky lady.   If I stay
here another two months with her I think I go crazy.   I was
very sick the other Sunday.   We had 8 people and so you
can immagine what work I had.   Only if you would see
me you would get frightened how I look ; I am only bone
and skin and pale in face.   You would say that I go by and
by in grave.   Everybody ask me what's matter with me
but you know I can't tell everybody I come from Bedford.   You know when I had these 8 people to table
and I have to wait on table and after they was through
I get such a cramp like I had in the Tombs.   My lady she
was so mad at me that I leave the dishes and I went to lay
down.   Friend you wouldn't know what it is when we have
our home again.   When anything hurts you we can get
help — but this way we are like dogs — don't you think
I'm right ?   If you can only see this and how I worry about
both of us how we should come free.   Friend, I didn't understand your letter.   You want I should write to Miss R. or
you do it ?

Friend, dear, I am sending you a letter.   Be so kind —
send it from Brooklyn or New York.   You know he [doctor]
ask me where I live, so I told him I am a dressmaker from
Newark but when the letter going to be sent from Brooklyn
or New York, but don't let you lady see that because that
doctor is only for bad sickness [venereal], only for women
which are sick from men ; otherwise you bring me in a
trouble more than I am.   He's known all over.   So soon

as you get the letter, mail it right away. Don't let the letter lay no place they shouldnt see it. If my lady should know this, so I know its only your fault. My lady told me that you show every letter you get from me to your people and they write one another, so if you be true to me you do what I ask you. He's the doctor what going to cure me. Dear Friend forgive me that I write such a short letter. I'm very tired. Answer right away will you and then I write to you one long letter and I come to see you soon as possible. With happiness and kisses from your true friend. Esther.

[Note by parole officer: When Esther was asked to translate the original of the foregoing letter . . . she omitted the sentence with the word "doctor" in it. . . . When she had finished the letter I asked her if she had not omitted a sentence, pointing out. She read it again and said: "Oh, yes, he is the doctor what's going to make me well, that is, my head well." I reminded her that she had previously said he was the doctor she was keeping company with and also a doctor for women's sickness. She was evidently quite confused but insisted that she meant all women's sickness, and that he treated women only, not men.]

Dearest Friend: I am letting you know I received your letter. I was very happy with it. Dear Friend I write to T. where is the lawyer. He went there and told him that he met us on the street, so see how T. is false; so lawyer ask my uncle where did we pick up the two boys, so uncle ask me how is it with the boys — where we met them, so I have trouble yet again. . . . When T. come to you so you tell him that he meets us on the street but we are not street girls; give him good but tell him we are innocent. Ha, ha, Dear M., Miss R. was here yesterday and ask me about trial, I didn't know what to say, she had so much to say [knew so much that Esther was surprised]. Friend why did you tell your lady that we going to have trial. I didn't tell mine nothing. You've got to say everything out before there's any start. You know she going to let it out to Bedford. Miss R. told me your lady wrote to Bedford — that she write there every

month, so realize how stupid you are.   Excuse me that I
scold you like that but I can't help.   I am very excited and
angry that you must tell everything you know.   I asked
Miss R. if I can go and see you and she told me "no."   So
I ask her if you can come see me and she told me she ask
your lady if she let you go.   I told Miss R. that I am willing to give you money for train if you havn't got it.   You
should come to see me soon as possible and then we going to
talk over. . . .

December 1914.   Dear Friend: I must say that I like
it here, because Miss R. asked me if I like it here.   If not
she will give me another place, but I would lose my good
references and that would make it very bad, as they might
say I do not know how to work — or then I could perhaps
not come out in the trial.

Tell me what to do.   The lawyer always wants money,
and I have none now.   My uncle gave me some or told him
he would give him later, but you know my uncle promised
to give it to him right away, if he himself had money, but
he poor fellow is in debt yet on account of his business that
he had. . . .   I cry every day and pray to God he should
help me.

I also went with one young fellow to have a good time and
earned $2 and what is that?   For that I bought stockings
and what I needed and the $2. were gone.   I am now the
same as you are, everything tires me.   I would rather not
see myself.

Let me know my dear what I must buy for you for Christmas or else I might buy something what you do not like.

[Note by parole officer: Esther herself translated this
. . . passage as follows: "I was in town for a good time and
I see the young man with the $2."   She then explained: "I
don't mean that as it sounds; it means that before in New
York I met a young man when I was getting off the car.   I
lost the heel from my shoe and slipped and this young man
picked me up and gave me $2. which I dropped out of my
pocket-book."   Then translates: "I was in town and I spent

$2. for stockings and other things which I needed." Explained: "I hav n't meant that I got $2. from the man the way you have taken it up."]

My dearest friend: I received your letter with happiness. I read letter about five times and I going to read it again. I laugh so much. You wrote, I were only fooling them. Ha, dear I think you know me already, how I know to fix things up. I want to make them jealous, Ha, ha. I go to laugh so much, so much. If you want to marry one of the officers, you know what they are, they are ever the other [army] men. They can't marry only a poor girl. If they want to marry they got to have a girl with lots of money 20,000 Kronen, and they got to put the money down for guarantee. If happens something to your sweetheart officer, then you get the money back. Do you understand me, Sunday School? But dear we hav n't got the mens yet, we have to wait for them. If we going to get mens like that, cause we not rich. What your boys says? Did you give them the letter to read. Ha. ha we fooled them. All right, my sweetheart, we going to go always together. You have a right just scold him enough, Italian T. Such a Italians! He did n't have to say that he meet us on the street. Listen friend, if my uncle ask you if that T. is my sweetheart, then tell him the truth. Otherwise he would n't help me out. He could be very mad. Tell that these are merely some acquaintance. Don't forget. Friend come to me, I am not allowed to go to see you. You come over and we going to have good time together. Here its lots of nice young men. Listen dear, my lady ask me if I 'm going to school and where I 'm going when I go out and I told her that I go to visit girls which I knows from school, but I 'm going to moving pictures and I have three nice young mens, that 's always so, ha? They said, say kid, how much do you want, one dollar? Then when he feels like to have something — and want to go some place, then I tell him $1.00 that is too cheap. I have no time, maybe next time, so I fool the boys there.

To us usually come one man with eggs. He brings me

eggs Wednesday, in the afternoon and Saturday. Always when he comes we kiss each other, but he isn't rich; that's nothing for us but when you can get a kiss from a man, its nice, isn't it? Ha, ha. I have always a good time with him. I wish you can be here with me, then you see what fun we can have . . . Sunday School.

Dear Friend: Just now I was at the P. O. and I get letter from you, so I am very happy again. Dear Friend, would you think that T. has a factory? You think if he is such a rich man he would not write like that. His handwriting is like when a cat scratches. T. he don't write to me, so I don't write to him either. So I wrote him today and I told him he would go to see you. Dear, we was in newspapers. My lawyer, he put us in and [it said] there we was innocent, that we forgot to pay it. Ha, ha, so we are innocent, don't you think so. That was nice newspaper. I got to laugh so much at that. I were laughing so much that I got stomach ache from it. So T. when he comes to see you, tell him enough and tell him about cheap watch what you have and pocket-book they say we took. . . . And don't forget to bring me my sweethearts picture and then I am going to put in — and I am going to show that picture to my lady to make her jealous. Don't forget to get receipt from the ring what I put in the pawn shop. Friend, I want you to pay for the ring. I like you should pay if you can do it for me. I going to send it to you but your sister should not know anything about it. Don't tell her nor my uncle either. You know what I should get from him. T. is nice, isn't he? I wrote to the lawyer and he answered me such a nice letter and he isn't married yet; he is only young yet. Maybe I going to make love to him. Ha, ha, friend, I got new sweetheart again. Ha, that egg man I don't like him no more. I don't kiss him any more because he is only egg man. I want something better, don't you think, friend? . . . I go home to see uncle and to see the lawyer. I must see him how he looks.

January 1915. My dearest friend: Your letter and present I received. I was so happy that we are so good friends always. My dear, how do you like that present what I sent you. You want to know something new. Today I am twenty years old, my birthday. When you going to have your birthday, dear, — I have big trouble about your dress; I did n't know what to do I should help you out with it. You know that time I put different name, now I could n't remember what kind name I put and after while I remember I put a name Reich. So they answer I should send first $4.40 so tomorrow I go to city. So dear I helping you out much as I can. . . . I send you receipt from that dress you should believe how much I paid. So darling right away tomorrow I take $4. from my lady's pocket bag and when you send me $4 I going to put them back. . . .

Dear Friend : . . . I going to have a trial this month or start of next month, so don't say anything about the hat, only about the stockings and about the belt. You must go through to see that you know how to speak in the court. Let your sister speak. I don't want to work for servant always. That going to cost $125. I have two lawyers; one ask $78, so if you come out would you pay half of it or don't you want to be with me on the trial? So let me know darling, I got to work too, but so much I take time to write to you. I am always so happy when I get letter from you. I got to go, for my letters to get them; to us don't come no letter-carrier; I got to go on the post-office. I usually go on the evening and no one think of me and you forgotten me too because you got fellow and you don't want me to know something about it. I have one too in Philadelphia. My lady told me she would not have taken me out from the Institution but she saw I was innocent; so she took, me. Here is nice blond man. . . .

Dear Friend : Just today I opened letter which made me very happy. I always can hardly wait till I can fool them. Dear Friend tell me what I can do. I just received letter from my lawyer that I have to go to N. Y. and he send me bill for $100. When I receive that I din't know where I am ;

I thought I faint when I saw the bill.   Listen dear tell me where I can get the money.   On 30th I have to have it.   They going to start the trial.   My lawyer he told it going to be bad, that we got to say the truth, but don't say anything about the pocket-book and the little things. . . .   But only the money, what I do about it.   My uncle said he hadn't any and no one to borrow from.   I can't fool any Jew, Ha, ha. I'm all broke down.   I am afraid when the day come when I come between those young mens [lawyers] how I going to stand there, I wouldn't have no money to pay, so I think the day come to take my life.   Now answer me what you going to do.   I going to wait for your letter.   Address, Franz Joseph, C. K. o. f. Wein, Kaiser Palace.

Dear Friend: . . . I know something new, if you want to do that.   I think you should dress yourself nice and put a veil on your face, nobody should know you, and go to the store where we took the things — that was on 2nd February 1914.   That was on Thursday and this time is on a Thursday again and 2nd of February.   If I were in your place I would buy one hat for spring and ask for a receipt and then I would buy two pair stockings and belt — and I pay you for it and the stockings and the hat would be yours.   And you should keep the receipt and when its our trial you could show the receipt of your lawyer and your sister and me too and those receipts it is going to say second of February, second month, Thursday.   That's the way we going to burn our people.   You need hat and I need 59 cents pair stockings.   Soon as you send me the receipts, my lady she have a machine, so I going to change it from 1915 to 1914, and then we going to win.   We wouldn't have to be ashamed about it.   You know she didn't see me when I took the belt, so we can say well we have receipts for the stockings and maybe they did not see us to take one belt and hat; and this I going to tell to the lawyer that I thought I paid already and I put that in my pocket-book and he's going to think that's how it is.   Friend, do that and you going to see how we come out.   I was awfully afraid when I received letter from lawyer and he say it would be very hard with us but I think [the foregoing story] be very good. With that we come out very nice. I can make another excuse. I can tell that we bought that [altogether] and when we get the receipts I was so nervous from those detectives when they catch us that I couldn't remember right away what we does with these receipts and I could put the receipts in my cuff of coat . . . . And I going to put the tickets in my cuff in the toilet — you know how we put our handkerchiefs in — and I going to forget the coat and maybe they going to examine the coat and find the tickets. We can play then innocent. So think over darling. I would do that if I only can have a chance to go to N. Y., like you. You get card from me but its only for fun.

P. S. Was it 4 o'clock in afternoon or 2 o'clock when we were in the store — Thursday, 2nd Feb., and we locked up at 5 o'clock.

Dear Friend: . . . I received letters from my sister and they were so happy; they want me to come home soon as I get that letter. But you know how can I go. I haven't got the money and I am not free and I don't want to ask them about money and now its the war; they need the money themselves. My sweetheart is not killed yet, so I going to take him when I get home. He always asks about me if I'm angry at him. I rather take him than American; they only want to have girl got to have money. The poor girl they don't want her and those which are not rich they are nothing worth. Don't you think so friend, I am right? Don't be angry friend. Love and kisses.

February, 1915: Dear Friend: Scuse me that I didn't write so long to you. I was so nervous and mad that I didn't know what to do — when I can't help you with the money. Friend I have something new to tell you, so now look out. Tonight lady sent me to P. O. for letters and one letter was there from Miss R., so you know what I does? I breathed on the letter so long till I opened it her letter. I get so frightened I didn't know where I am or what I am doing. Miss R. writes that if I am not . . . satisfied on parole it would be better to take me back to the institution. . . . Please send me the money $4. I took them from my lady so I should pay your dress. Otherwise I couldn't pay them right away and you wouldn't have your dress, and I had only $1. and when I think on you so you know what heart I have, and I took the money out and now I'm ready. When you send them I put them back where they was. You know what Miss R. have another girl for my lady but she don't know how to cook and she is 28. She come from the institution. She was ther 14 months. She be more satisfied than me. See friend, Miss R. I would give her a kick if I can — don't you think angel. So my angel maybe we wouldn't see one another any more. Back again to the institution.

. . . Dear we going to have another girl upstairs with us. If you could come to us that would be nice and we would enjoy it much better. Last night I was to school and when I returned home on the train I saw very nice young fellows. They make lots of fun with me — such nice gentlemen. They went from some kind of parade and when I went down from the train they took their hats off and next Wednesday I am going to see them again. Dear Friend. . . . I need the money I have only a nickel and that got to be enough for one week. — so you can imagine how I got to save and I need new hat — so I would like to buy me a hat for my money. You look very nice in that hat, Ha, ha. Friend, if we could only help us to run away to the West. I ask my lady at the school — she comes from California. She tell me if I have carfare, I should go there. Dear, if we can be only free then we know how to use the world. I'm not so any more like what I was in the institution — I'm now such a devil that you wouldn't believe it. That man promised to lend me money but if he wouldn't lend it I don't know what I am going to do. I have not got even for the doctor and you know what it is with me? Friend, I would like to have picture from my sweetheart, but send me [back] the money, I going to send you money some other time for him because I only wanted to make my lady jealous. She thinks we are only so-so. Sunday School. Friend, you write to T. ? I don't, I don't care. Wait, I going to fix myself up and I going to wait for him and then I going to wipe my nose and then I going away from him. Friend, I am so happy now that we are going to go West. We are going to take other girls with us. We go like soldiers — hurrah, hurrah, like soldiers to the war. Friend, if you answer me right away I going to answer too. When you don't answer on four letters so I don't think you care for me. Goodnight, Sunday School. Let the bed-bugs bite you? Friend you have fellow in the bed. You go with him to sleep? In the night when bite me some I kill him so blood runs. Write right away.

. . . I am crying so much — I have such a hard work. Everything hurts me; I am all broke down. If I can only come free I wouldn't mind to have not even a shirt. I would give everything if we can be free. Friend, if you only know how I feel bad but don't say anything to your lady. You know what Miss R. wrote, that I always ask you to come over. You must told something to your lady or you wrote something to Miss R. Now I don't care any more if no one comes to see me. Forgive me if I write such a letter. I don't know what to say — I want to go to bed, its 10 o'clock. I want you to get the letter right away Monday. Answer me right away what you think if you want to be with me. If you like your sister better, so stick to her and I go my way and worry about myself and save my money for trip to go home and I never will return. I stay with my sweetheart. When you go there friend, if you give me every month a dollar for your dress, like a friend. Answer right away.

[March, 1915] . . . My lady told me everything be much better next winter. I going to have a nice warm room. This winter I had awfully cold room. I went to bed with my cloths. She didn't give me no blankets, so I sleep in my clothes and I used to take hot iron with me to warm up the bed, so bad I have here. Friend, I got to go to school every Wednesday but next Wednesday I would n't go, I go to the dance. I have white dress under the black skirt and long coat and she going to think that I go to school. I leave my skirt and my books in my friends house and I go to the dance, ha, ha, ha. Come with me ha, ha, I have there lots of nice young boys and the man who brings me the eggs and lots of other nice young man, so I going to have nice time. Dear, I went Sunday out and I went to the girl, her sister have a boarding house there where nice 3 young mans, and all ask me to go with them to the dance, so I going to have big fun. I be very glad if you can come with me, but don't tell on me that I'm going to the dance. My lady she don't know anything about it. She think I am innocent girl, No 1. I am, don't you think friend? When I think I have three years, I start to cry, I don't know what to do. But when I think of nice mens, I start to jump in the kitchen and singing. [Writes the song she sings.] Only if you see me you would burst from laughing. . . . I ask my garbage man if he can lend me money, he said he help me with much as he can. . . .

So friend have a good time and maybe on Tuesday I be back to the institution. This year I get new trial, so don't worry and don't cry. You know we have one God and he see everything. He must punish Miss R. sometime. She is old enough but she could n't get married. Nobody wants her who is rich and poor man she don't want. . . . I like to have the money by Tuesday. I should be sure that nothing is missing from her. So take care of yourself. I going to eat beans for supper, ha, ha, but I going to be all right. Now I be so bad that everyone is afraid of me. I don't care if they put me in the disciplinary in the cellar — I going to have there friends — you know what kind — red ones, bed bugs, and roaches and mouses. Ha, ha, I'm going to have good time, I won't cry. You friend, when you send the money don't say nothing to your lady and send them so

that my lady would'n't know nothing about it, my lady. I
suppose Miss R. wrote that I receive dress from pawn shop.
See, don't tell on me — when I be in the institution. Tell
that your J. that he put them [dress] there, that it should n't
get lost. Otherwise they would laugh at us that we did not
have any money and we had to put our dress in pawn shop —
that be a shame.

Miss R. wrote that they would n't let me go to you — and
if I ask again she would give me a good scolding, so write to
the old fortune-teller. So good-bye friend, have a good time.
Don't forget to answer me right away. Don't say to no
one what happen — write right away. You know in the
institution maybe they would n't give me your letter. Good
night and good-bye forever. I think if I come to the institution I take my life there.

[June, 1915. From Esther to parole officer, Miss R.]
. . . I am letting you know I am back in the same place
— institution. I'm letting you know why and I wrote you
letter about my head and I like to get rid of that. Doctor
told me that he [saw] no other help, that I got to have an
operate on my nose. If not then I get a inflamation thro
my nose. So I wrote that to my friend, that one what we
was together locked up, but I didn't tell her that I got this
sickness, but I wrote to her in English that I got disease,
but I did n't know that she gave the letter to her lady and
they sent them to the institution. So they read that I
getting disease that I stole $4 and one young man gave me
$2, so they make me very dirty, but I'm not afraid of them
— you know that, when they start with such a story, so I
know that I'm in heaven. They only want have me back.
I should stay here the three years, so they come and get me
on Sunday, afternoon. So how I was, I went. They didn't
give me only chance to put on my dress, shoes and hat and
put me in a auto and so that was we took the train to the
institution and there they start to ask me questions, why
they took me back and when I come down here. I got to
let them examine myself and when she examine me, she said

everything is all right.   You know what a disease is — so explain to her about my head and my nose.   So she said if girl say she have a disease, they take it that its girl bad from a man, but I did n't know that a girl get sickness from a man.   The lady doctor told me about how. the girl get sick. . . . But where is the right?   And on account of the $4, that this way : That girl is a Croation and I'm a Czech, and we used to write, and sometimes we did n't understand the letters from each other.   And so about the $2.   Once in N. Y. I went down from car, I lost heel from shoe, I dropped the hand bag, and so real man come out and pick up my bag [and gave me $2.00].

[Letter to Superintendent of institution from parole officer; June 4, 1915, after Esther had been returned to the institution] :

. . . It is very difficult to tell from the letters [of Esther] whether or not she has actually broken her parole.   The worst she has done, according to her own statement, is (1) to borrow $4 from employer's purse to pay for a dress with fullest intention of returning it (and employer is sure she would have missed it had it not been returned); (2) opened a letter addressed to employer from writer; (3) went to picture shows sometimes when she was supposed to be in class; (4) flirted with men on train; (5) wrote T. T. whom she knew before coming to the Institution; (6) kissed the egg man; (7) probably had sexual relations with a man in Philadelphia for $2 (Esther denies this).

Her letters refer also to plans to go to a dance secretly and to go to New York secretly.   There is nothing in the letters to indicate that she ever put her plan about coming to New York into effect.   Esther denies emphatically that she has been to New York and her employer thinks it very unlikely that she could go without her knowledge.   They show also she thought she was diseased and had been to a doctor about it before she came to the institution.   She still worries about it whether or not there is any cause.   (First blood test was S— G —.)

Subject's attitude expressed in these letters is far more serious to my mind than anything she has done, but it is a question whether it is anything for which she should be blamed or punished. She is unquestionably abnormally sensitive, suspicious and secretive and these traits have been unfortunately emphasized by her arrest and commitment here. She evidently suffers bitterly and constantly because she is on parole to the institution and that resentment poisons everything she does and thinks. She must have been under a frightful strain during these months while she was working with the lawyer to win her freedom, with the constant pressure he put on her for money and to come to New York to see him. Then too the conflict of what may be merely normal and natural sex interests and her fear of breaking her parole by expressing these in any way has probably been bad for her and has emphasized these sex interests. I think all of the references in the letters to "nice young mens" who smiled at her and tipped their hats to her on the train, to the nice young mens she sees at picture shows, to the men who invited her to a dance, may be explained as a boastful desire to appear bad and to be having attention and a good time, arising from a regretful realization of how much she is missing in these lines. Possibly she was just beginning to have a taste of "gay life" before she came to us and the institution may have done much to whet her curiosity. She seems to ridicule the idea of being considered "innocent and good"—"Sunday School girls"—and asks co-defendant to send her the picture of her (Esther's) Bohemian sweetheart (she has always claimed to be engaged to a man now fighting in the Austrian army) so she can show her employer she has a sweetheart, "make her employer jealous" as she puts it.

Certainly if she had not been determined to keep her parole, with such a demand on her for money from the lawyer and such an interest in men, she would have solicited long before this. I think it is to her credit that she has worked so steadily and satisfactorily and has tried to keep, as she understood it, the letter at least of her parole.

I feel, however, that if the interest we have taken in her in giving her an early parole under such good conditions and her employer's never failing efforts to understand and help her have not won her confidence, we can scarcely hope to break down her attitude of misunderstanding and suspicion of us, which breeds deceit in her so readily. After what has happened she will probably be more antagonistic than before; the strain on her of keeping parole might easily become too great at any time. It would seem to be a very great risk both for us and for Esther to have her out on parole again, particularly in another state.

I hope you will be able to make her see, even if you decide she has not actually broken her parole, that she has not even understood its spirit when she tried to buy her freedom through a lawyer and deceived us and her employers as to her real intentions.

I think much of subject's suspiciousness and deceitfulness is racial and there is small chance of her adjusting to American customs. I remember that you considered deporting her in the first place and while I still think it would be very bad for subject to have the stigma of deportation added to that of arrest, I do feel that her own country is the best place for her and that she will be far more apt to live a straight, normal life there with the restraints of her family and their standards to help her than she will here. Do you think it may be possible to send her back on her own money when conditions of war permit?

From certain standpoints this girl seems to be almost ideal human material. The institution called her "intelligent, conscientious, and, far beyond our girls, sensitive to fine distinctions of right and wrong." All her wishes are strong and social. She craves pleasure, association with "nice young mens", dancing, pretty clothes, but is an industrious worker. Her letters to Lilian are overflowing with the desire for response — both to give it and to receive it. In a letter after her return to the institution, not printed here, she refers to the child of her former employer: "Oh, I was glad to hear about Max. How often I think about the times he used to pull my hair, and that was a great joke. Yes, I often think and talk about him. Give him my love and see if any of my flowers are up. If so, put one on him for me." And she is always thinking of improving her position in the world. "We are," she says, "going to look for some nice man, but something better, not only working men." She is ashamed of her relation to the egg man, "because he is only egg man." She does not want it known that she pawned a dress. In her reference to Austrian army officers and a sweetheart in Bohemia, she wishes to claim before her mistress that she has some social standing. During the whole of her parole she is working on the problem of her life. She is working alone, and she leaves no stone unturned. She is in a village, not allowed to visit New York. She plans her campaign for a new trial by letter, working through a stupid friend who unintentionally betrays her. Her lawyer is exploiting her, her doctor also; her Italian friend is not loyal, her uncle promises help but is poor. She even appeals to the garbage man. Like many who have sought to reconstruct a broken life, she plans to go west.

And she is very able. She has a mind adapted to the law, and she could write scenarios. Note how she plans in one letter to have something "up her sleeve" for the trial — to have her friend buy duplicates of the articles stolen on the anniversary of the theft, to change the date of the receipt from "1914" to "1915" on her employer's typewriter, to put the receipt in the

cuff of her wrap and leave it in the toilet room of the
court to be found.   This would be indeed a dramatic
vindication.   She is thoroughly cunning and she lies
a great deal.   But she is in a fight with organized society.   She feels that there is a disproportion between
her offense and her punishment, and that she is being
wronged and defrauded of life.   Cunning is one of the
forms which intelligence takes in a fight.   And in
general people become cunning when they are oppressed or do not participate on an equal footing
in their society.   Esther is a Jew, and the "racial"
cunning of the Jew has the same origin as the particular cunning in this case — exclusion from recognition and participation.   Any successful scheme of
education, reëducation or reformation must recognize
the wishes expressed by Esther and will involve an
active participation of the subject in the plan.   Esther
was not bad enough to be committed to the institution to which she was assigned, but once there we
note her complete psychic isolation from the officials
and from the family in which she was placed.   She was
directed toward no interesting and creative work, and
was not included in any form of society in which she
completely participated and in which she could have
recognition and the gratification of the other wishes.
And this is characteristic both of the penitentiary and
of the older type of reformatory for adults and for
children.

But some years ago the juvenile courts were established.   It had become apparent that numbers of
disorderly children, mainly from broken homes, were
being brought into the criminal courts for escapades
and sexual offenses, placed in jails with hardened criminals and thereby having the possibility of the for-

mation of a normal scheme of life destroyed once and forever. Certain women were the first to protest and to act, and the result was the formation of a court for children which dispensed with lawyers and legal technicalities, and treated the child as far as possible as an unruly member of a family, not as a criminal. The first of these courts was established in Chicago, and in 1908 provision was made for the study of the child by endowing a psychological and medical clinic, — a practice which has been followed by other juvenile courts. During the past decade some of these courts have reached a high degree of elaboration and perfection. Their service has been very great in checking the beginnings of demoralization. The court is wiser than the parents of the children and incidentally does much to influence home life. These courts have also focused attention on the general questions and methods of reform and have begun to influence both penal institutions and general education. There are many successful formulations of influence developed by women of insight and personality connected with the juvenile courts in numerous localities. An important review of these conditions has recently been made by Miriam van Waters.[1] But perhaps the highest perfection of procedure has been reached in the juvenile court of Los Angeles where Dr. van Waters is herself the referee.

87. In the treatment of juvenile delinquency that comes before the court and involves change in status there should be an integration of the forces that seek to establish new social relationships. . . . Some mechanism of passing the threshold from ward of the state to the threshold of normal

[1] "Where Girls Go Right", *Survey Graphic*, June, 1922.

citizenship should be devised with sufficient strength to endure over the period of crisis.

An attempt to meet the problem of socialization has recently been begun in behalf of the juvenile court of Los Angeles County. For the girl whose normal relation to the family group has been severed by reason of the permanently broken home, parents dead, imprisoned, incuraby ill, or defective and the like — a girl whose behavior-difficulties make it impossible for her to be absorbed in the neighborhood group — there is usually no provision but the reformatory institution. A place of adjustment, a link between the court, the detention home and the community is an important phase of diagnosis and treatment. El Retiro, a school for girls of Los Angeles County, is an experiment toward such solution.

The method of adjustment is as follows: Preliminary tests and examinations are made in the detention home and a more or less homogeneous group of girls in their teens are selected for El Retiro. An intensive program of work, study, play and expression has been provided. Student government, that is to say, student participation in the conduct of affairs of group life, not a formal organization based on the least satisfactory elements of our government, the municipality and the police court, but rather a flexible, club-like organization of team work and community responsibility is maintained. After another period of observation at El Retiro a conference is held concerning the girl. At this conference all available sources of information are brought together.

The referee of the court, the probation officer, physician, psychologist, superintendent of El Retiro, the principal of the El Retiro school, the recreation director (who later directs the program of the girl and directs the accomplishment of her project), and one of the girls chosen from the student-body to represent the student-body knowledge and opinion — all these persons with specialized information meet to form a many-angled diagnosis. Traits of personality and the reaction to group life are stressed especially. In this field of research no opinion is more competent than that of the girl who represents the student-body point of view — a mine of information hardly touched as yet by social research. The objective of the conference is the formation of a project or activity-goal for the new student, a task suited to her strength and personality and for which she will be responsible and receive the reward of recognition. On the completion of this project, usually from eight to ten months, the girl is ready to leave El Retiro; that is to say, she has succeeded in some phase of group life and important clues for the adjustment of her personality in the larger community outside have been formed.

Since these results have been attained largely as the result of social relationships formed within the group at El Retiro, and by the use of the project method and student government, the girl is likely to have developed both self-confidence and group loyalty. The next essential was to form some social relationship for the complete passage of the girl into the community.

A Girls' Club was organized and a club house secured in the city for about eighteen girls and their field secretary. The girls pay their board and work in stores, industries, etc. The housework is done by one girl, who is paid by the others to act as home-maker. It is called the Los Angeles Business Girls' Club and is sponsored by the Los Angeles Business Women's Club not as a charity, but as an act of coöperation on the part of the business women with the younger and handicapped working girls of the city. Not all the residents are wards of the court, the chief requirement being that girls be under twenty-one years of age and receiving the minimum wage. The club serves as meeting place for organization of young people, business girls, college girls, etc. Thus any element of isolation, or unlikeness, is at an end for the girl who may be a ward of the court and she is brought into relationship with the normal forces of the community.

The following four cases, selected because they serve to illustrate the integrating processes at work in a socialized court procedure, may be presented.

Evelyn is one. She is an orphan of Canadian extraction. Placed by a children's aid society in some six temporary homes, she readily drifted into delinquency. For two years for her it was a succession of institutions, tempered by probation, after she came under the court. Then El Retiro was established. Her health was so delicate that she was sent there for observation for anæmia. There her central ability was discovered — leadership, and her chief interest the design and manufacture of clothing. On graduation she became president of the alumnæ group of girls and went to live at the club house. She began earning $22.00 per week as designer and shortly plans to open a shop of her own. As president of the alumnæ organization she has succeeded in doing what no probation officer has done — the voluntary reporting of each girl's change of work, address, and new friends. If they are out of work through indifference or indolence, her fluent scorn and her own stylish costume act on them as a spur. Her activity has two major outlets, leadership and craftsmanship.

Margaret is another: She was the oldest in a large family headed by a dissolute factory operative and a quarrelsome, complaining mother. Her home life was marked by coarseness and obscenity of language, and her personality by alternate melancholy and violence. At El Retiro it became apparently probable that her behavior was the reaction made by her organism in seeking that which it really craved most, peace and security. She became an El Retiro homemaker. A troublesome asthma yielded to treatment based on quiet and contentment. She is now an officer of the alumnæ club and she has returned to her own home, which has largely become rehabilitated through her efforts. The club life apparently affords her all she needs of contact with the outside world.

Geraldine is a girl of eighteen, wrecked on the moving

picture industry. She was seduced by an under-director in attempting to sell a scenario, and was passed from hand to hand until her health broke. Her experiences were unbelievably tragic and unbelievably common. Her health, self-confidence, and charm were restored at El Retiro. She took to nursing but the key to her interest in everything was affection. A professional man understood her real and genuine capacity and married her. She is an exceptional wife and mother. She too is a club member, proud of her school and eager to assist.

Maggie was a rollicking, buxom girl of seventeen. Her parents were dead and her living relatives of doubtful reputation. Indeed all the female members of her family had "gone to the bad." Maggie's own escapades were many. At El Retiro she was rough, noisy, daring, fearless, impetuous, in short filled with the spirit of adventure. She did not graduate but was returned to the custody of the probation officer. While on probation she became pregnant. She refused to tell who was responsible but concocted a story of nameless attack. The court commented on her strength, her bravery, her resourcefulness, and gave her two weeks in which to find the man and bring him herself, unaided to court. Surprised but not daunted the girl succeeded. The man proved to be a soldier with a temperament much like her own; on careful examination, physical, mental, and social he was proved to be a fit husband and was permitted to marry Maggie. This social rehabilitation has restored her to club life, much to her delight. For several months she has been happy and successful.[1]

In the meantime another important step has been taken,— the attempt to forestall delinquency by working on the maladjusted, neurotic, predelinquent child, or to adjust the delinquent child without resort to the

[1] Miriam van Waters: "Juvenile Court Procedure as a Factor in Diagnosis", "Papers and Proceedings of the American Sociological Society", Vol. 16.

court and the consequent court record.   In the larger
cities departments of child study, children's welfare
committees, bureaus of children's guidance, institutes
for vocational guidance have been formed in the public
schools or working in connection with the schools.   In
this work the object has been to work by cases, bringing the girl under the influence of the social worker,
improving the home conditions and the attitudes of
the parents, placing the girl in a better environment,
moving her from one situation to another until one
is found to which she responds, and developing in her
some activity interests.   The ideal is to coördinate the
girl immediately with the large society in which she
lives instead of building up a complete institutional
community about her as in the case of El Retiro.

The possibilities of this type of approach to the problem are illustrated by the following cases reported by
Doctor Jessie Taft of Philadelphia.

88. Ruth, fourteen, Irish, pink-cheeked and blue-eyed,
in her first year of High School, the picture of attractive,
innocent girlhood, had been taken to the house of detention
for stealing a diamond pin and taking money from a teacher's
desk.   When her denials were finally broken down by proof,
she confessed to a long history of petty thieving, hitherto
unpunished and for the most part undiscovered. . . .

Ruth was an intensely egotistic person, desirous of social
recognition, approval, personal success; but due to lack of
training, unfavorable conditions and an impulsive, impa-
tient make-up had never learned to work for her satisfactions or make her impression on society in constructive ways.
She was quickly discouraged and resentful in the face of
failure or hardship and at once turned to some pleasure experience as a compensation — something which could be
obtained immediately and easily.   She used boastful stories
and even her own misdeeds to heighten the impression of her

importance and superiority. This is a natural reaction in childhood, where immediate gratification is obtained through crying, tantrums, day dreams, purely subjective methods; but they are not appropriate to a developing organism and must be abandoned for an objective dealing with the facts of life. All of Ruth's normal cravings had been thwarted by her environment. She had lost her love object in the death of her mother. Her family ideals had been shattered. Her father had been exposed as unfaithful to her mother, and a weakling in the battle between the stepmother and Ruth. He was a failure as a provider and did not pay his debts. Ruth was forced to live in a home situation which had for her none of the elements of a home, nothing to be proud of, no loving approval and overlooking of faults, no faith, no support and assurance of safety. She was forced not only to give up her love object but to see it supplanted by an enemy, who also usurped her place and influence with the father. Undoubtedly her sex ideals also met with shock. She became convinced that her father was interested in another woman before the death of the mother. Father and stepmother quarreled and made up — separated and came together repeatedly. She saw marriage as a series of endless petty conflicts. Both of them were church-goers, given to religious interests. Ruth's disillusionment with life was complete. There was nothing genuine, no real satisfaction. The father and mother who constitute the bridges over which the emotional life of the child may cross to a more and more social development had blocked normal growth and thrown the child back upon subjective or anti-social satisfactions. One of the defense reactions to such a thwarting of fundamental needs is that taken by Ruth — a cynical, suspicious, critical attitude toward everything and everybody. To want and never get satisfaction is too painful a state to keep up, so the individual criticizes every possible love object that he may make himself and others believe he would n't have it if he could. The reason he has no love object is that none are worth having; thus he defends his inferiority. Also he undermines any criticism from others by showing up the inferiority of the source. He is protected by having already discredited the other person. Moreover, there is a sense of power and superiority in being able to criticize everything, so it offers a natural compensation for the inferiority from which the critical or cynical person suffers. Not having admirable loving parents one must remember is a source of tremendous inferiority. A child of eight has no intelligent weapons with which to combat a hostile family situation. It has no chance against the egoism of the adults around it. All it can do is to react blindly in ways that offer some temporary solace. Stealing from the stepmother is a way of satisfying the needs to fight with or injure or destroy the pain-giving stimulus. It gives the child a tremendous sense of power and victory. Here is something which he can do secretly and effectively. It really hurts the hateful object and it supplies pleasure-giving stimuli, such as candy, which are otherwise denied. . . .

Ruth . . . was so absorbed in the injuries done her by life that she thought of nothing but pleasure compensations. She would face nothing that demanded effort or any unpleasantness. She had a right to take things because life owed her reparation. She saw nothing in school or work, or the ordinary habits of daily hygiene but hardship to be avoided. She wanted nice clothes and felt she had a right to take them, but she saw no reason why she should take any care of them. If a garment was torn or dirty, get a new one. She thought she ought to be placed where there were servants so she would have no housework and no laundry to attend to. She had no loyalty to any one. She played one person against another and used everything to her own advantage as she saw it. As soon as an effort was made to give her insight she reacted to protect herself from the painful revelations by criticizing the worker and taking the attitude that there was a game going on between her and the worker in which each was trying to get ahead of the other. She could not believe in disinterested effort on her behalf.

Ruth was turned over to a child-placing agency with the foregoing interpretation of her behavior and suggestions for working on the problem, but with great doubt as to the outcome. She was to be given as much gratification of her pleasure wants as possible in order to reduce the struggle to satisfy them and leave some of her energy and interest free to be developed along other lines. She was to be placed with a really superior person whom she might finally come to respect as genuine and her best chance would be to find some one person, the worker or the foster mother, who had real faith in her possibilities.

The social worker who took her over was young and enthusiastic, undaunted by the impossible and full of faith in her own ability to get results. She transferred this faith to Ruth. She never wavered in her belief that Ruth could change her ways. She lived through stealing episodes, truancy periods, every kind of discouragement and finally found a home which did some of the things we had hoped for. Ruth's first experience in this home was a summer trip and a glorious good time. When she came back there was little housework and a doctor's important business to help with after school. There was social prestige in this home. The mother was a good disciplinarian and insisted on the formation of certain daily habits of living, but she took Ruth in as a member of the family and had, like the worker, supreme faith in her own ability to make Ruth go to school every day, study her lessons and keep going in the path of righteousness.

Ruth responded surprisingly and for six months all went well. Then she began to be unhappy and ask to be removed, saying that she would make removal necessary if something were not done. Finally she had her way. It seemed evident that this home, while successful in many ways, lacked the thoroughly admirable personality which we thought Ruth needed. The woman was hard, set and self-centered. Another home was found in which there proved to be serious marital conflicts in which Ruth was forced to be a party.

Here the stealing broke out again. Then a high school teacher became interested in the girl and invited her to her summer home for vacation. This was the great turning point in Ruth's life. Here her desires for social superiority and pleasure were satisfied, and she was surrounded by real people for whom she felt at last the whole-souled genuine devotion and admiration which was essential for her socialization.

From that moment there has been no trouble with Ruth. No more stealing, no more truancy, no shirking of lessons. She has gone to live with another teacher for whom she keeps house. Six months have passed and there has been no complaint. To complete this treatment and make it permanent, Ruth ought to be given insight into her own behavior and understand just what has happened to her. Then she would be armed against the accident of circumstance.[1]

89. . . . Mary was an alert, boyish, attractive girl of eighteen . . . at work in a department store after having reached first year in High School and reported to have been living with her weak, immoral mother, sharing the mother's young paramour, a boy only a little older than herself. . . .

The following case history was obtained: Because of the mother's promiscuity, Mary's paternity was uncertain. As a child in her mother's home she had known only loose living, good-natured, easy-going neglect and poverty. Illegitimate births were common in the family. There seems to have been complete lack of ordinary sex morality and social standards. The family lived a roving, hand-to-mouth existence. When Mary was ten, the Court removed her and gave her to a child-placing agency. She was tried out unsuccessfully in several homes and finally made a good adjustment in a country home where she had excellent school opportunities, finishing grammar school at the head of her class. She entered High School with a continuing interest in school, ac-

---

[1] Jessie Taft: "Some Problems in Delinquency — Where Do They Belong?" "Papers and Proceedings of the American Sociological Society", Vol. 16.

companied by an increasing interest in boys. Her late hours, love for good times and her rebellion against restraint worried the foster parents so that they gave her up. She was accepted by a city institution where she was under strict supervision and was sent for the first time to a city school. She tried to enter the second year of High School with inadequate preparation, failing quite completely in every subject. Accident entered at this point in the shape of a new matron at the institution. The girls were trying her out and in her effort to control the situation she threatened to expel the next girl guilty of insubordination. Mary happened to be the victim. She was returned to the Court and discharged to a married and apparently respectable sister. The sister, unequal to disciplining Mary, allowed her to go to her mother, then living in a wretched little house in another town with a young man by whom she was pregnant. There was only one bedroom containing a bed and a cot. Mary shared the cot with the younger brother, a boy of fifteen. For about a year this situation continued. Mary broke away once only to return again. The mother finally went out to work with the new baby, leaving Mary to keep house for her brother and the man. Finally Mary came to the city a second time and got a job. She wandered from one position to another and came in contact with a social agency just as she was about to give up and go home again because she saw no work ahead and was unable to support herself on what she was earning.

The social worker took the matter up as a vocational guidance problem and . . . . with the psychologist worked out the following picture of Mary :

In earliest childhood she had known little or no restraint and had been familiar with the freest sex life and complete absence of ordinary social standards as regards sex. But there had been affection, easy-going, good-natured attitudes and a great deal of personal freedom. The loose living, the roving, unsettled existence had made it fairly easy for Mary to accept and adjust to varying conditions so that foster-home placement to her was not the agonizing experience that it is to some children. Moreover, she seems to have been from the first an objective, eager, alert, social youngster who most fortunately compensated for her family inferiorities by a complete going over into school life and active energetic expression in work and play. . . .

The dismissal from her foster-home seems to have been caused by behavior which was natural enough on the part of a developing adolescent girl. She merely carried over too much of her superabundant energy into parties and good times with boys. . . . The dark side of her life here was her introduction to sex experience through the foster father. These experiences, shocking at first, were finally accepted as a matter of course and sank into the background of an existence in which objective interests — school, companions, good times, farm work, held first place. There seems never to have been any deep conflict nor any marked feeling of shame or inferiority. It was taken as part of the day's work, something which went along with living in this foster-home which for the most part was desirable. She wanted to keep on with her school. She was afraid to tell the wife. She had none of the ordinary sex morality which most of us have absorbed from infancy on. The easiest way was to keep still and adjust. When Mary was asked how she felt about sex, she replied characteristically and cheerfully: "Well, the world is made that way, you just have to accept it. It is n't any use to worry about it, you might as well take people as they are."

Although these years in Mary's life apparently left no scar, they did break down completely any sex inhibitions she might have had, aroused sex needs and accustomed her to the habit of sex expression. It meant that when she went to live with her mother, she experienced no particular shock and was illy prepared to offer resistance to the advances of her mother's paramour who found her so much more attractive than her mother and with whom she was thoroughly infatuated. . . .

The really critical experience was the transfer to the city institution and the city High School. In neither situation was she at home and for the first time in her life she experienced failure and disgrace in her studies. She now had a genuine inferiority, a discouragement which undoubtedly reacted on her behavior at home. She grew indifferent and reckless, would not respond to scolding or appeal. The objective work and play expressions, as well as the customary sex life, were cut off. There was nothing left but breaking rules to get a good time. Expulsion from the institution meant the final break with school and she thinks it was then that her ambition died. She had no technical training, she could get only underpaid, uninteresting jobs. Where was she to find an outlet for her young energy? The sister, less intelligent than Mary, had no influence and was only a source of irritation. Then in her restless seeking for something more satisfactory, she went to her mother who was living in another city. There she was disturbed chiefly by the mother's jealousy and feeling she was doing her wrong; also the presence of the younger brother. Finally the glamour wore off and she began to see the man in his true character. He was lazy, unreliable, disloyal, weak. He had none of the straightforward, eager, active attitude which Mary had toward life. Gradually she turned against the kind of person he was and after many struggles, finally broke away.

It was at this point, when her courage was giving way once more, that she was found by the case worker.

It seemed to the psychological examiner that the problem here was not the so obviously indicated sex situation, but the blocking of Mary's work and play interests and the complete quenching of her egoistic ambitions. The psychometric tests showed her to be well up to average in intelligence. She was as interested in taking the test as the examiner was in giving it. Her intellectual curiosity was a delight. In the course of the interview she brought out a slip of paper with two long words on it which she had been treasuring, waiting for an opportunity to look them up in a dictionary. She thought the examiner was a good substitute. Throughout she exhibited a frank, straightforward attitude, an honest, unsentimental facing of facts, a complete freedom from cynicism or critical reactions. She put no blame on other people, used no evasive mechanisms. She had a certain pride and independence. When consoling herself for her lack of good clothes she remarked: "My clothes are n't much but no man is paying for them, and at least I have a contented mind." There seemed to be every basis for a satisfactory adjustment to life if the environmental opportunities could be provided so that her work and social interests would have a chance to develop and help to organize a more socialized sex expression.

The social worker was reassured and determined by this analysis of the problem. Mary herself was allowed to go over every detail of the intelligence tests and was told that ability like hers had a right to a better training. She faced what lack of education would mean in underpaid, uninteresting work. Her faith in her own power and ability was restored and her ambition revived. Her former failure in High School was explained and she became convinced that it was not too late even now to achieve success in school work.

Meantime the case worker built up the social background, finally raised scholarship money and Mary went into the second year of the commercial course in a good High School.

There was never any attempt to deal with the sex side by repressive methods, never any interference with her social life, nor any form of restraint. When she wanted to go to visit her mother, the whole situation was talked out with her and she was given the worker's attitude frankly and honestly but decision was left to her. She did not go. She has continued to associate with boys on an unusually free basis. She will go to see a boy friend at his home exactly as she would visit a girl. She could not be made to see why she should not accept a boy's invitation to go to New York City for a sightseeing excursion. She was willing to stay home to please the worker but she was told she must decide on another basis. Only accident in the shape of the boy's illness prevented the escapade. Everything she does is talked over with the worker with the utmost freedom. Her standards are changing rapidly with her developing tastes and interests. She has made good in her school work consistently. She has been rash and unconventional in the extreme but has never, apparently, overstepped the boundaries of morality on the sex side. For a year and a half she has made steady progress and there is no indication that she will ever again become a delinquent.[1]

The most disheartening condition which we have to face in connection with the delinquent child is the demoralized home. It appears in one study (document No. 58, p. 100) that nine tenths of the girls and three fourths of the boys who reach the juvenile court come from bad homes. Case No. 83 (p. 152) is an extended description of such a home and the following summary of some cases may be taken as representative.

90. A family of 13 children; father a drunkard who deserted them; mother scrubs and cleans; "a very poor, dirty, and crowded home."

Family "very degraded"; father, a drunkard, criminally abused two little daughters (who later became delinquent wards of the court) and then deserted the family to avoid prosecution. Mother married again, but stepfather also drank and was so abusive that wife and children left him.

Father, a man of bad habits, deserted; mother drank; she said girl had inherited unfortunate tendencies from father.

A family of fourteen children, six of whom died; father was immoral and cruel to his wife, and very unkind to his

[1] Jessie Taft: "Some Problems in Delinquency — Where Do They Belong?" "Papers and Proceedings of the American Sociological Society", Vol. 16.

children; he deserted, leaving family to charity; the girl left home because of ill treatment and became immoral.

Father, professional gambler, utterly irresponsible, deserted his family; one boy was always "wild" and one girl went to a house of prostitution.

Father and mother, both shiftless, begging people who will not work; father periodically deserts family, who were all in Home for the Friendless at one time and who are often destitute and a public charge. Father is now in old soldiers' home and three of the children are in a soldiers' orphans' home.

A family of six children, one girl delinquent; home dirty and untidy with two beds in parlor; mother has a bad reputation, drinks habitually and always has the house full of men. Father deserted at one time, and family has been helped by a charitable society constantly for two years.

A family of seven children; father, an habitual drunkard, supposed to be a fruit peddler but really a common tramp; deserts periodically but always comes back; very brutal to wife and children when he is at home, and responsible for demoralization of two older girls; family a county charge and on records of three relief societies.

A very degraded home; father drunken and immoral, abused girl's mother shamefully before her death; criminally abused girl when she was only seven and then abandoned her. Girl brought to court at the age of twelve on charge that she was "growing up in crime.". . .

Lillie, a German girl, seven years of age, whose father, now dead, is said to have been as near a brute as a human being could be, whose mother is insane, and whose sister is abnormal, was brought in as incorrigible and immoral.

Vera, a seventeen-year-old girl, whose father's address is unknown, and whose mother is insane, found employment as a barmaid in a concert hall, and afterwards became a prostitute.

Rosie, a sixteen-year-old Russian Jewess, whose mother is in the hospital for the insane, and whose father abandoned her, was brought into court on the charge of immorality.

Annie, a fifteen-year-old girl, whose father was frozen to death and whose mother is of unsound mind, has two brothers who are imbeciles. She is herself feebleminded, and has been the mother of three illegitimate children — probably the children of her imbecile brothers.[1]

The gradual realization of this condition through the experience of the juvenile courts and the schools and also the desire to avoid any court procedure in connection with a child whose morals are endangered has led many teachers and social workers to the view that the child should be taken in charge by society as soon as it shows any tendency to disorganization and that the school should have this function and should gradually displace or incorporate the juvenile court, or such functions of the juvenile court as remained would be transferred to the court of domestic relations. Eliot took this position as early as 1914,[2] and the conviction has been expressed frequently in various forms. The following is an extract from one of the most systematic proposals.

. . . Each city, probably each county would require an extension or reorganization of its personnel to include a department of adjustment to which teachers, policemen and others could refer all children who seemed to present problems of health, of mental development, of behavior or of social adjustment. For good work this would require the services of doctors, nurses, psychiatrists, field investigators, recreational specialists. . . .

The ideal would be to have the school act as a reserve parent, an unusually intelligent, responsible and resourceful parent, using whatever the community had to offer, making up whatever the community lacked. . . .

[1] Sophonisba P. Breckenridge and Edith Abbott: "The Delinquent Child and the Home", p. 102.

[2] Thomas D. Eliot: "The Juvenile Court and the Community."

All neglected, dependent and delinquent children, whether of school age or not, would fall within the province of [the department of adjustment]. For these children we would have the authority of the school extend from infancy to adult life. . . . We should [thus] get entirely away from the conception of penalizing children for their offenses and from the stigma of courts and reform schools. . . . We should establish our thinking firmly on an educational basis. The fatal gradation of reform school, work-house, county jail and state prison would be broken. . . . Wherever possible we would have dependent children sent to public schools. Homes for "friendless" or "destitute" children belong with scarlet letters, stocks and debtors' prisons. . . .

With the clearing away of old names and associations should come better opportunity to meet the needs of girls before they reach an advanced stage of incorrigibility.

[Arrangements should be made for] pooling the juvenile court's probation officers, the truancy department's numerous officers, the school nurses, the medical instructors, the special schools and reformatories, and all the rest of the specialists on the physical, mental and social troubles of school children into one department of adjustment. . . . Only the most determined blindness could prevent [the school board member] from seeing how the school truant officer and the probation officer overlap. . . . He could surely see the waste of having the schools, on the one hand, build up a staff of doctors and nurses and the juvenile court on the other trying to duplicate this machinery — both sets to serve the same group of children.[1]

These writers argue also that the juvenile court does not afford so good an opportunity as the school for the study of the child and for record-making, that the stigma placed on the child by an appearance in court deprives him of the chance of future favorable recogni-

[1] Henrietta Additon and Neva R. Deardorff: "That Child", *The Survey*, May 3, 1919.

tion, that the court cannot prevent delinquency, that the child is frequently incorrigible before he reaches the court, that the courts have a very limited range as propaganda and general educational agencies, since they have no power over the child's life before he comes actually before the bar of justice, that the power of the probation officer is relatively slight and casual, and that vocational placement should be connected with the school.

Further than this, the depraved family conditions which I have emphasized are due not only to bad economic conditions but to the failure of community influence. You may have very good family life with bad economic conditions but you cannot have good family life without community influence. [I have shown in Chapter II how strong was the influence of the community on the family. It is not too much to say that the community made the family good. Human nature often appears at its worst in connection with pair marriages and small families. The records of the societies for the prevention of cruelty to children are filled with sickening details of the brutality of parents. An organic connection with a larger community is necessary to the maintenance of moral standards and fine sentiments. If we look, therefore, as we are forced to look, for a social agency whose influence may penetrate the family we find it in the school. The school is not a natural organization like the family, but an artificial organization capable of rapid changes and adjustments. In this respect it has almost the freedom of a scientific laboratory. It receives all children early and keeps them a relatively long time. Its function is the setting and solving of problems and the communication of information. Its representatives are far superior to the average parent in intelligence and understanding. If we invented any device to replace social influence lacking at other points it would be the school. It is probable that the school could be a sort of community forming the background of the family and the child and could supply the elements lacking in the home, at least to the degree of preventing in a large measure delinquency and crime, if it exercised all the influence it could conceivably exercise, and that it could, more than any other agency, socialize the family. From this standpoint the appearance of the visiting teacher in the school has the greatest importance.

The first visiting teachers began work in the year 1906–1907 in New York, Boston and Hartford, Connecticut. In these cities, and later in other places, as has frequently happened in other educational experiments, the impulse came from outside the school system. Private organizations — in Boston, settlements and civic organizations; in New York, settlements and the Public Education Association; in Hartford, the director of the Psychological Laboratory — saw the need of providing a specially equipped worker to help the schools, and developed and privately maintained the work until the school board became convinced of its value and incorporated it as part of the school system. In other cities, like Rochester and Mt. Vernon, New York, and Cleveland, Ohio, the work was introduced directly by the board of education. At present in all but four cities the work is part of the city public school system. The movement has grown until at present the work has been extended to twenty-nine cities in fifteen states. In some of these "school visitor" or a similar term is used instead of visiting teacher. . . .

"Through individuals to the group" is the approach of the visiting teacher, and as the result of her knowledge, derived from case work, new types of classes have been organized, school clubs, or other means to make the school fit the newly discovered need. Study rooms have been opened, school recreation centers organized; parents' clubs, courses in domestic training, special trade courses, school lunches and other extensions have been started as a result of the visiting teacher's view of the neighborhood. In this way her work becomes of value to the school as a whole. She acts as a scout bringing back a more definite knowledge of the lacks in the neighborhood, educational, social and moral, and of newer demands on the school that have arisen because of changing social and industrial conditions. This relation accords with the ideas of modern educators who believe that the connection between the school and the community life cannot be too closely integrated.

On the other hand, the visiting teacher's acquaintance with the families and the neighborhood brings about social results. Through her work, various communities have been stimulated to provide scholarship funds, nurseries, community houses, homes for neglected children and other social activities. Hidden danger spots are not infrequently brought to her attention by parents who have not known what to do about the situation or have been afraid to report to the proper agency or official. In this way the work assumes an additional preventive aspect, and results in such improvements as better policing and lighting of parks, better provision for playgrounds, closing of improper movies, etc., checking of traffic in drugs to minors and the removal of similar insidious conditions.

The visiting teacher's position as a member of the school staff makes for certain advantages. She gets in touch with cases at an earlier stage than would an outsider. Teachers and parents consult her about suspicious cases which they would not feel justified in referring to a social agency. As representative of the school, the visiting teacher is free from the suggestion of philanthropy, and of all visitors she has, perhaps, the most natural approach to the home, going as she does in the interests of the child. It is a very rare thing for a visiting teacher to experience an unpleasant reception. Further, she is in a position to follow the child in school from year to year. Where the home carries a serious handicap, she may anticipate the difficulties of the younger children, help them avoid the false starts made by the older brother or sister, and also assist the school to reinforce the children against the inroads of the family handicap. . . .

The following case shows how, out of a bad family situation, real educational capital was made for a headstrong, irresponsible girl of fourteen who hated school and thought she wished to go to work to help her family. Knowing the reaction of the home situation on the girl's school life, the visiting teacher worked out a special plan with the family agency to which she had referred the family. She advised that the money required for the family budget be paid in the form of a weekly scholarship to the girl. The conditions stipulated were that she attend school regularly and keep a budget. She was transferred to a special class and given a special course providing an unusual amount of household training — the one school subject which seemed to her to serve any useful purpose. The personal interest of the domestic science teacher was enlisted in the girl's home situation, and she not only advised about the budget but encouraged the girl to make the most of her scanty home furnishings. A tutor was provided to help with the academic subjects. Through this weekly-payment plan the girl was made a partner in the family situation, and her sense of responsibility developed. Her budget book served as the most effective arithmetic text book she had ever used. Incidentally, she learned much about food values and purchasing.[1]

But while in the present condition of society there is no point at which the prevention of delinquency and the socialization of the family can be undertaken

[1] Jane F. Culbert: "The Visiting Teacher", *Annals of the American Academy of Political and Social Science: Child Welfare*, November, 1921, pp. 85, 87, 88.

so successfully as in the school, the school itself has very grave defects of character, and the question of its adaptation to the welfare of the child involves at the same time the question of change and reform in the school itself. [Many educators will agree that if we attempt to measure the influence of the school with reference to its efficiency as a factor in personality development we are confronted at once with the following conditions:

1. The average school, like the old community, works on the assumption of uniformity of personality and presents the same materials and plans in the same order to all. [The assumption is that children react in the same way to the same influences regardless of their personal traits or their social past, and that it is therefore possible to provoke identical behavior by identical means.] "Nature," says Doctor Jennings, "has expended all her energy in making our little flock of children as diverse as she possibly can; in concealing within it unlimited possibilities which no one can define or predict. It sometimes seems as if we parents in our process of educating them were attempting to root out all of these diversities, to reduce our flock to a uniform mass. . . . The only way in which appreciable progress can be made in the attempt is by cutting off, stunting, preventing the development of the special and distinctive qualities of the individuals. Unfortunately this can be done to a certain extent, but only by a process which may be rightly compared with the taking of human life." [1]

2. The creative or plan-forming interest of the child is an expression of the phase of new experience which

[1] Herbert S. Jennings: "The Biology of Children in Relation to Education", in "Suggestions of Modern Science Concerning Education", p. 15.

is based on curiosity and appears very early in the
child. The child expresses his energy and secures his
recognition, favorable or unfavorable, mainly along
this line. Response and security do not mean so
much to him as yet. The fact that the school work
is detached from activity and not related to the plan-
forming and creative faculty explains its failure to
interest the child. An investigator took five hundred
children out of twenty factories in Chicago and asked
them this question: "If your father had a good job
and you did not have to work, which would you rather
do, go to school or work in a factory?" Of the five
hundred children, between the ages of fourteen and
sixteen, 412 said they would rather work in a factory.[1]

In 1920 the White-Williams counselors in the Junior Employment Service of the Board of Public Education interviewed 908 of the 10,674 children who came that year to
the Board of Public Education for general working certif-
icates. Forty-seven per cent of these did not want to go
on with their school work. They gave as reasons: "I was
'left down'"; "I didn't like arithmetic"; "I was too tall
for the other girls in the room", etc. Many of these difficulties might have been adjusted if some one could have
made plans with the children while they were still in school.[2]

3. There is therefore a question whether as a device for plan-forming by presenting the right material
and definitions at the right moment, the school is not
inferior to the world at large, at least when its influences are protracted. The school presents indispen-

---

[1] Helen M. Todd: "Why Children Work", *McClure's Magazine*,
April, 1913.

[2] Anna Beach Pratt: "The Relation of the Teacher and the Social
Worker", *Annals of the American Academy of Political and Social Science:
Child Welfare*, November, 1921, p. 90.

sable information, a technic for handling problems, such as reading, writing, and ciphering, and presents the solution of the innumerable problems which are already solved and which it is unnecessary to solve again. But the school works injuriously on personality development and creative tendencies. By presenting the whole body of cultural values in a planless way, planless so far as schemes of personal development are concerned, it tends to thwart and delay the expression of the plan-making tendency of children until physiological maturity approaches and the energetic, plan-forming, creative period is passed. The lives of creative men show that they began their work early and did it by hook or by crook sometimes by evading the schools, often by being the worst pupils. The chemist Ostwald in his interesting book "Grosse Männer" has pointed out that the precocity of such men as Leibnitz and Sir William Thomson would have done them no good if the schools had been "better" in their time.

In measuring the influence of the school we must recognize two types of success in the adaptation of the individual to life, the one based on his assertion and realization of wide and original claims, the other on contentment with limited claims. If he is contented with claims which are more limited than his powers justify, his adaptation is success through relative failure. To the degree that the school treats children as identical it produces a maximum number of relative failures. To some extent the genius is regarded as a prodigy because so much spontaneity is repressed by the school.

4. Clinicists and case workers who handle successfully difficult children taken from the schools report

that the schools tend to accentuate rather than obviate the difficult features. Some of them feel that where unsocial and neurotic tendencies have begun to appear through bad family conditions the school is an additional influence for evil to be overcome.

The school reaches practically every child and does its part in deepening or lessening the neurotic tendencies. At present we are safe in assuming that for the most part it deepens these tendencies. It drives the neurotic child into truancy, vagrancy, anarchy, invalidism and every form of delinquency or hardens its emotional reactions into permanent moods, and it does all of this without in the least being aware of it. . . .

If our public schools really educated, if they understood that education involves a training of the instinctive and emotional life as well as of the intellect, if they saw that they cannot even develop intellect as long as they ignore desire, we should have an agency for adjusting the neurotic girl and boy second only to the home in its power. There is proof for this statement. Enlightenment is coming into education in spots. There are visiting teachers who work on the problem children in a school and get wonderful results. There are experimental schools whose methods are based on an understanding of the new psychology as it applies to educational theory. These schools are able to deal with the able but neurotic child who cannot get along in the public school. Those of us who work with difficult children are defeated constantly, not so much by the impossibility of the cases, as by the impossibility of finding any public school that understands or has time to act on its understanding. I am constantly trying to straighten out the children the public school can't handle. Our school is not primarily educational but is a place to observe and get acquainted with difficult, dependent, or destitute children whom the various children's agencies of Philadelphia are trying to place satisfactorily in homes. They are children who do not get along anywhere. Nobody wants them because they are so hard to manage. The thing that constantly surprises us is how easy it is to manage their behavior. They are not set like adults and a little understanding, a little insight, and patience, a mere approach to real educational methods gives immediate results that are almost like magic.[1]

It is desirable that the school should eventually supersede the juvenile court and replace other welfare agencies concerned with the child, but in adapting itself to this task and to the task of general education it will be compelled to make provision for the development of the emotional and social life of the child as well as the informational, and in doing this it will inevitably approach the model of El Retiro as described by Doctor van Waters.

[1] Jessie Taft: "The Neurotic Girl", *Modern Medicine*, Vol. 2, p. 162.

CHAPTER VI

THE MEASUREMENT OF SOCIAL INFLUENCE

In the last chapter we have seen the development of definite methods and very positive successes, but everybody who deals with human beings professionally — the educator, the criminologist, the statesman — feels that he has no certain method for the control of behavior, that there are obscure and incalculable elements, that the same procedure does not secure the same results when applied to different individuals, that the successes are often as unintelligible as the failures, and that such successes as there are depend on common sense, personality, and trial and error rather than on any known system of laws.

For example, among the social sciences criminology has a larger amount of concrete material bearing on behavior, more printed and unprinted cases than any of the others. Certainly there is the strongest possible motive for understanding the criminal and reforming him, and preventing crime in general. But a recent appeal to the public by the President of the American Institute of Criminal Law and Criminology for funds to study the effects of criminal procedure indicates how far criminology is from being a science :

. . . . The institute asks that special inquiry be made of the wisdom and success of probation, parole, indeterminate sentence and the entire handling of criminals after conviction; that present acute differences of opinion among equally public-spirited citizens be clarified and sound conclusions reached as to the treatment of convicted criminals, neither in the interests of sentimentality nor of vindictive vengeance, but for the better protection of the public and the promotion of law and order. The public may be shocked to know that no one now has facts to answer the above inquiries.[1]

[The whole criminal procedure is based on punishment and yet we do not even know that punishment deters from crime. Or rather, we know that it sometimes deters and sometimes stimulates to further crime, but we do not know the conditions under which it acts in the one way or the other.]

Similarly the most successful workers with delinquent children report that sometimes their charges reform themselves spontaneously and, so to speak, in spite of the efforts of the institution.

In analyzing the process of our successes among the so-called delinquent girl two types are of special interest — those who "make good" without any special kind of treatment, who get well by themselves, that is to say, those who would have succeeded in any case; and second, those who have succeeded by some accident, some course of the girl's own that ran counter to our wishes, our routine and our expectation; in short, those who "make good" in spite of us.

The second type, those who unexpectedly make good by their own plan, which is not of our making, is of profound sociological significance. "We possess only that which we set free", said an old Chinese philosopher. How many of us know girls whom we have not set free, but who have taken the bit in their teeth and run away from us, later to emerge decently clothed, resourceful, industrious, successful and adjusted to life beyond our fondest hopes. Recently I visited some thirty state institutions for the training of de-

[1] James Bronson Reynolds: Communication to the *New York World*, March 6, 1922.

linquent girls. Most of the superintendents reported stories of rebellion, escape, followed by the inexplicable "making good." Many commented on fortunate marriages contracted because the girl strayed in forbidden paths, dance-halls, piers, rinks, cafés and other loafing places of Prince Charming. We are more familiar with this type of fortuitous success in boys than in girls, boys who flee from us to navy, army or wild west. Many a candid probation officer will tell you that she has met with it in girls.[1]

Detective Burns, speaking of the counterfeiter Wilken, says below (document No. 92, p. 236): "I have often wondered whether his talents would have been smothered by convention if he had been kept in the straight and narrow path. The most common-place man becomes sometimes the most startlingly original crook. The reformed crook, on the other hand, turns to honesty and becomes duller than ditch-water."

In the paper quoted above as document No. 88, p. 200, Jessie Taft says:

The intimate psychological or psychiatric interpretation, the individual intensive treatment, are fundamental for solving the problems of delinquency. No matter how ideal the social conditions, no matter how farsighted the laws, there will always be compensatory behavior in the lives of individuals, and some of this behavior is bound to be unwholesome and socially undesirable. Instinctive protective reactions on the part of society, even the more enlightened mass treatment in institution, will bring results only by accident.

What we need is a treatment of behavior so scientific that results instead of being accidental will be subject to intention and prediction. Biology studies the life-history

[1] Miriam van Waters: "The True Value of Correctional Education." Paper read at the 51st American Prison Congress, November 1, 1921.

of individual forms and explains any particular details of
their behavior in the light of the life of the organism as a
whole from birth to death. Where does a similar case study
of human beings belong? Without it there can be no scientific solution of the problems of delinquency.

Our best efforts to reform the delinquent, or even
to control the behavior of the young child in such a
way as to secure a balanced, efficient, creative, and
happy schematization of life are very imperfect. The
juvenile court and the experimental schools do not
completely realize the hopes they inspired. The most
careful methods may result in failure and the most
imperfect methods and even neglect of method may
result in, or at least not prevent success. We sometimes see a poor, obscure, and underfed boy assuming
a definite life-direction, planning to be something,
and pursuing his aim with the certitude of the homing
instinct, while a boy with the choicest opportunities
of life — money, schools, tutors, and travel — remains
a nonentity or becomes demoralized.

Now the example of the physical and biological
sciences shows that the human mind has the power
to work out schemes which secure an adequate control over the material world and over animal and plant
life by a series of observations and experiments which
have been sufficiently thorough and detailed to discover series of facts and their causal connections which
lead to the establishment of general chemical, physical,
mechanical, and biological *laws*, and the same objective methods will lead to similar results in the field
of social theory and practice.

There is, indeed, no sharp line between the common-
sense method of the average man in determining facts
and causal relations and the method of the scientist.

When we have found that a certain effect is produced by a certain cause the formulation of this causal dependence has in itself the character of a law; we assume that whenever the cause repeats itself the effect will necessarily follow.   The agriculture of the peasant and of the old-fashioned farmer was scientific to the degree that they had observed a causal relation between manure, lime, moisture, seasonal changes, varieties of soils, animal and plant pests, and the success or failure of their crops.   But science is superior to common sense in its methods of experimentation, measurement, and comparison, in its isolation and intensive study of problems from mere scientific curiosity, without regard to the practical application of its results.   Science is called cold because it is objective, seeking the facts without regard to whether they confirm or destroy existing moral and practical systems.

But science is always eventually constructive.   A large number of specialists working in many fields, upon detached and often apparently trivial problems — primroses, potato bugs, mosquitoes, light, sound, electricity, heredity, radium, germs, atoms, etc. — establish a body of facts and relationships the social meaning of which they do not themselves suspect at the time, but which eventually find an application in practical life, — in agriculture, medicine, mechanical invention.

Science accumulates facts and principles which could never be determined by the common sense of the individual or community, and of so great a variety and generality that some of them are constantly passing over into practical life.   The old farmer has learned the value of soil analysis, though with reluctance and suspicion, and he has learned to spray his orchards to preserve them from pests whose existence he did not suspect. At this moment science is advising him to put a bounty on the head of the turkey buzzard instead of imposing a fine for killing it. His common sense had told him that the vulture was valuable as a scavenger. Now science tells him that it is an ally of the paralysis fly and carries cattle, hog, and other diseases over the country. "Probably more than the income from a million dollars is spent each year in the several marine biological institutions for the study of three lowly forms, — the sea urchin and its progeny, the coral, and the jelly-fish." An American entomologist has spent many years in measuring the influence of physical environment on potato bugs. He established colonies of these insects in Mexico, moved them from one temperature to another, one degree of humidity to another, one altitude to another, and recorded the changes shown in the offspring. He then moved the new generations back to the old environment and recorded the results, — whether the spots and other acquired characters changed or remained. His object was to determine certain laws of heredity, — whether and under what conditions new species are produced, whether acquired characters are hereditary. To common sense this procedure seems trivial, almost insane. But assuming that a biologist determines a law of heredity, this will presumably have a practical effect in the fields of agriculture, eugenics, crime, and medicine.

These examples show that a science which results in a practical and efficient technic is constituted by treating it as an end in itself, not merely as a means to something else, and giving it time and opportunity to develop along all the lines of investigation possible, even if we do not know what will be the eventual applications of one or another of its results. We can then take every one of its results and try where and in what way they can be practically applied. We do not know what the future science will be before it is constituted, and what may be the applications of its discoveries before they are applied.

But, on the other hand, the scientist will naturally be influenced in setting and solving his problems by the appreciation that if discoveries are made in certain fields practical applications will follow. He may know, for example, that if we can discover the scarlet fever germ we can control this disease, and he may work on this problem, or he may suspect that if we knew more of the chemistry of sugar we could control cancer, and may work on that problem.

There is no question that a more rational and adequate control in the field of human behavior is very desirable. And there are no powers of the human mind necessary to the formation of a science in this field which have not already been employed in the development of a science and a corresponding practice in the material world. The chief obstacle to the growth of a science of behavior has been our confidence that we had an adequate system for the control of behavior in the customary and common sense regulation of the wishes of the individual by family, community, and church influences as outlined in Chapter II, if only we applied the system successfully. And the old forms of control based on the assumption of an essential stability of the whole social framework were real so long as this stability was real.

But this stability is no longer a fact. Precisely the marvelous development of the physical and biological sciences, as expressed in communication in space and in the industrial system has made the world a different place. The disharmony of the social world is in fact due to the disproportionate rate of advance in the mechanical world. The evolution of the material world, based on science, has been so rapid as to disorganize the social world, based on common sense. If there had been no development of mechanical inventions community life would have remained stable. But even so, the life of the past was nothing we wish to perpetuate.]

Another cause of the backwardness of the science of society is our emotional attachment to the old community standards or "norms." I described in Chapter II how much emotion enters into the formation of everyday habits. It is well known that men have always objected to change of any kind. There was strong condemnation, for example, of the iron plow, invented late in the eighteenth century, on the ground that it was an insult to God and therefore poisoned the ground and caused weeds to grow. The man who first built a water-driven sawmill in England was mobbed; the man who first used an umbrella in Philadelphia was arrested. There was opposition to the telegraph, the telephone, the illumination of city streets by gas, the introduction of stoves and organs in churches, and until recent years it would be difficult to find a single innovation that has not encountered opposition and ridicule.

This emotional prepossession for habitual ways of doing things enters into and controls social investigations, particularly social reforms. The Vice Commission of Chicago, for example, which undertook an investigation of prostitution, was composed of thirty

THE UNADJUSTED GIRL

230

representative men, including ministers, physicians, social workers, criminologists, business men and university professors. In the introduction to its report it was at pains to state that it was anxious to make no discoveries and no recommendations which did not conform to standards accepted by society. "[The Commission] has kept constantly in mind that to offer a contribution of any value such an offering must be, first, moral; second, reasonable and practical; third, possible under the constitutional powers of our courts; fourth, that which will square with the public conscience of the American people." This commission made, in fact, a very valuable report. It even included items of scientific value concerning prostitution which led the federal authorities to exclude the report from the mails (the decision was later reversed) but it had determined beforehand the limitations and character of its investigation and results, and excluded the possibility of a new determination of behavior norms in this field.

[A method of investigation which seeks to justify and enforce any given norm of behavior ignores the fact that a social evolution is going on in which not only activities are changing but the norms which regulate the activities are also changing. Traditions and customs, definitions of the situation, morality, and religion are undergoing an evolution, and a society going on the assumption that a certain norm is valid and that whatever does not comply with it is abnormal finds itself helpless when it realizes that this norm has lost social significance and some other norm has appeared in its place.] Thus fifty years ago we recognized, roughly speaking, two types of women, the one completely good and the other completely bad, — what we

now call the old-fashioned girl and the girl who had
sinned and been outlawed. At present we have several
intermediate types, — the occasional prostitute, the
charity girl, the demi-virgin, the equivocal flapper,
and in addition girls with new but social behavior
norms who have adapted themselves to all kinds of
work. And some of this work is surprisingly efficient.
Girls of twenty and thereabouts are successfully competing in literature with the veteran writers. But
no one of these girls, neither the orderly nor the disorderly, is conforming with the behavior norms of her
grandmother. All of them represent the same movement, which is a desire to realize their wishes under
the changing social conditions. The movement contains disorganization and reorganization, but it is the
same movement in both cases. It is the release of important social energies which could not find expression
under the norms of the past. Any general movement
away from social standards implies that these standards are no longer adequate.

A successful method of study will be wide and objective enough to include both the individual and the
norms as an evolving process, and such a study must
be made from case to case, comparatively and without
prejudice or indignation. Every new movement in
society implies some disorder, some random, exploratory movements preliminary to a different type of
organization answering to new conditions. Individualism is a stage of transition between two types of
social organization. No part of the life of the individual should be studied as dissociated from the whole
of his life, the abnormal as separated from the normal,
and abnormal groups should be studied in comparison
with the remaining groups which we call normal.

There is no break in continuity between the normal and the abnormal in actual life that would permit the selection of any exact bodies of corresponding materials, and the nature of the normal and the abnormal can be understood only with the help of comparison. When we have sufficiently determined causal relations we shall probably find that there is no individual energy, no unrest, no type of wish, which cannot be sublimated and made socially useful.   From this standpoint the problem is not the right of society to protect itself from the disorderly and anti-social person, but the right of the disorderly and anti-social person to be made orderly and socially valuable.

But while we have prepossessions which have stood in the way of an objective study of behavior there is no doubt that the main difficulty at present is the lack of a concrete method of approach.   This method will have to be developed in detail in the course of many particular investigations, as has been the case in the physical sciences, but the approach to the problem of behavior lies in the study of the wishes of the individual and of the conditions under which society, in view of its power to give recognition, response, security, and new experience, can limit and develop these wishes in socially desirable ways.

Correlated with the wishes of the individual are the values of society.   These are objects directly desired or means by which desired objects are reached, — immediate values or instrumental values.   Thus a coin, a foodstuff, a' machine, a poem, a school, a scientific principle, a trade secret, a dress, a stick of rouge, a medal for bravery, the good will of others, are values which the individual wishes or uses in realizing his wishes.   Money is the most generalized value;   it is convertible into many values which may be used in turn in pursuing the wishes. A value is thus any object, real or imaginary, which has a meaning and which may be the object of an activity. The sum total of the values of a society is its culture. Any value may provoke in the individual a variety of tendencies to action which we may call mental attitudes. Thus money as a value may provoke one or another of the attitudes: work for it, save it, borrow it, beg it, steal it, counterfeit it, get it by gambling or blackmail. The attitude is thus the counterpart of the social value; activity, in whatever form, is the bond between them.

The problem of society is to produce the right attitudes in its members, so that the activity will take a socially desirable form. In Chapter II we saw that society is more or less successful to the degree that it makes its definitions of situations valid. If the members of a certain group react in an identical way to certain values, it is because they have been socially trained to react thus, because the traditional rules of behavior predominant in the given group impose upon every member certain ways of defining and solving the practical situations which he meets in his life.

It is, of course, precisely in this connection that the struggle between the individual and his society arises. Society is indispensable to the individual because it possesses at a given moment an accumulation of values, of plans and materials which the child could never accumulate alone. For example, a boy can now construct a wireless plant or build an engine, but he could never in his life accumulate the materials, devise the principles alone. These are the results of the experience of the entire past of a cultural society. But the individual is also indispensable to society because by his activity and ingenuity he creates all the material values, the whole fund of civilization. The conflict arises from the fact that the individual introduces other definitions of the situation and assumes other attitudes toward values than the conventionalized ones and consequently tends to change plans of action and introduce disorder, to derange the existing norms. A new plan may be merely destructive of values and organization, as when a counterfeiter imitates a bank note or a girl destroys her value and that of her family by prostituting herself, or it may be temporarily disorganizing but eventually organizing, as when an inventor displaces the hand-loom by the power-loom or the biologist introduces a theory of evolution which contradicts the theory of special creation. Society desires stability and the individual desires new experience and introduces change. But eventually all new values, all the new cultural elements of a society are the result of the changes introduced by the individual.

If now we examine the plans of action carried out by children and men with reference to social values, whether they are good or mischievous, we find that the general intellectual pattern of the plan, the quality of ingenuity, is pretty much the same in any case. When, for example, children have escapades, run away, lie, steal, plot, etc., they are following some plan, pursuing some end, solving some problem as a result of their own definition of the situation. The naughtiness consists in doing something which is not allowed, or in ways which are not allowed. The intellectual pattern is the same whether they are solving a problem in arithmetic, catching a fish, building a dog house, or planning some deviltry. And the psychological pattern followed is the same as that involved in the desire for new experience which I illustrated in Pasteur's pursuit of a problem, document No. 6, p. 10. From the standpoint of *interest* the nature of the problem and the means of its pursuit and solution make no difference. The latter are moral questions.

The celebrated *Himmelsbriefe* (correspondence with heaven) may be taken as an example of an immoral scheme which is intellectually beyond reproach. These letters are a pathetic and comic expression of the ingenuity, artistic imagination, business enterprise and desire for recognition of a young peasant girl. It will be seen that this "correspondence" has a remarkable resemblance to the pages of Anatole France; it lacks only the irony and the elaboration.

91. Cölestine Wurm, aged 13, was sick, bedridden, afflicted with boils and oppressed by the feeling that she was a burden to her parents. A neighboring family named Korn had lost a daughter named Ursula. Cölestine represented that she had had a letter from the dead daughter, who was then in purgatory and needed money to get out. A sum was provided, 1,000 marks, and committed to Cölestine for transmission. A letter was then received from Ursula describing paradise, the joy of the saints, and how Mary, mother of Jesus, was overjoyed with an oven Ursula had bought for her. In later letters it appeared that Ursula was desirous of improving her status among the saints and she requested money to buy a fine bed, some golden buckets, kitchen utensils, etc., which were for sale dirt cheap. Mary herself wrote a letter of appreciation to the parents of Ursula informing them that they had been in danger of losing two valuable cows through the machinations of the devil, but that out of gratitude to Ursula and themselves, she had sent twenty angels to guard them. Jesus also sent a letter, sign-

ing himself, "Your Son of God, Jesus Christus." First and last Cölestine collected 8,000 marks on her enterprise.[1]

In more mature minds the socially unregulated scheme may be admirably elaborated and executed, corresponding in ingenuity with the most complete business or scientific plan and yet remain dangerously immoral because its application is in a form not sanctioned by society. In the following astonishing case we have an anti-social pursuit of a problem executed with all the ardor and resources of a Pasteur. I call the case astonishing because working under such handicaps, clandestinely, stealing the values of society, this boy yet knew how to use these values, the materials accumulated by society — the paper mill, the library, the printing office — so much better than we have been able to use them in an organized system of education. Pasteur's scheme, and his later schemes of the same pattern, were socially organizing because they contributed to the development of medicine, agriculture, grape culture, etc., while Wilken's scheme was socially disorganizing and personally demoralizing.

92. Henry Russell Wilken is the only man who has ever successfully counterfeited the fabrics on which we print our paper money. He did that so well that the people who make it for the Government accepted it as genuine. Now that I'm out of the Government service I can grin at what happened at that paper mill. He was a clever boy and a nice one. You'd like him.

There have been counterfeiters and counterfeiters. Some were almost brilliant. Others were plain dubs — clumsy lowbrows, who were clowns at work that required delicate artistry. But here you have a boy who had never seen an engraver at work, who knew no more about the engraving

[1] Based on E. Wulffen: "Psychologie des Verbrechens", Vol. 1, p. 173.

and printing industry than he did about paper making and chemistry. I assure you his knowledge of these industries, prior, of course, to launching upon his great enterprise, amounted to nothing at all. In fact, he told me, and I verified it, that he had never been in an engraving or printing plant in his life before he decided to compete with the United States Mint. . . .

One morning in February, 1910, he came across a small item in a Boston newspaper wherein it was stated that a milkman out in Dorchester had found a packet of one dollar bills. The milkman took them to a bank. The bank informed the milkman that the bills were counterfeit, and very obvious counterfeits at that.

And there, on that morning in February, 1910, the criminal career of Henry Wilken was launched. As he told us afterward, he gave the matter much thought. Here he was earning $25 or $30 a week. There was a girl he liked and who liked him. There were certain relations who looked upon him as something of a castoff, a misfit, a ne'er-do-well, a drifter. And there were clubs that rich young men belonged to — rich young men who were not particularly top-heavy with brains, but who had money, and lots of it. There was but one thing for him to do — make money. . . .

The boy was ambitious for success, for wealth, for position, for luxury. At that particular moment Boston was being pestered by a youth who lacked everything but several million dollars, and the city knew him as "The Millionaire Kid." Wilken had scraped acquaintance with the Kid and the sight of the latter's spending orgies merely added fuel to the fierce desire for wealth.

I have told you that Wilken knew nothing about chemistry, paper-making, engraving, printing, dyeing, and photography — all of them necessary arts of the counterfeiter. I assure you he knew absolutely nothing about any one of those things. But he did the thing that must commend itself to all successful men.

He stuck to his advertising job by day and spent his

nights in the public libraries.   He read every available technical volume treating on engraving.   Then he went out and bought the tools of the engraver.   Next he practiced until he became an engraver quite as clever as any man in the Government service.   That's likely to stagger you.   There are folks who will not believe that.   But here we have the records and the confession.   In a moment I shall tell you facts that will indicate just how clever he really was. . . .

He read chemistry and paper making until he was something of a magazine of information on the subject.   He limited his chemistry to that part of the science that has to do with paper making.   He read volumes on dyeing and struck up an acquaintance with a well-known printer in Boston.   This printer did the better grade of work and was so amused by Wilken's enthusiastic desire for knowledge on the subject that he permitted the young man to browse about his plant of nights watching the various processes.

I merely mention all this detail to show you how, when Wilken set out to make his first counterfeit bill, he had mastered every phase of the complex industry.   And all this studying took time, although not so much time as you would think.   Certainly it was not more than a year.   At any rate, he devoted himself for twelve months to the study of how to make a one-dollar bill.

There is just one firm making bank note paper for the Government.   That firm turns out this paper in one factory.   Government inspectors are there to check up the product and there is never any surplus.   The mints [Bureau of Engraving and Printing] consume it as it is turned out; or, rather, it is turned out as the mints need it.

This mill is located in Dalton, Mass.   The firm takes a certain amount of pride in it.   Visitors are quite welcome, and there are guides to take callers through the plant.   In one batch of visitors to this plant came Wilken.

He was about 26 years old at the time.   I am ready to believe that he could see more in a given time from a given point than any man I ever knew.   He had two exceedingly sharp eyes and a retentive memory. He told me that he could read faster than most men he knew and collect more in his fast reading than the majority of his acquaintances could by attentive study. I don't think he was boasting. His was a remarkable mind. . . . It seems as though he had been built by nature for the job. I have often wondered whether his talents would have been smothered by convention had he been kept in the straight and narrow path. The most commonplace man becomes sometimes the most startlingly original crook. The reformed crook, on the other hand, turns to honesty and becomes duller than ditch-water.

Wilken went to that paper mill in Dalton three times. On each occasion he went as a visitor, of course, and spent inside the mills only the comparatively few minutes it takes the visitor to be ushered from process to process and room to room. If you have ever been conducted through an industrial plant you will realize how little you actually see of processes. . . .

Wilken left the paper mill convinced that he was quite ready to start business. He moved to New York City and set up a studio at 250 West 125th street. To make everything appear regular he got a job with an advertising firm. He drew pictures of soap and suspenders, and so on, and did rather good work arranging display type for posters. That required only a small part of his time. . . .

First he made the necessary paper. Just how well he worked will be apparent in a few minutes. Then he set about utilizing his book-learned etching and engraving. Little by little he added to his equipment. He never used a camera. In this fact alone he stands conspicuous among counterfeiters. So far as I know, he was the only counterfeiter of any ability at all who did not first photograph the bank note he was about to counterfeit and work from that. . . . . [Then he made one-dollar bills.] I must say to begin with that not all the Wilken bills were detected. Really relatively few of them came into our hands. We took several of the bills to the paper mill in Dalton. They de-

clared the paper to be genuine! We looked back over the
production records and checked them against consumption.
The two figures balanced! In other words, the United States
Mint had used all that had been produced. There seemed
to be nothing to do but watch the factory. For six months
we hung around and nothing happened.

In a month or so Wilken, so we learned later, decided it
was time to go to work again. He did. He set up a studio
in West Twenty-third Street, New York City, and began to
turn out ten dollar bills that passed the tellers of some of
the most important banks in America. They even passed
the scrutiny of experts in the Treasury Department. I
have samples of them here. They are magnificent frauds.
I have never seen finer engraving.

And to think that he learned this engraving in a public
library.[1]

And there are many cases in the records of courts
and prisons showing a high degree of imagination, ingenuity, constructive intelligence, artistic ability, and
careers as long continued in crime as legitimate life
careers in physics, engineering, or art.

93. Adrian Gorder, born in Holland, the son of a night
watchman, set about making of himself a counterfeit priest
with as much thoroughness as Wilken set about making
counterfeit money. He learned all the technique of the
church service, including music and church history, celebrated Mass perfectly, posed as member of various religious orders, dressed richly, was poetic and plausible. He
visited, for example, Budapest, made certain representations
of himself to the clergy there, showed pictures of eminent
ecclesiastics and spoke of them as his friends. Talked intimately about church affairs, celebrated Mass, borrowed
money or cashed worthless paper and disappeared. He

[1] William J. Flynn, Former Chief of the United States Secret Service:
"My Ten Biggest Man Hunts", *New York Herald*, January 29, 1922.

was not so perfect a counterfeit as Wilken's bills because he had not completely mastered Latin as a spoken tongue, but in spite of frequent incarcerations he operated for twenty-five years over a large part of the world.[1]

All the types of wishes coexist in every person, — the vague desire for new experience, for change, for the satisfaction of the appetites, for pleasure; the new experience contained in a pursuit, as in the cases of Pasteur and Wilken; the desire for response in personal relations ("there was a girl Wilken liked and who liked him"); the desire for recognition (Wilken was "ambitious for success, for wealth, for position, for luxury"); and the desire for security, — the assurance of the means and conditions for gratifying all the wishes indefinitely. And all of these classes of wishes are general mental attitudes ready to express themselves in schemes of action which utilize and are dependent upon the existing social values. These values may be material, as when Wilken used the library, the printing office, the paper mill, or they may be the mental attitudes of others, as when a bogus nobleman imposes on the desire for recognition of a bourgeois, or a scientist appeals to a philanthropic person to endow an institution for medical research. That is, the attitudes of one person are among the values of another person.

The attitudes of a given person at a given moment are the result of his original temperament, the definitions of situations given by society during the course of his life, and his personal definitions of situations derived from his experience and reflection. The character of the individual depends on these factors.

Any mobilization of energies in a plan of action means that some attitude (tendency to action) among

[1] Based on E. Wulffen: "Psychologie des Verbrechens", Vol. 2, p. 320.

the other attitudes has come to the front and subordinated the other attitudes to itself for the moment, as the result of a new definition of the situation. This definition may be the counsel of a friend, an act of memory reviving a social definition applicable to the situation, or an element of new experience defining the situation. Thus in Wilken's case the newspaper item stating that a package of counterfeit money had been picked up identified itself with a wish that was present and seeking expression; the fact that Wilken already had some skill in drawing entered into the definition of the situation, and the result was an attitude and a plan: get money by counterfeiting.

The definition of the situation by Cölestine was determined by the death of Ursula, and the scheme was made possible by the current theological definition of heaven and the credulity of Ursula's parents, used as values by Ursula. In Gorder's case we may assume that his observation of the life of priests, and certainly some particular expression of this, caught his attention and defined the situation for him. It may be remarked that this whole process is similar to the steps in a mechanical invention, — a particular datum working on a body of previous experience, producing a new definition of the situation and a plan or theory.

The moral good or evil of a wish lies therefore not in the cleverness or elaboration of the mental scheme through which it is expressed but in its regard or disregard for existing social values. The same wish and the same quality of mind may lead to totally different results. A tendency to phantasy may make of the subject a scientist, a swindler, or simply a liar. The urge to wandering and adventure may stop at vagabondage, the life of a cowboy, missionary, geologist, or ethnologist. The sporting interest may be gratified by shooting birds, studying them with a camera, or pursuing a scientific theory. The desire for response may be expressed in the Don Juan type of life, with many love adventures, in stable family life, in love lyrics, or in the relation of the prostitute to her pimp. The desire for recognition may seek its gratification in ostentatious dress and luxury or in forms of creative work. That is to say, a wish may have various psychologically equivalent expressions. The problem is to define situations in such ways as to produce attitudes which direct the action exclusively toward fields yielding positive social values. The transfer of a wish from one field of application to another field representing a higher level of values is called the sublimation of the wish. This transfer is accomplished by the fact of public recognition which attaches a feeling of social sacredness to some schemes of action and their application in comparison with others, — the activities of the scientist, physician, or craftsman on the one hand and the activities of the adventurer, the criminal, or the prostitute on the other. This feeling of sacredness actually arises only in groups, and an individual can develop the feeling only in association with a group which has definite standards of sacredness. Practically, any plan which gets favorable public recognition is morally good, — for the time being. And this is the only practical basis of judgment of the moral quality of an act, — whether it gets favorable or unfavorable recognition.

The problem of the desirable relation of individual wishes to social values is thus twofold, containing (1) the problem of the dependence of the individual upon social organization and culture, and (2) the problem of the dependence of social organization and culture upon the individual. In practice the first problem means: What social values and how presented will produce the desirable mental attitudes in the members of the social group? And the second problem means: What schematizations of the wishes of the individual members of the group will produce the desirable social values, promote the organization and culture of the society?

The problem of the individual involves in its details the study of all the social influences and institutions, — family, school, church, the law, the newspaper, the story, the motion picture, the occupations, the economic system, the unorganized personal relationships, the division of life into work and leisure time, etc. But the human wish underlies all social happenings and institutions, and human experiences constitute the reality beneath the formal social organization and behind the statistically formulated mass-phenomena. Taken in themselves statistics are nothing more than symptoms of unknown causal processes. A social institution can be understood and modified only if we do not limit ourselves to the study of its formal organization but analyze the way in which it appears in the personal experience of various members of the group and follow the influence which it has on their lives. And an individual can be understood only if we do not limit ourselves to a cross-section of his life as revealed by a given act, a court record or a confession, or to the determination of what type of life-organization *exists*, but determine the means by which a certain life-organization is *developed*.

In connection with this problem we may again refer

to the natural and biological sciences. These have obtained their results, the establishing of laws, by the use of experiment. Having isolated a problem, say the problem of heredity, they make conjectures as to what would happen under changed conditions, and consciously introduce all changes which are conceived as having a possible meaning for the problem. In these sciences the experimenter is not hindered from introducing changes by the consideration that he may spoil his materials. The chemist or entomologist expects to spoil many materials in the course of his tests. Human material is, however, so precious that the experimenter is not justified in assuming the risk of spoiling it. The child is more precious than the problem. The only field in which experiment on the human being is recognized, or rather practiced without recognition, is medicine, where the material is already threatened with destruction through sickness, and the physician introduces an experimental change, say the use of a serum, which gives a chance of preserving life and restoring health.

Nevertheless, as the result of a series of experiments on the behavior of animals, one of the psychologists assumed that similar work might be done on the newborn child with no more discomfort than he suffers in having his ears scrubbed and certainly no more damage than he receives from the strains and distortions suffered in the act of being born. I quote from the record of these experiments :

On the psychological side our knowledge of infant life is almost nil. . . . A prominent professor of education once said to us, "You will find when you have taught as many children as I have that you can do nothing with a child until it is over five years of age." Our own view after studying many hundreds of infants is that one can make or break the child so far as its personality is concerned long before the age of five is reached.   We believe that by the end of the second year the pattern of the future individual is already laid down.   Many things which go into the making of this pattern are under the control of the parents, but as yet they have not been made aware of them.   The question as to whether the child will possess a stable or unstable personality, whether it is going to be timid and beset with many fears and subject to rages and tantrums, whether it will exhibit tendencies of general over or under emotionalism, and the like, has been answered already by the end of the two year period.

There are several reasons why the minute psychological study of infant life is important. . . .   (1) There are no standards of behavior or conduct for young infants.   Our experimental work, which even at the end of two years is just beginning, has taught us that the study of infant activity from birth onward will enable us to tell with some accuracy what a normal child at three months of age can and should do and what additional complexities in behavior should appear as the months go by.   Psychological laboratories in many institutions ought to be able to make crosssections of the activity of any infant at any age and tell whether the streams of activity are running their normal course, and whether certain ones are lagging or have not even appeared.   After sufficient work has been done to enable us to have confidence in our standards we should be able to detect feeble-mindedness, deficiencies in habit, and deviations in emotional life.   If a proper analysis of the activity streams can be made at a very early age the whole care of the child may be altered with beneficial results. . . . At present we simply have not the data for the enumeration of man's original tendencies, and it will be impossible to obtain those data until we have followed through the development of the activity of many infants from birth to advanced childhood.   Children of five years of age and over are enormously sophisticated. The home environment and outside companions have so shaped them that the original tendencies cannot be observed. The habits put on in such an environment quickly overlay the primitive and hereditary equipment. A workable psychology of human instincts and emotions can thus never be attained by merely observing the behavior of the adult. . . . (2) By reason of this defect the study of vocational and business psychology is in a backward state. The attempt to select a vocation for a boy or girl in the light of our present knowledge of the original nature of man is little more than a leap in the dark. High sounding names like the constructive instinct, the instinct of workmanship, and the like, which are now so much used by the sociologists and the economists, will remain empty phrases until we have increased our knowledge of infancy and childhood. The only reasonable way, it would seem to us, of ever determining a satisfactory knowledge of the various original vocational bents and capacities of the human race is for psychologists to bring up under the supervision of medical men a large group of infants under controlled but varied and sympathetic conditions. Children begin to reach for, select, play with and to manipulate objects from about the 150th day on. What objects they select day by day, what form their manipulation takes, and what early habits develop upon such primitive instinctive activity should be recorded day by day in black and white. There will be marked individual differences in the material selected, in the length of time any type of material will be utilized, and in the early constructive habits which will arise with respect to all materials worked with by the infant. Without instruction one infant (eighteen to twenty months in an observed case) will build a neat wall with her blocks, with one color always facing her. If the block is turned while she is not looking she will quickly change it and correct the defect. In other children such a bit of behavior can be inculcated only with the greatest difficulty. Still another child cannot be made to play with blocks but will work with twigs and sticks by the hour. Variations in the selection and use of material are the rule in infancy, but until we have followed up the future course of such variations upon *infants whose past we have watched day by day* we are in no position to make generalizations about the original tendencies which underlie the vocations. (3) Finally, until we have obtained data upon the emotional life of the infant and the normal curve of instinctive and habit activity at the various ages, new methods for correcting deviations in emotional, instinctive and habit development cannot be worked out. Let us take a concrete example. A certain child is afraid of animals of every type, furry objects, the dark, etc. These fears are not hereditary. Our experiments will be convincing upon that point. What steps can we take to remove these fears which, unless they are removed in infancy, may become an enduring part of the child's personality? [1]

It will be seen that the Watsons are here studying attitudes — what ones appear, in what order they appear, what ones are universal, and what ones are particular to certain children. They introduce values — the materials and influences — only as means of determining the presence of attitudes, of calling them into action, of modifying them, and of giving them application in different fields. They consciously introduce change on the basis of some hypothesis and measure the effect of the new influences on personality development. Already in this brief passage and this unfinished experiment they indicate methods of determining (1) occupational aptitudes, (2) defective mental efficiency, (3) the age levels at which influences are to be presented and the order of their presentation, and (4) the conditions of stable or neurotic personalities.

[1] John B. Watson and Rosalie Rayner Watson: "Studies in Infant Psychology", *Popular Science Monthly*, December, 1921, pp. 494, 515.

Their task is the measurement of influence under conditions which they prepare and control. All scientific experimentation involves the measurement of influence. The chemist measures the influence of a material, say coal tar; the technician uses this influence in preparing a dye or a medicine. The measurement of the influence is the definition of the situation preliminary to action.

Now the world in which we live presents to the child influences comparable with those artificially prepared in this experiment, and the first task of behavior studies is to measure these influences as shown in their effect on personality development.

There are in society organized sources of influence, institutions, and social agencies, including the family, the school, the community, the reformatory, the penitentiary, the newspaper, the moving picture. These are sources of mass influence and will naturally be the main objects of study and change. But in order to supplement and make scientific these studies and to give them an adequate method it is necessary to prepare at the same time more complete records of the personal evolution of individuals. Eventually the life of the individual is the measure of the totality of social influence, and the institution should be studied in the light of the personality development of the individual. And as we accumulate records of personal evolution, with indications of the means by which the wishes seek expression and of the conditions of their normal satisfaction, we shall be in a better position to measure the influence of particular institutions in the formation of character and life-organization and to determine lines of change in the institutions themselves.

The "human document", prepared by the subject,

on the basis of the memory is one means of measuring social influence. It is capable of presenting life as a connected whole and of showing the interplay of influences, the action of values on attitudes. It can reveal the predominant wishes in different temperaments, the incidents constituting turning points in life, the processes of sublimation or transfer of interest from one field to another, the effect of other personalities in defining situations and the influence of social organizations like the family, the school, the acquaintance group, in forming the different patterns of life-organization. By comparing the histories of personalities as determined by social influences and expressed in various schemes of life we can establish a measure of the given influences. The varieties of human experience will be innumerable in their concrete details, but by the multiplication and analysis of life records we may expect to determine typical lines of the genesis of character as related to types of influence. It will be found that when certain attitudes are present the presentation of certain values may be relied upon to produce certain results.

Human experience and schemes of personal behavior are the most interesting of all themes, as is evidenced by fiction, the drama, biographies, and histories. And works of this kind contain materials which will be given a scientific value as we analyze, compare, and interpret them. Even fictitious representations are significant when viewed as showing the tendency at a given moment to idealize certain schematizations of life. The autobiography has a more positive value for the student, but usually tends to approach the model of fiction, idealizing certain situations and experiences and repressing others totally. Incidentally

one of the largest and most important bodies of spontaneous material for the study of the personality and
the wishes passes through the mails. The letters of
the Bedford girl, for example (document No. 86, p. 172)
appeal to me as the most significant document in this
volume, in spite of the fact that they relate to one incident and cover a relatively short time. The short
life-histories of approximately six thousand Jews
printed in the New York *Forward*, and representing
the effort to find new definitions of new situations on
the part of the million and a half Jewish immigrants
in New York City, and to some extent of the three
million Jews in America, are a rich contribution to the
study of the wishes. These records, hidden from the
eye of the "*goi*" behind the Hebrew alphabet, have
the intimacy and naïveté of personal confessions.

Another type of behavior record is now being prepared by those social workers, psychologists, and psychiatrists who have to handle the problems of maladjustment in the courts, schools, and reformatories and
in private practice. Under the pressure of practical
needs they have already assumed the standpoint I
have outlined and are studying the evolution of personal life-organization and making the record as complete as possible. They meet the individual at the
point of some crisis, some experience or breakdown
calling for readjustment, but from this point they
work backward into the history of the case and follow
its development into the future. In the beginning
they over-determined the value of the psychometric
test, because this was the only method psychology
had put in their hands, but at present the measurement of intelligence is recognized as having a limited
usefulness. "Feeble-mindedness" is partly a classi-

ficatory term for those personalities whose behavior
we have not been able to conform to the usual standards because of lack of knowledge and method. We
shall not know what conditions to call feeble-minded
until we have determined the limits of the social influences which we can apply. Certain social workers
are taking case after case pronounced subnormal by
the clinicists and developing in them activities which
enable them to live in a society where they could not
live before, while a large proportion of those now pursuing peaceful callings would be called morons if they
were rounded up and gathered into some of the clinics.
The government records determined that 47.3 per
cent of all Americans called out in the draft for en-
listment in the war were mentally deficient. They
showed the mentality of a twelve-year-old child or
less.[1] A report of this kind really loses all significance, because it makes no provision for lack of uniformity in the social influences. There are certainly
cases of constitutional inferiority, but the clinical
psychologists are now realizing that these must be
studied, like the cases of the maladjustment of the
normal, in connection with life records showing the social influences tending to organize or disorganize the
personality. These institutional records obtained
by testing, observation, and inquiry should be sup-
plemented by a life-record written by the subject. In
many cases it is not difficult to obtain this, and wherever the subject of the study participates, giving the
incidents of life which have been determining factors
the record gains in value.

[1] "Psychological Examining in the United States Army". Report
prepared by Charles M. Yerkes, in "Memoirs of the National Academy
of Sciences", Vol. 15.

From this standpoint the merit of the psychoanalytic school of psychiatrists consists in the study of the personality. I do not refer to theories or cures but to the method of studying the life-organization by an analysis of the wishes, by enlisting the participation of the subject, and using a special technic to revive all possible trains of memory. The defect of this particular practice has been its lack of objectivity. The operator has been using an interesting theory — sex as the basis of life-organization — and his methods have been adapted to the confirmation of the theory. More recently "recognition" has assumed a prominent place in the theory, lack of recognition being indicated as the source of the "inferiority complex." But taken simply as cases the psychoanalytic records are increasingly important for the study of behavior. And the general method of psychoanalysis, or at least methods inspired by it, are being used with the best results in connection with delinquent children in the psychological clinics and by case-workers, as in documents No. 88 and No. 89.

But we cannot rely entirely on the spontaneous production of autobiographies nor upon the efforts of practical workers who make records with reference to equilibrating maladjusted personalities. Research into behavior problems through the preparation of records, including life-histories, should be associated with every institution and agency handling human material from the standpoint of education or reform, but in addition specialists in behavior, psychologists, social psychologists, sociologists, psychiatrists, social workers, should isolate and study selected personalities as the biologist studies selected organisms. Ordinary and extraordinary personalities should be included, the dull and the criminal, the philistine and the bohemian. Scientifically the history of dull lives is quite as significant as that of brilliant ones. The investigator may, of course, select cases having special significance; for example, secure the life-histories of the girls mentioned at the beginning of this chapter who were not influenced by the institution but made good in spite of the institution. The analysis, comparison, and publication of the various records would continuously influence social practice, as in the case of medical and technological research.

We saw in the records given at the end of the last chapter that very rapid and positive gains are being made in the treatment of delinquency, but for a fundamental control and the prevention of anti-social behavior a change in the general attitudes and values of society will be necessary.

Up to the present, society has not been able to control the direction of its own evolution or even to determine the form of life and relationships necessary to produce a world in which it is possible and desirable for all to live. Common sense has not been adequate to these problems. We have evidently overdetermined certain values and underdetermined others, and many important situations are undefined — without policy. The most general and particular studies of the wishes and the determination of the laws by which attitudes are influenced by values and values by attitudes, the development of a technic for the transfer of the wishes from one field of application to another, and the development of schemes by which not only the wishes of the individual may be sublimated but the attitudes and values of whole populations controlled will be necessary before we are able consciously to control the evolution of society and to determine an ideal organization of culture.

Among the general problems involved in the study of attitudes and values — the history of personality development and the measurement of social influences — are the following:

1. The problem of abnormality — crime, vagabondage, prostitution, alcoholism, etc. How far is abnormality the unavoidable manifestation of inborn tendencies of the individual, and how far is it a matter of deficient social organization, — the failure of institutional influences? There is a quantitative difference of efficiency between individuals, but if there is hardly a human attitude which if properly controlled and directed could not be used in a socially useful and productive way, must there remain a permanent qualitative difference between socially normal and anti-social actions?

2. The problem of individualization. How far is individualism compatible with social cohesion? What forms of individualism may be considered socially useful or socially harmful? What forms of individualism may be useful in an organization based on a conscious coöperation in view of a common aim?

3. The problem of nationalities and cultures. What new schemes of attitudes and values, or what substitute for the isolated national state as an instrument of cultural expansion, will stop the fight of nationalities and cultures?

4. The problem of the sexes. In the relation between the sexes how can a maximum of reciprocal response be secured with a minimum of interference with personal interests? How is the general social efficiency of a group affected by the various systems of relations between man and woman? What forms of coöperation between the family and society are most favorable to the normal development of children?

5. The economic problem. How shall we be able to develop attitudes which will subordinate economic success to other values? How shall we restore stimulation to labor? The bad family life constantly evident in these pages and the consequent delinquency of children, as well as crime, prostitution and alcoholism, are largely due to the overdetermination of economic interests — to the tendency to produce or acquire the largest possible amount of economic values — because these interests are actually so universal and predominant and because economic success is a value convertible into new experience, recognition, response, and security.

The modern division and organization of labor brings a continually growing quantitative prevalence of occupations which are almost completely devoid of stimulation and therefore present little interest for the workman. This fact affects human behavior and happiness profoundly, and the restoration of stimulation to labor is among the most important problems confronting society. The present industrial organization tends also to develop a type of human being as abnormal in its way as the opposite type of individual who gets the full amount of occupational stimulation by taking a line of interest destructive of social order, — the criminal or vagabond.

The moralist complains of the materialization of men and expects a change of the social organization to be brought about by moral or religious preaching; the economic determinist considers the whole social organization as conditioned fundamentally and necessarily by economic factors and expects an improvement exclusively from a possible historically necessary modification of the economic organization itself. From the viewpoint of behavior the problem is much more serious and objective than the moralist conceives it, but much less limited and determined than it appears to the economic determinist. The economic interests are only one class of human attitudes among others, and every attitude can be modified by an adequate social technic. The interest in the nature of work is frequently as strong as or stronger than the interest in the economic results of the work, and often finds an objective expression in spite of the fact that actual social organization has little place for it. The protests, in fact, represented by William Morris mean that a certain class of work has visibly passed from the stage where it was stimulating to a stage where it is not, — that the handicrafts formerly expressed an interest in the work itself rather than in the economic returns from the work. Since every attitude tends to influence social institutions, we may expect that an organization and a division of labor based on occupational interests may gradually replace the present organization based on demands of economic productivity. In other words, with the appropriate change of attitudes and values all work may become artistic work. And with the appropriate change of attitudes and values the recognition of economic success may be subordinated to the recognition of human values.]

INDEX

Abbott, Edith, 102, 211.
Abnormality, problem of, 255.
Addams, Jane, 31.
Additon, Henrietta, 212.
Alcoholism, problem of, 255.
Anger, emotion of, 2.
Attitudes, mental, 233.

Bedford Hills Reformatory, 172.
Behavior, a science of, 228.
Bentley, Mary Ide, 86.
Bohemian, 12.
Breckenridge, S. P., 102, 211.

Cabot, Hugh, 92.
Cadet, the, 141.
Character, definition of, 241.
Charity girl, 119.
Chicago Vice Commission, 229.
Church, Irish Catholic, 159;
    Polish Catholic, 159.
Code, the social, 50.
Common sense vs. scientific procedure, 225.
Community, 43.
Crime, problem of, 255.
Crime and punishment, 223.
Criminology, procedure of, 222.
Culbert, Jane F., 216.
Cultures, problem of, 255.

Davis, Katherine B., 116, 117, 118.
Daydreaming, 35.
Deardorff, Neva R., 212.

Delinquency, beginning of, 109.
Delinquent, proportion of foreign born, 152.
Demi-virgin, 231.
Demoralization of girls, 98, 150.
Dostoievsky, F., 10.

Economic Determination, 118.
Economic interests, overdetermination of, 256.
Economic problem, 256.
Eliot, Thomas D., 211.
Ellis, Havelock, 100.
El Retiro, 200.
Emotions, 2.
Engelgardt, A. N., 45.
Epithets, 49.
Experience, desire for new, 4.
Exploitation of girl by parents, 108.

Family, 43.
Fear, emotion of, 2.
Feeble-mindedness, 251.
Flapper, 231.
Flynn, Wm. J., 240.
Flynt, Josiah, 7.
Folkways, 44.

Gang, Influence on Girl, 142.
Girls' Protective Bureau, 160.
Gossip, 49.
Group and individual, 70.

Hapgood, Hutchins, 21, 24.
Healy, William, 35.

259